D1565721

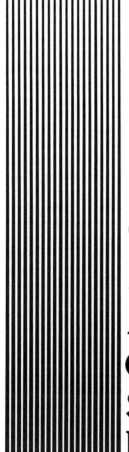

The Strategic Approach to QUALITY SERVICE IN HEALTH CARE

Kristine Peterson

Laventhol & Horwath
Chicago, Illinois

AN ASPEN PUBLICATION®
Aspen Publishers, Inc.

1988

Rockville, Maryland
Royal Tunbridge Wells

Library of Congress Cataloging-in-Publication Data

Peterson, Kristine.
The strategic approach to quality service in health care.

Bibliography: p.
Includes index.
1. Hospitals--Administration. 2. Hospital patients.
I. Title.
RA971.P5   1988   362.1'1'068   88-6269
ISBN:0-87189-764-4

RA971
P5
1988

Editorial Services: Marsha Davies

Library of Congress Catalog Card Number: 88-6269
ISBN: 0-87189-764-4

Printed in the United States of America

1 2 3 4 5

Table of Contents

Foreword

At the time I wrote *Service America! Doing Business in the New Economy* four years ago, the health care industry's fascination with service quality was well evidenced. Over time, this fascination has grown. As competition gets tougher, the resolve to transform hospitals and other health care provider organizations into customer-driven, quality-obsessed businesses becomes even stronger.

Hospitals have been spending thousands of dollars in the pursuit of quality service and the success they hope will follow. In general, however, the returns on these investments have been less than satisfactory. The problem stems from defining the issues too narrowly and addressing them primarily through training programs to improve relationships between the organization's employees and the various customers it serves. In most instances, what is missing is a model for service that will enable the hospital to manage the customer's entire experience in the service delivery process.

In this book, Kristine Peterson presents a model for structuring health care service delivery to achieve customer satisfaction. The service management approach that she describes is an excellent tool for building and maintaining a service culture. These methods will enable executives and managers to translate the concepts of service into actions that will produce results for the organization.

Quality service is the new standard by which patients, physicians, and other health care customers will measure organizational performance. The process demands a concerted, consistent, and persistent organization-wide commitment to help people in health care organizations focus on service. Master the art and science of managed service delivery and you will create a successful future for your business.

Karl Abrecht
Author
At America's Service

Preface

In 1978, I was hired by Lifemark Corporation, an investor-owned management corporation in Houston, Texas, to develop a guest relations program for their 35 owned and managed hospitals. Although I was thrilled with Lifemark's offer, I was somewhat unaware of the need for such a program and its vast future implications for the entire health care industry.

I was certainly aware that service in America had begun to erode. I am old enough to remember when milk was delivered to the back door and when full service at gas stations meant that someone would wash your windshield, check your oil, and give you Green Stamps. I could even recall the days when asking a department store clerk to send the packages did not imply that I would pay a delivery charge to receive them 4 days later. In those days, a truck would deliver the purchases the next day at no charge and even pick them up for return.

Yet, I had never heard about a search for excellence. I thought of culture as something pertaining to a foreign country and had never heard the words "high tech" and "high touch" juxtaposed.

The idea to create a guest relations program was not merely a lapse into nostalgia by a Lifemark executive. The decision made good business sense. Back in the 1970s, the for-profit segment of the health care industry was predicting a new competitive era, and its members were forging ahead to assume strategic positions. Moreover, they needed to dispel the emerging perception that they were "for-profit bad guys" who would sacrifice quality for their shareholder's dollar. In reality, what Lifemark recognized was that their future profits were dependent upon sound financial management and relationship management. Profit at the expense of dissatisfied customers would accelerate their demise.

Once I was hired, I set about trying to find out what other companies did to create customer satisfaction. I contacted several, and most politely answered my inquiries, but few revealed anything of great significance. I wrote Delta Airlines a particularly long and persuasive letter, asking their officials to share with me the reasons why I had come to think of their flight attendants, ticket agents, pilots, reservations agents, and baggage handlers as friends, whereas I viewed the employees of another major airline as enemies. A Delta representative wrote back to say that they really did not have a program, per se; they simply hired the right people. I didn't believe him. It seemed too easy. I have since learned that Delta Airlines accepts 40 to 48 of the more than 20,000 applicants for flight attendant jobs who inquire each month.

I also contacted the Marriott Corporation seeking assistance. As a frequent traveler, I had always been impressed with the way in which I was treated at Marriott hotels. No matter which Marriott hotel I stayed in, I noticed a perceptible difference—in the attitudes of employees, in the ambience of the environment, and in the quality of the experience. Somehow, I got the feeling that the Marriott staff really cared about me as a person and that the corporation cared about me as a customer. I hired several executives from Marriott, seeking all the answers. I hoped that they would be able to bottle up and sell to me the "Marriott Mystique" so that I could repackage it for our 35 Lifemark hospitals. What I discovered was that Marriott's magic potion is formulated, not by programs and posters, but by the fundamental values and priorities of its corporate culture.

That is why I have written this book with some trepidation. I simply cannot package all of the answers within these pages. Success does not come in a set of trade secrets or in an assortment of videotapes, workbooks, and manuals. It does not come bottled up in a book. Although the following chapters outline strategies, systems, and structures to create service excellence, they can, at best, merely start you on your own quest.

Since 1978, I have worked with over 500 hospitals. It has been a richly rewarding experience, and I have learned much along the way. Some of these hospitals have experienced fantastic success and growth in the area of guest relations. Others have failed. The success or failure of any hospital has had little to do with the quality of their videotapes, discussion exercises, recognition programs, or publicity efforts. It has had everything to do with the strength of their leadership, substance of their culture, and the depth of their commitment.

In 1981, I left Lifemark Corporation and started my own firm, K. E. Peterson & Associates. In July of 1987, we merged with Laventhol & Horwath, a consulting and accounting firm with over 50 offices nationwide. Since that time, many have questioned why I undertook the merger. The answer was apparent to me when I had lunch in Chicago with one of the partners of the Organizational Consulting Division of Laventhol & Horwath. I learned that they had entered into a co-venture with Karl Albrecht, co-author of the book, *Service America! Doing Business in the New Economy,* which was published in 1985 by Dow Jones Irwin. I found the theories presented in that book to be totally consistent with what my experience had taught me. Unless you have a multidimensional approach to creating service excellence that is built on a strong commitment to create customer satisfaction, you cannot succeed. Laventhol & Horwath had developed compelling technologies for putting the theory of service excellence into practice. They were working with industry giants to transform the ways in which service was conceived, managed, and delivered. There was powerful synergy in what our respective firms were doing. We are now developing new technologies for the health care industry. Together, we are moving in directions that I could never have predicted in 1978.

Our merger took place as the final pages of this book were being edited. What I have attempted to do is to incorporate as much state-of-the-art information as is possible, but as is true of any evolving technology, the seeds from which new ideas and innovations grow are planted every day. It is for this reason that I encourage every reader to realize that your quest is as evolutionary as mine has been. Foster its growth by continually seeking answers but recognize that fewer than half will be contained in this book, and the majority will be revealed to you as you proceed on your own journey.

Although the language used in this book is directed to the hospital audience, there is no reason why the same strategies, systems, and approaches cannot be used within any health care organization. Nursing homes, home health agencies, physician clinics and group practices, health maintenance organizations, etc., are facing similar issues and challenges as are hospitals. I encourage those who are not within the acute care setting to adapt the concepts and to implement the strategies that would be applicable to their situation and circumstance.

Acknowledgments

I would like to gratefully acknowledge those who have generously contributed to this book. To my associates—Betty La Porte, Rosalie De Marte, Rosemary Marks, Sharon Noel, Gaylene Melashenko Johns, and Karen Quinn—to whom I dedicate this book with heartfelt appreciation for their faithful support; To my partners and colleagues at Laventhol & Horwath, especially Barbara Shomaker, Ed Crego, Ed Kazemek, Dennis Lombardi, and Ken Solomon; To Karl Albrecht for his insight and wisdom; To my friendly competitors—Norm Burns, Rita Fritz, Wendy Leebov, Doug Mosel, Kathleen McInerney, and Paul Roelofs—who willingly submitted excellent contributions to this book; To Mike Scott, Anne Doll, and the staff at Aspen Publishers, Inc. for their contributions and patience; To family and friends—too numerous to mention—who were there when the demands of running a business, running to planes, and running the word processor were all-consuming activities. And last but not least, to our clients—our valued customers—you have made this book possible.

Chapter 1

Excellence: A Fad or Phenomenon?

Ever since the excellence phenomenon descended upon the health care industry, we have witnessed hospitals across the nation adopting its principles. In small towns and large cities, on university campuses and in the inner city, in profit, not-for-profit, and public hospitals alike, the visions of health care executives have evolved from myopic to expansive as they have endeavored to peer into the future and identify excellence strategies for survival and prosperity. It has been fascinating to observe the degree to which the emphasis on excellence has transformed the organizational mindset, created innovations, and improved the quality of health care services.

Competition has been the impetus for change. As competition has become widespread, patients more discerning, payers more cost conscious, and physicians more entrepreneurial, hospitals have reached deeper into their pockets to fund their retaliation. They have recruited marketing specialists from other industries, hired a host of consultants for services ranging from market research to guest relations, and sent staff to seminars and conferences that promise the latest innovations in marketing warfare.

These new initiatives, however revolutionary and exciting, are now beginning to wane. Enthusiasm is becoming clouded by skepticism and doubt. Participants are experiencing culture fatigue and strategic shellshock. As one administrator has been heard to say, "If I hear one more time that the future success of my hospital depends on my becoming a customer-obsessed, wandering and blundering megalomaniac with a mission, I'm going A.W.O.L."

The wave of any sociocultural phenomenon is bound to crest. When the tide recedes, we clean up the debris and wait for the new rush. It has happened over and over again, as one business fad replaces another. We move from Theory X to Theory Y to Theory Z. With no more letters in the alphabet, we move to searches and then to passions. And when our passion subsides, we use our marketing imaginations to reinvent our corporations.

Is there a lesson to be learned? Perhaps one. If we are to ride the crest of emerging trends, it is important not to get battered against the rocks.

Health care is in the midst of a powerful maelstrom that, for the most part, keeps it in a constant state of flux. The industry experiences times of tranquility and purposeful direction, but these times are literally the calm before the storm. To manage change amidst such turbulence, we seek answers. It is not unlike twisting and turning the Rubik's Cube a thousand different ways trying to solve the puzzle. After countless configurations and as many failed attempts, we give up. The Cube is abandoned on the shelf.

And that is exactly where guest relations programs are being found in increasing numbers.

WHERE DO WE GO FROM HERE?

Guest relations, a concept so amazingly simple and delightfully fresh, was embraced from its beginning as holding a promise too good to be true. Many hospital administrators sincerely believed that, by training employees to be more courteous to guests, their organizations could achieve greatness and sustain a competitive advantage. Their intentions were noble, but their expectations were far too high. Training is not the magic ingredient in the excellence formula.

Certainly there are hospitals whose service programs go beyond training. Some have implemented recognition programs to identify and applaud "situational heroes" for their episodic contributions. Others have redecorated their lobbies and redesigned their patient questionnaires. Many have incorporated guest relations standards into their performance appraisal systems. Yet for all of these efforts, frustration has been the principal result. The bugles that had sounded so clearly at the launching of guest relations programs have turned flat, if not sour . . . and the banners have come down.

Where do we go from here? It is a question that is asked frequently. Were it not for the fact that guest relations was, is, and forever will remain one of the most vital and essential strategies for positioning a hospital in a competitive marketplace, for managing risk, for creating excellence, and for providing a workplace in which employees can be challenged, productive, and fulfilled, our response might indeed be to retire the program to the shelf, dismantle the committees, and move on. Yet those who thoughtfully ask the question recognize that the effort cannot be abandoned.

The first step is to go beyond thinking of guest relations as a program, and more specifically as a training program. Far too many hospitals have initiated *and* concluded a guest relations program. Yet, few, if any, hospitals have ever initiated and concluded a quality assurance or risk management program. If guest relations is to provide hospitals the same competitive advantage that it has achieved for a host of service-driven, customer-oriented companies, we must think of it as a multidimensional approach for delivering quality care that is directed at meeting the needs and exceeding the expectations of customers. We must steer our organizations beyond the limited vision of one more "excellence" program to a broader vision of service management, to a strategic approach for defining the hospital's services in a manner that differentiates it from its competitors. Service management calls for targeting market segments and needs, conceptualizing how the service will be perceived by customers, defining operation strategies, and designing efficient and effective service delivery systems. It also calls for a service strategy that is built on core organizational values that presume superior service performance from every person and system. Service management requires enormous effort and commitment because, to succeed, it must ultimately burrow into the very marrow of the organization, shaping the manner in which business is conducted in every corner of the hospital. The potential benefits of such a foundational change are equally enormous.

BENEFITS OF CUSTOMER SATISFACTION

The goal of service management is to create exceptional satisfaction among both external customers and internal providers. External customers can be defined as patients, physicians, and payers. Internal providers include employees, physicians, and volunteers. Service management success can be measured by the satisfaction that is experienced by these groups.

Patient Satisfaction

By far, institutional reputation is the dominant factor shaping people's preferences, and in turn, reputation is shaped to a large degree by perceptions. Consumers' beliefs about your hospital and their perceptions of your strengths are shaped principally by personal experience, word-of-mouth advertising, and/or information shared from someone who works there. These three factors account for approximately 67 percent of consumers' awareness of hospitals. Another 26 percent are influenced by paid advertising. Therefore, two of the most powerful forces in shaping consumer perceptions of competency in medical, emergency, and humanistic care—personal experience and word-of-mouth advertising—result from satisfying patients.[1]

Satisfied patients talk; so do dissatisfied patients. A Washington D.C. consumer research group, the Technical Assistance Research Programs (TARP), has uncovered telling statistics about customer satisfaction: satisfied customers will tell between four and five other people about their satisfaction, dissatisfied customers will tell between nine and ten other people about their dissatisfaction, and 13 percent of the dissatisfied customers will tell over twenty people.[2] These statistics are not health care specific. Therefore, based upon the usual severity of a hospital stay and in light of the fact that hospitalization is a significant lifetime experience, it is not unrealistic to assume that patients will recount their positive experiences to far more than five other people and their negative experiences with even greater frequency. For this reason, word-of-mouth communications have a critical impact on the hospital's image. The current extensive investments in health care advertising and marketing are of little value if the *internal* marketing does not support the external effort.

One of the more tangible ways to measure the benefits derived from customer satisfaction is to track the donations that are made by former patients or memorials that are made to the hospital. Many people express their gratitude for the special care and attention that are extended during hospitalization by making contributions to the hospital. As fund raising continues to be an important source of revenue for most hospitals, the value of patient satisfaction cannot be overstated.

In the United States, the number of lawsuits filed against companies is reaching epidemic proportions, with hospitals and physicians particularly hard hit by this trend. One of the best defensive strategies against malpractice suits is good customer relations. Patients who feel ignored, dehumanized, and uncared for are far more likely to become legally aggressive. Although risk managers and patient representatives can help ameliorate volatile incidents after the fact, these incidents can be far less threatening if the quality of caring is in line with the quality of care.

Finally, satisfied patients are more likely to comply with treatments and participate in their health care. When patients are housed in a positive, healthy environment that does not provoke frustration and anxiety, they tend to recover faster. Given that the primary mission of a health care institution is to restore a patient's health and well-being so he or she can be discharged, this benefit is of primary importance.

Physician Satisfaction

In the truest sense of the word, the physician is the hospital's customer. It is he or she who makes the purchase decision. Although physicians have relinquished some control over provider selection, it is the physician who retains admitting privileges and influences, to the greatest degree, the choice of hospital to which the patient will be sent.

Physicians and hospitals are mutually dependent, and that dependency can both strengthen and weaken their relationship. To strengthen the bond, hospitals must respond in ways that keep physicians satisfied. Physician bonding programs are emerging, but regardless of how innovative these incentives are, if a spirit of service does not prevail, no amount of bait or number of "perks" will capture the undivided loyalty of the physician. Loyalty and satisfaction affect service utilization. You can enhance physician satisfaction by keeping patients happy—and you can keep physicians loyal by responding to their needs and their expectations.

Employee Satisfaction

Although we have acquired unparalleled technological capabilities within the past decade, one fact remains—we still need human beings to achieve quality in the delivery of health care services.

Employees are your greatest resource, and it is vitally important to ensure that they will be productive, satisfied, and involved members of your health care delivery team. You cannot satisfy your customers if those who comprise your service delivery team are not satisfied. Whether they are paid or not, every employee must contribute.

Unquestionably, it is becoming more difficult to attract qualified employees as the available pool of health care workers dwindles. And just as it costs five times more money to recruit a new customer than to keep one, it is similarly more expensive to recruit than to retain employees. An organizational climate that fosters satisfaction among internal providers as well as external customers accrues value in employee recruitment and retention.

Such a climate also leads to higher productivity. When patients and physicians are satisfied, they complain less. Employees and their managers spend less time putting out fires and are able to spend their time more productively. When employees are happy, they are more likely to invest themselves fully in their jobs. Departments work together more cooperatively and productively when members are vested in a unified purpose.

SUMMARY

The potential gains that will result from a strong commitment to achieve excellence and superior service far outweigh the investment. That is not to say that the cost is not high. It takes an enormous commitment to make it work.

Guest relations is quickly becoming a fad merely because too many hospitals have quickly admitted defeat. The time has come to mobilize the troops and to reinstate the commitment. Keep asking the question, "Where do we go from here?" If you are smart, you will never stop asking the question. Excellence is more a state of mind than a state of being.

NOTES

1. Joyce Jensen, "Advertising Helps More Consumers Select Hospitals," *Modern Healthcare* (February 14, 1986): 62-63.

2. Technical Assistance Research Programs (TARP), "Consumer Complaints Seminar" (Presented for the Nippon Cultural Broadcasting Company, Tokyo, Japan, September 4, 1981).

Chapter 2

The Service Challenge: Back to the Basics

The technological explosion of the early 1950s essentially lit the fuse of modern consumerism. A major evolution in personal values that began in part as compensation for the impersonal nature of technology eventually spread to a generalized distrust of institutions. As people grew less trustful, they also grew more self-sufficient. Nowhere is this evolution more apparent than in the health care industry, where loss of faith in the medical establishment has prompted assumption of greater responsibility for personal health and well-being. These societal shifts, identified as megatrends by John Naisbitt in his book of the same name, contributed to transforming the lives, attitudes, and behaviors of the American public.[1]

In part, these changes also transformed the lives, attitudes, and behaviors of American health care providers. Changes in payment systems, the emergence of managed care and of alternative delivery systems, and the interest in guest relations are all outgrowths, to some degree, of consumerism.

CONSUMERISM

The effects of consumerism are being experienced in all service industries. The "Phoenix phenomenon" is nowhere more evident than in the hotel industry, where increasing demands made by the American consumer have led to the introduction of amazing amenities. Hotels are now resurrecting personal service. Although the hotel industry was among the first to implement the concept of personal service, the provision of such service began to wane a couple of decades ago. As hotels attempted to be more efficient and profitable, services were withdrawn. The valets, who in the middle of the night would collect the guest's suit from inside the hotel room door and press it, were retired. Hotels no longer polished the shoes that the guest left outside the door before going to bed. With the exception of a very few facilities, hotels focused on delivering comfortable lodging for a reasonable cost. And the value-driven, cost-conscious consumer accepted the changes graciously.

Our intense longing for "the way things used to be" has its roots in deprivation. Once the level of service declines below their threshold of comfort, consumers begin to demand more. They will begin to pay a little more for it, justifying the additional expense for the extra measure of comfort, convenience, and care they feel that they need. Once one service business recognizes that it can compete on the basis of value, rather than cost, it takes full advantage. Service increases and others follow suit. Service decreases only when customers decide that the level of service does not justify the cost. The pendulum begins to swing the other way.

Consumers' desire for personal service, their demand for convenience and accommodation to their busy schedules and lifestyles, their revolt against high costs, and the expressed need to humanize the frightening technology, have come together to create a demand for service in the health care industry. The industry has now discovered its own version of what some call "burger wars" and others refer to as the era of the "hotel for the sick." Take notice of the little bottles of shampoo that are being packed inside the emesis basins, and you discover that, to the chagrin of many, hospitals are now adopting the hotelier's tactics. Although the issues at hand are more far reaching and complex and the solutions are not found in creating a hotel facade, the hospital can benefit from treating patients as guests.

THE PATIENT AS GUEST

Ten years ago, if you had referred to patients as "guests," reactions would have ranged from amusement to indignation. After all, the word "patient" was derived from the Latin word *patic*, meaning "to suffer or endure." Webster defines the word as an adjective meaning "bearing or enduring pain without complaining or losing self-control; calmly tolerating delay, confusion, or inefficiency." How well the word fitted the mentality of a decade ago! We wanted our patients to be passive and compliant so that we, in our all-knowing omnipotence and loving maternalism, could care for them best.

When providers recognized that patients were becoming intolerant of delays, confusion, and inefficiency, they knew that it was time for change. They could not call patients "impatients," and the term "customer" was too cold and implied that health care was a business, rather than a benevolent provision of service to the sick and infirm. Therefore, the health care industry adopted the term "guest."

In areas more substantive than nomenclature, hospitals further recognized the advantages of modeling their institutions after hotels and prepared to view themselves as hospitable innkeepers. Over time, the identity of "guest" was substituted widely—a small step that produced an entirely new perception and attitude about patients. And although we may want to pat ourselves on the backs for generously redefining the relationship, we truly cannot take credit for the change. It was really the patient who forced us to change the way we think and relate.

THE GUEST AS CUSTOMER

Where has this evolution taken the health care industry? The wise among us are finally becoming customer-driven. We have accepted the fact that we are in the *business* of providing services that have value to various *customers*. We realize that we can no longer create the services we want to deliver and expect the customer to consume them. We now scientifically assess the needs of our target audiences and then strategically set out to provide those services that will satisfy those needs. We have awakened to the realization that health care is, first and foremost, a service enterprise requiring a customer-oriented approach to the design, development, and delivery of service.

In some hospitals, the results of this customer-oriented approach are testing the bounds of traditional health care management's credulity. Chauffeured limousines transport patients to and from their homes for outpatient surgical procedures. Hotels are built adjacent to hospitals to accommodate family members. Valet parking and 24-hour room service are offered. Lobbies and reception areas are lavishly redecorated, and "guest relations representatives" appear in tailored uniforms to welcome and admit their guests warmly while concierges stand by to handle any problems. Yet, hotel-like services notwithstanding, hospitals should not delude themselves that they are merely "hotels for the sick." The hospital that simply adopts the surface appeal of a hotel will soon find that it has solved the superficial problems to the neglect of the substantive, underlying systems and attitude changes required to deliver consumer-driven quality service and superior care.

Leah Curtin, RN, the profound and prolific editor of *Nursing Management* magazine, wrote in an editorial entitled "Courtesy: Rescuing Patients from the Me-Generation":

> To quote Elwood Hubbard: "Every man is a damn fool for at least five minutes every day; wisdom consists of not exceeding the limit." This (ostentatious hotel amenities) exceeds the limit. Worse, it falls short of the mark. Hospitals provide *health services*, not merely *hotel services*. And the public expects the difference. . . . To develop an effective (guest relations) program, one must nonetheless know a good deal about patients. . . . The promise of professional attendance—not the clink of crystal chandeliers—lures anxious patients into hospitals.[2]

UNIQUENESS—BOTH A BLESSING AND CURSE

In our enthusiasm to emulate hotels, airlines, and other superb service models, we must not forget that there are characteristics of our business and the climate in which we operate that make us unique. It is inherently more difficult to achieve customer satisfaction and service excellence in the health care industry for a number of very valid reasons—some of which are within our power to change immediately and others of which may be modified over time.

First, the nature of the customer's experience is different. On more than one occasion, I have stood before a group of sullen managers who have converged in the auditorium for a guest relations kickoff meeting. They listen as their administrator introduces me by saying, "Betty and I took the kids to Disney World this summer and I have to tell you, it was a fantastic experience! We were overwhelmed by the hospitality. Everyone, from the ticket takers to the guy cleaning the streets, bent over backwards to make sure we were having a great time. I decided then and there, that when I came back to the hospital, we were going to investigate guest relations programs. We did and today I am pleased to introduce . . ."

I cringe as I watch those managers sink deeper into their seats. They face what they perceive to be insurmountable obstacles in managing their department's operations and keeping employees, patients, physicians, and other departments happy. Is it any wonder that they resent the suggestion that we acquire the marketing acumen of Mickey Mouse?

Although we may return from Disney World with zeal for creating that special kind of guest relations, the fact of the matter is that we will never be able to create the same kind of magic because our hospitals are quite different places from amusement parks.

Our guests are sick, their families are apprehensive, and our doctors are demanding. Moreover, our guests enter the hospital with very different expectations about their impending experience. For this reason, the challenges our employees confront differ vastly from those of Disney employees. It is easier to help people have fun when they are having fun already. It is not at all easy for caregivers to feel good about their jobs while inflicting pain on a patient or performing procedures that patients fear and detest. It is not easy for food service workers to feel good about their jobs when they constantly hear complaints and jokes about "hospital food." Nor is it easy for nurses to feel good about their achievements and competencies when they are degraded by some physicians and made to feel that assessing a patient's condition is not their "place," even though they spend more time with the patients than do the physicians.

By contrast, however, few Disney employees probably realize the great moments of satisfaction experienced by health care professionals whose care and concern touch profound needs. Kind gestures mean infinitely more to persons in dire need of kindness and compassion than to those enjoying an afternoon at an amusement park. And a single expression of thanks from patients is perhaps all the more meaningful because they know their care made a difference in their lives.

Another reason why customer satisfaction is difficult to achieve is that we ignore the fact that quality service has a price. As an industry, we are becoming increasingly consumed with productivity and the notion that, to succeed in light of the prevailing cost reimbursement philosophy, we must do *more with less*.

It seems that we are not alone. In a recent *Time* magazine article entitled, "Why Is Service So Bad?," the authors noted: "The simple reason that service workers have so little attention to give is that businesses often overwork them, to save labor costs and keep prices low."[3]

To maximize productivity, many service companies have established productivity standards that force workers to speed up transactions. According to that article in *Time* magazine, "If a phone operator spends too much time with one customer, it spoils his or her average and standing on the job. Operators have been known to fake a disconnection when customers ask questions that are too complicated."[4] That action results from placing an employee in an untenable position when he or she is only trying to do a good job for the customer. And just as unrealistic productivity standards exist at the phone company, so do they exist in hospitals.

We cannot ignore the subtle indications of our service orientation or lack thereof. Customers are perceptive. I shall never forget the conversation I had on a plane with a man who was sharing his observations about the state of service in hospitals. He commented: "One thing that I have always found interesting is that, when I telephone IBM, Xerox, or Sears, they answer my telephone call right away. But when I call a hospital, the phone rings and rings and rings. Do you know what I interpret from that? IBM, Xerox, and Sears are interested in my business but the hospital couldn't care less." There was little I could say to change his perception.

Try this experiment. Call your hospital several times during the day and count the number of rings before the phone is answered. Repeat it five more times during the next 5 days. I hope that your experience is better than that of my plane companion. And I also hope that you will be able to hear clearly the name of your hospital when an operator answers and that you receive a simple "thank you" before the call is transferred.

When a patient calls for a nurse because he or she is in pain, it is no consolation to the patient that the nurse is smiling and friendly if the nurse appears 15 minutes later. Pain demands immediate relief. To be responsive to guests, we need to staff for service. I am not certain that industry leaders are ready to recognize that, despite their declining patient days and understandable fiscal struggles, human resources need to be allocated to achieve superior service. Yet without adequate levels of staffing and an appropriate mix of staffing, it is unlikely that the image of hospitals will improve, regardless of their commitment to service.

We must establish methods for measuring productivity that are realistic. It is easier to attain predetermined productivity levels when you are serving up telephone numbers or turning out widgets on a production line than when you are responding to the unpredictable and sometimes life-threatening needs of sick patients. Time and motion studies make little, if any, allowance for the extra measure of care and attention delivered along the way. Although there is admittedly a need to achieve productivity, caring does take time.

One trend that has, in some ways, enhanced the quality of care while at the same time diminishing the quality of service has been primary care nursing. Some argue that placing a registered nurse in charge of all of the patient's needs and clinical care has greatly enhanced quality—but has it necessarily done so from the patient's perspective? Registered nurses are paid higher wages than are licensed vocational nurses and aides. If you staff your units with fewer, more clinically qualified nurses but they are involved in time-consuming tasks that others are just as qualified to perform, you are not utilizing your resources optimally. Aides can provide backrubs to bedridden patients just as expertly as nurses can. If too few nurses are too busy administering medications and charting, they cannot always administer those special touches.

If a service motivation does not ultimately change the staffing mix on nursing units, the shortage of qualified nurses may. And herein lies another potential obstacle for our industry.

We face a severe shortage of qualified, caring professionals. Although Disney World is in the enviable position of receiving over 40,000 resumes a year, recruiters in some hospitals are frantically trying to identify qualified, able-bodied candidates. It is easier to follow a policy of "hiring the right people" when there are people to hire. Health care recruiters face the major challenge of hiring the right people with the right values, people who are humanistically and clinically (or technically) competent, from an increasingly limited pool of applicants.

How severe must the situation become before we realize that the shortages in nursing and allied health professions can be attributed, in some part, to the exodus of professionals who have simply found the demands too high and the pay too low? McDonald's, the fast-food chain, has turned to senior citizens to help solve their staffing problems. Hospitals do not have the benefit of such an approach.

The U.S. Department of Health and Human Services predicts that by the year 2000 there could be a shortage of 1.2 million nurses.[5] This trend is also affecting other allied health professions. These shortages threaten not only the quality of service, but also the quality of care.

Another obstacle to creating consumer satisfaction is the constraints placed on service delivery by rules and regulations. Rene McPherson, chairman of the Dana Corporation, threw out all of the policy and procedure manuals soon after he was hired. He reasoned that if values guide the decision making, rules and regulations are not needed.

Throw out your policies and procedure manuals as Mr. McPherson did and you'll probably lose your accreditation, to say nothing of compromising the safety and well-being of patients. Yet, it is a good idea to take a close, hard look at your policies and procedures. To serve whose best interests do they really exist?

If we were really honest with ourselves, we would probably see that many of our policies exist to serve our needs and not those of our customers. We do a good job of cloaking the rationale for a policy in terms of what is "good for the patient." For example, I wonder whether visitation rules were drafted to protect the patient or protect ourselves from the bothersome interruption of the patient's family and friends.

There are some legitimate reasons why we cannot cast away many of these rules, but a prevailing sense of conformity to rules that inhibit an employee's actions in behalf of the customer is potentially devastating for service. It is easier to allow your employees special latitude for individual decision making in behalf of customers when they are not regulated at every turn by policies and procedures.

Think of how many times you have heard these phrases—"I'm sorry, but it's hospital policy," "That's not my department," "That's not my job," "That was the evening shift," "I can't," "You can't"—and you will begin to understand just how powerless employees are made to feel when it comes to independent decision making.

Another reason why achieving service excellence is difficult is because we do not share our success. Although there are at least 800 for-profit hospitals in the United States, we are principally a not-for-profit industry. Therefore, we are, for the most part, restricted in what we can and cannot do to share financial success with employees. Profit-sharing and stock purchase plans are an option for relatively few hospitals.

Few of us would invest our money in a company's stock if there was not some potential for dividend payment and value appreciation. Few employees feel vested in the mission of a hospital if they cannot see how it will reward them. Even without shares and dividends, you can achieve a similar organizational mentality if you look for ways to share success. Remember that hospitals are not reluctant to ask people to share in the downside. When your employees are asked to work harder and to do more with less because your hospital is going through a difficult period of adjustment, they expect to be rewarded when it turns around. Lee Iacocca was only taking a salary of $1 a year when he asked his workers to make concessions. They made those, and together they turned the company around. But when Chrysler was back on its feet, management moved quickly to reinstate its salary increases and perks. The unions were disgruntled, and the workers felt betrayed when they discovered that their compensation was slow to increase.

When a hospital exchanges red ink for black, debt retirement often becomes a higher priority than wage increases, and employees are quick to draw conclusions about the administration's support of them. One Eastern hospital was beset by fires 2 years ago when, after laying off hundreds of employees, the lobby was redecorated before jobs were reinstated and employees received nominal pay increases. Perhaps employees would not have been so touchy if one of the employees laid off during the hard times had been the driver of the president's car.

One hospital in the West did a noble thing several years ago by rewarding employees for pulling together during a time of downsizing. Following a particularly encouraging report of earnings to the board, hospital executives negotiated with a large retail store to provide $35 to $50 gift certificates for each employee, based upon the number of hours worked. The gift certificates were mailed to the employees' homes with a letter thanking them for their support during a difficult year. The following day, the hospital was filled with employees who had received their gift certificates and were ecstatic. The program cost the hospital $120,000, no little amount in the aggregate, yet some were amazed to witness the powerful effect that this gift had on boosting morale.

A willingness to support employees with sound management, professional development, and rewards has a payoff. Few organizations have enjoyed the levels of tangible employee support that Delta Airlines has. Their employees voluntarily contributed funds to purchase a multi-million dollar airplane, which they presented to Delta management in 1985.

Delta has received its share of bad publicity lately, but my personal belief in and devotion to the airline have never faltered. In my opinion, an organization that treats its employees well—and whose employees have always treated me, their customer, very well—deserves my vote of confidence.

A sense of pride and ownership promotes the employees' investment of their time, energy, and commitment.

Few businesses have the customer equivalent of doctors. Actually, hospitals serve several target customer groups, each of which is somewhat dependent upon the other. The one who makes the purchase decision (physician) is not the one who consumes the service (patient) and is usually not the one who pays for it (payer). In terms of service and customer satisfaction, it is clearly difficult to be attentive to the needs of multiple groups. These needs compete when there are limited resources. Dealing with limited resources is familiar to the majority of corporate, governmental, academic, and charitable organization leaders, but with the possible exception of politicians who must keep multiple constituencies happy, few other leaders have quite as a demanding and politically charged job as that of a hospital executive.

It is especially difficult to keep physicians happy, primarily because they have power and can, to a great extent, control the distribution of business. Although this power is shifting away from the physician, their influence on your decision making must still be considered. Consider the following hypothetical situation. You have invested heavily in image advertising and guest relations. Your feedback indicates that you have improved many service dimensions and have enhanced your image. Yet, you find that one group has sluggish performance: your physicians. What are you going to do? Withdraw their admitting privileges until they participate in a guest relations program? Rather doubtful.

You exercise little control over the behavior of your physicians. If one of your employees continually displays inappropriate behavior that contradicts the culture you are trying to create, you can always suggest that he contribute his time and talents to the competing hospital across town. It is unlikely that you will want to suggest this alternative to a physician. No matter what the charter of your hospital is, physicians are your customers. They are also members of your service delivery team and are seen by employees as integral players who should not be excluded. It is also difficult for many patients to distinguish between physician provider and hospital provider as two separate entities.

In the new environment of health care, managing hospital/physician relationships poses major challenges to the hospital leadership team. They are complex relationships that few other service industries encounter.

ON THE HORIZON

If we can rise above the obstacles that are part of our way of doing business and can assume a more progressive and innovative stance in the ways in which we conceive, manage, and deliver service, the future holds great things. The industry has changed greatly in just one decade, although we still have a distance to go. Here are some predictions for the future.

- Market/consumer research will become increasingly important. As the marketing warfare has taught us, the battleground of competition is in the minds of customers. That terrain is tricky and difficult to negotiate. Market research will become increasingly important because of what it reveals about customers' attitudes, perceptions, needs, and expectations. Long-standing industrial market research techniques, such as focus groups, telephone interviews, and personal, face-to-face interviews, will be employed with greater intensity and frequency. As health care organizations become more knowledgeable about the demographic and psychographic characteristics of their targeted markets, they will package their services more precisely. Product and market segmentation will result in greater innovations in service delivery that will have a positive impact on the perception of service quality.

- Customer satisfaction feedback systems will be improved. As hospitals become more attentive to research, they will scrutinize their services more carefully to determine whether customer expectations have been met. Questionnaires will no longer simply be a ''nice thing to do'' or a ''public relations gimmick.'' More time and money will be spent designing questionnaires, distributing them in a way to achieve higher percentages of return, tracking satisfaction levels, and isolating problems to be addressed.

- Departments will be held accountable for customer satisfaction. Because every department in the hospital produces and delivers a service that has essential value to a primary customer group, customer satisfaction will be a measure of accountability in service performance. It will become a key component of departmental goals and objectives, as well as a criterion for a manager's compensation and bonus. Quantitative feedback from customers, whether these customers are patients, physicians, or other departments, will determine whether goals have been met.

- Departments within the hospital will view their services as ''product lines.'' The resulting decentralization will force managers to think of themselves as chief executive officers of their own companies. They will work harder to create their own service cultures within the context of the overall corporate culture, to solicit the cooperation of others on whom they rely to produce their final product, to motivate those who deliver it to be more responsive, to gain customer acceptance and satisfaction, and to generate profits in which they will share. Performance bonuses will be based on measures of service excellence.

- Employee commitment to service will be strengthened. Employees will learn that taking part in the organization's excellence effort is not a matter of personal preference; rather, that it is an explicit expectation of their roles. The department managers will make that obligation clear to their employees through job descriptions, performance reviews, and pay policies. Recruitment, orientation, education, and training will become powerful tools in promoting the desired behavioral traits. Service performance will trigger promotions, rewards, and recognition.

- Systems for delivery will be designed and redesigned for flexibility. Employees will be given the autonomy to exercise good judgment, to challenge rules, and to make decisions in the interest of their customers.

These predictions steer us in a new direction—toward service management. Service management is the strategic approach that will infuse staying power to consumer-directed organizational change. Service management is a structured, systematic approach for planning, organizing, and controlling the design, development, and delivery of a product and/or service that promotes superior consumer satisfaction and results for the organization. We have already come a long way—from patients to guests to customers. We are now moving from unidimensional training programs to comprehensive systems that will enable us to create and sustain service excellence. The past is prologue.

SUMMARY

In the past decade, the health care industry has endeavored to become more consumer-driven. Yet, it will continue to cope with unique challenges to achieving excellence in service delivery. Acknowledging that these challenges exist should cause you to be even more committed to achieving superior service and performance within the hospital setting. Do not necessarily minimize your expectations or compromise your visions. Becoming a customer-driven hospital will enable you to fulfill your mission and enhance your reputation as the quality provider in the marketplace. That is the position that can make all the difference.

NOTES

1. John Naisbitt, *Megatrends* (New York: Warner Books, 1982), 1.

2. Leah Curtin, "Courtesy: Rescuing Patients From the Me-Generation," *Nursing Management* (May 1986): 7–9.

3. Stephen Koepp, "Why Is Service So Bad?," *Time* (February 2, 1987): 51.

4. Ibid., 51.

5. Dan Richman, "Nursing: An Endangered Profession," *Modern Healthcare* (March 27, 1987): 33.

Chapter 3

Service Management: Aligning Strategies, Systems, and People

Virtually all of the developed nations are evolving from industrial economies to service economies. This evolution has led to an emerging focus on the new technologies that will be required of businesses that are service-focused rather than product-driven. In contrast to a product-oriented company in which decisions are motivated by product and manufacturing considerations, the service-oriented business begins with the market and lets it guide every decision and investment.

SERVICE CHARACTERISTICS

Service-focused businesses face special challenges. The product is intangible, and hence, the quality is highly variable because the value of the service depends on a customer's personal experience. Unlike products that are manufactured long before the customer purchases them, services are produced and consumed simultaneously. Unlike most products, which can be inspected after production for defects and failure to conform to quality standards, services cannot be centrally inspected or warehoused; nor can they be demonstrated before delivery. Measures to ensure quality must be implemented before delivery.

Other characteristics also distinguish businesses that are service-focused, particularly health care services, from product-driven businesses. Services cannot be returned for a refund. A hospital or physician may apply a credit to compensate for customer dissatisfaction; however, the service itself cannot be recalled or returned. As a result, the customer's final recourse for a defective service is often legal action.

Because service cannot be tested before delivery, customers tend to rely heavily on word-of-mouth advertising to assist them in decision making. In fact, some health care market research studies have demonstrated that word of mouth has more influence on hospital selection than all other forms of promotion. Even when patients cannot exercise discretionary choice because of immediate need or physician practice patterns, they nonetheless will form preferences for various hospitals based on what others tell them about their experiences.

In addition, service delivery requires human interaction. The larger the number of people with whom the customer must interact during the delivery of service, the less likely the customer will be satisfied. Although hospitals have stringent quality assurance standards, perceptions of quality vary, and service is variable because it is delivered by people whose performances cannot be consistently monitored or controlled.

Not only is the frequency of interaction high in a hospital but also no one person manages the patient's experience. The patient is, rather, dependent on the collective efforts of many departments and employees. Some come to the patient to deliver services. He or she goes to others to receive other services. There is no coordinated effort to see that the services are delivered effectively and efficiently from the patient's standpoint. No one person is responsible for the patient from the time he or she enters the hospital until the time of discharge.

However, service quality *can be* achieved in the minds of your customers when you manage the patient's experience from beginning to end. To do this, you must manage the moments of truth.

MOMENTS OF TRUTH

Jan Carlzon, president of Scandinavian Airlines Systems (SAS), captured the essence of managing service by adopting the concept of "moments of truth." A moment of truth, by his definition, was any instance when a customer came into contact with the organization and formed an impression—no matter how insignificant. If you isolate the people-to-people interactions that are encountered at a moderately sized airline, such as SAS, the numbers are staggering. In Carlzon's words:

> Last year, each of our 10 million customers came in contact with approximately five SAS employees, and this contact lasted an average of 15 seconds each time. Thus SAS is created in the minds of our customers, 50 million times a year, 15 seconds at a time. These 50 million "moments of truth" are the moments that ultimately determine whether SAS will succeed or fail as a company.[1]

Think of the moments of truth in your health care organization. First, you are managing many more moments of truth than is SAS. A patient's average length of stay is 7-11 days. Compare this with a guest's length of stay in a hotel or the degree to which a passenger is exposed to airline employees, whether in an airport or in the air. Many of your employees are not interacting in 15-second increments of time; it is more likely that their interactions are in 15-minute increments.

When customers confront your organization, they come into contact with your physical facilities and your systems as well. Moments of truth are also formed when:

- A visitor enters your public restroom and finds that it is dirty.
- The phone rings 15 times before it is answered.
- A patient is wheeled down to physical therapy at excessive rates of speed.
- A visitor cannot find a parking space.
- The meal ordered by the patient is not what is received on the tray.
- A guest waits for over an hour to be registered for an outpatient procedure.
- A patient receives the bill!

Whenever an organization performs a service for a customer, that customer makes both conscious and unconscious assessments of service quality. The sum total of these assessments creates an image of the organization's overall service quality. The secret to success is to manage the moments of truth. If you allow that basic message to permeate your organization, you will soon find that employees, managers, and executives alike will begin to think differently about their roles. They will not be as focused on the tasks within the very limited scope of their job—rather, they will view themselves as having multidimensional roles and responsibilities that revolve around creating positive impressions and experiences for their customers.

THE SCANDINAVIAN EXPERIENCE

Reorienting employees and restructuring the organization were two primary needs that Jan Carlzon felt he had to address when he took over the helm at Scandinavian Airlines Systems (SAS). Recruited to SAS when the airline was suffering an $8 million operating loss, Carlzon initiated an energetic campaign of creative business strategies to change company attitudes.

To accomplish this turnaround, Carlzon turned the organization upside down. He restructured the organization by inverting the traditional pyramid. In doing so, the organization began to respond differently to situations and to people.

The prototypical corporate structure resembles a layered pyramid; those at the top make decisions, and those at several intermediate levels communicate those decisions to the front-line employees. Although it is these lower-level employees who know the most about front-line operations, they are relatively powerless within the organization. They carry out management's decisions, but they are not given much opportunity to be involved in formulating new policy or much authority to respond to individual situations as they arise; nor do the decision makers seek them out and ask for their ideas and advice.

Carlzon believed that the pyramid was a defective structure on which to rely for carrying out the airline's mission. Therefore, he reinvented the corporation and distributed the roles in a radically different manner. He decentralized the operation and delegated responsibility for creating customer satisfaction to those who were close to the customers. Middle managers became responsible for analyzing problems, managing resources, and supporting the needs of front-line employees. Authority to respond to the needs and problems of individual customers was given to the employees. In terms of managing the "moments of truth," this reallocation of responsibility was the only way that Carlzon could envision success.[2]

Eliminating the hierarchical structure produced astounding results. By defining clear goals and priorities and communicating them to his employees, Carlzon created a working environment that fostered flexibility and innovation. The front-line employees' efforts were imbued with greater value and purpose within the company. All the employees received special training on how to provide service. They were encouraged to act in behalf of the customer and to take initiatives that would improve the quality of the customer's experience.

At SAS, Carlzon pioneered new strategies and systems to create superior service and performance. He not only restructured the organization but he also changed the ways in which the airline's services were conceived, developed, and delivered. His broad-based approach to make the airline more pleasing to customers included:[3]

- increasing investment $45 million and operating expenses $12 million in the face of a $20 million loss the preceding year
- initiating more direct flights and closing some hub flights
- convincing Boeing to build a "people pleasing" airliner to be available in the 1990s
- empowering front-line employees with the authority to solve most customer problems without management approval or robotic policies
- reallocating resources to achieve a new, "flatter" organization, which was closer to the customer in all respects
- making the airline the most punctual in the industry
- modifying all support systems and facilities to be "customer friendly," by redesigning them from the customer's perspective
- requiring all 20,000 employees to participate in an intensive two-day training program so that all changes and redefined roles could be fully included for implementation

In just 2 years, his organization achieved a gross profit of $71 million on sales of $2 billion. This was done at a time when the entire airline industry was losing a total of $1.7 billion.

With the dismal prediction that over 1,000 hospitals will close their doors within the next decade, those who wish to survive should heed the call to become more service-driven and customer-oriented.

SERVICE MANAGEMENT

Service management has as its foundation many of the concepts, principles, and theories that were used by Jan Carlzon when he confronted the threat to the survival and prosperity of SAS.

The future is promising for those who are bold and willing to sift through the changes and re-evaluate their priorities and values. The challenge is to take hold of the internal culture and to place a premium on innovation, service, and people— both those who produce the service and those who avail themselves of it.

To manage service delivery successfully, health care organizations must have these elements:

- Strategies that make quality service and customer satisfaction the highest priorities in creating, managing, and delivering services.
- A decision-making and implementation process designed to determine what business the hospital and each of its service delivery departments are in; this is known as a business mission. Once the hospital managers have defined their business, they must analyze their service(s) to determine what components are most desirable and attractive to customers. Next, they must decide how the service(s) they offer will meet the needs and exceed the expectations of customers. Finally, to achieve the intended results, managers will need to define the values that will transform the internal culture to be more service-oriented and customer-driven.
- Values that demonstrate a strong commitment to employee satisfaction, as well as customer satisfaction; the key to success is to regard the employee's satisfaction, well-being, and fulfillment as primary, not secondary, to customer satisfaction.
- Methods to analyze the service delivery systems to ensure more efficient and customer-oriented services; systems must allow service to be provided easily and quickly. Policies and procedures should be conceived for the ease of the customer, rather than the ease of the organization, and employees must be given a latitude that enables them to make decisions in behalf of the customers.

- Feedback systems that enable the hospital to know if it is meeting customers' needs and expectations and that give it the ability to act decisively and quickly to analyze, solve, and prevent sources of recurring dissatisfaction.
- Efforts that are extended by each department manager to recruit, motivate, and reward employees to achieve more effective service delivery performances; these efforts must be aimed at making the personal interactions between the hospital, its employees, and the customers conducive to achieving satisfaction. They must also be aimed at producing and maintaining a motivated and satisfied staff that vigorously contributes to service excellence.

Just as Jan Carlzon championed the cause of service management for SAS, leaders who can define and communicate the visions and goals for the organization and ignite a radical change in the culture of the hospital are needed. It is not essential that these leaders be charismatic in terms of their personal style and personality. Rather, it is essential that they be totally committed to achieving their visions. They can no longer be content to sit back and simply respond to the changes. They instead must grasp ahold of the situation and begin to chart new directions. As futurist Leland Kaiser has said, "Tomorrow's winning organizations will be the ones that can think in the biggest terms and imagine the greatest possibilities."[4] The key to success is not adaptation, but invention.

THE SERVICE TRIANGLE

The principles of service management have been practiced to varying degrees by many service businesses, but the concept as a business strategy for transforming an organization was brought into focus by Karl Albrecht and Ron Zemke in their book, *Service America! Doing Business in the New Economy.*[5] Much of their work was based on the SAS experience.

In their book, the authors illustrate the key elements of quality service and their interrelationships in the service triangle shown in Figure 3-1. At the top of the triangle is the service strategy which embraces the culture of the organization. If customer satisfaction is a core value, executives can work to integrate it into the marrow of the organization by establishing a strategic plan that is customer-focused.

The left side of the triangle portrays the systems that are constructed to deliver the service to the customer and to manage the internal operations and resources of the hospital.

The right side of the triangle represents the people who perform the services. It includes not only front-line employees but also the support staff who may or may not have contact directly with the customer and the management staff who oversee

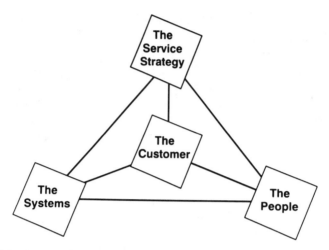

Figure 3-1 Service Triangle. *Source:* © 1984 Karl Albrecht. Reprinted by permission.

the entire service operation. It also includes the physicians, who are also represented at the center of the triangle.

At the center of the triangle is found the most important element in the model: the customer. Its position at the center of the triangle indicates that the strategies, systems, and people must be focused on the customer's needs and expectations.

The connecting lines of the service triangle indicate that there is interplay among the four elements. Systems have to support employees, as well as the customer. The service strategy must be clear to the employees, who must work well within the system and with the customer. The strategy must incorporate not only the customers' needs but also the employees' and the systems' needs.

To manage service successfully, organizations must follow three basic rules:

1. Communicate a clear vision about the concept of service. This service concept directs the attention of the employees in the company toward the priorities of the customer, and influences all that the people in the organization accomplish. It becomes the message that is transmitted to the customer. In every transaction, service-driven organizations relay this important concept, and customers who interact with them feel the difference. They feel understood as customers. They receive the distinct message that the company and its people understand not only their basic needs but also their expectations of service.

2. Design the delivery system for the convenience of the customer, rather than for the convenience of the organization. The systems must *assist*, rather than *insist*. The physical facilities, policies, procedures, methods, and commu-

nication processes all say to the customer: "The system is here to meet your needs."
3. Hire and develop customer-oriented employees. Excellent service organizations provide incentives to create customer satisfaction and recognize and reward those individuals who contribute to this goal. They provide training and support to help people who deliver services. They do not tolerate those employees whose attitudes and actions run counter to what the organization is trying to achieve.

WHAT ABOUT GUEST RELATIONS?

In reality, a strategic, systems-oriented guest relations program is a service management program. It is for this reason that the terms "guest relations" and "service management" will be used interchangeably throughout the remainder of the book. If you think of guest relations as a multidimensional approach to managing the delivery of quality service that is geared to meeting the needs and expectations of the customers, you should have no problem understanding the synonymous meanings. If you think of a guest relations program as a training program designed to achieve a more customer-responsive, caring, and courteous staff, you will not understand the interchangeability. Guest relations is essentially the internal marketing strategy that complements the external marketing strategy. When broadly defined and competently executed, guest relations is service management.

SUMMARY

The goal of service management is to create exceptional satisfaction among both external customers and internal providers. Service management requires communication of vision and values, fluid and flexible delivery systems, and responsive employees who will work toward the organization's goals.

Through a coordinated program of service management, hospitals are better able to meet the needs and exceed the expectations of customers—creating moments of truth that are magic, rather than mediocre.

NOTES

1. Jan Carlzon, *Moments of Truth* (Cambridge, Mass.: Ballinger Publishing Company, 1987), 3.
2. Ibid, 3.

3. Karl Albrecht and Edwin T. Crego, Jr., "What Every Customer Wants," *Perspective*, 13, no. 2: 3-5, 31–32.

4. Leland Kaiser, "Organizational Mindset," *Healthcare Forum* (March/April 1986): 7, 8, 10.

5. Karl Albrecht and Ron Zemke, *Service America! Doing Business in the New Economy* (Homewood, Il.: Dow Jones-Irwin, 1985), 41.

Chapter 4

Customer Expectations: The Baseline Measure

Years ago, syndicated columnist Bob Greene published a short essay entitled, "Why Must a Jerk Always Be Right?" He began his column by stating: "For years, a basic tenet of business has been 'the customer is always right.' What that means is that even when merchants disagree with a customer's complaints, it is good business to go along with the customer and try to rectify the situation." He went on to share his observation of an unruly, inconsiderate, and downright rude passenger on a commercial airplane. The flight attendant was impressively polite and responded with restraint. Greene concluded that perhaps it would be healthier for businesses and for other customers if companies adopted a different slogan: "Sometimes the customer is a total jerk. When he is, we don't want his business. We don't even want him around here."[1]

This is a rather irreverent way to introduce this chapter. After all, without customers a business would not exist, much less survive. Yet, Greene's observations and conclusions will strike a chord in those who, on a daily basis, experience the ecstasy and agony of working with the public. Their jobs have a multitude of rewards and a share of intense frustrations.

Any service business has customers who are frequently unreasonable, occasionally obnoxious, and seldom satisfied. Obsession, however, is all consuming. If you are to be truly obsessed with the customer and with achieving the customer's satisfaction, exceptions are not allowed. To suggest that any customer is any less deserving of an employee's best effort minimizes the "customer first" value.

One hundred percent satisfaction should be the goal. To set that goal at any less than 100 percent would mean that you tolerate a measure of dissatisfaction. As expressed appropriately in an IBM advertisement: "If your failure rate is one in a million, what do you tell that millionth customer?"

You might shrug it off and console yourself by reasoning, "The customer was a jerk." But do not go around shouting "The customer is king" from the rooftops if you turn around and dethrone him when *you* have not been successful in meeting *his* expectations.

Customers are not always right. Sometimes they are dead wrong. Their perceptions or expectations are very real to them, however. They think they are right; therefore, they are right. The situation cannot be changed; the perceptions and expectations can be.

Customer expectations are highly variable and unpredictable, yet they are integral to the resulting levels of satisfaction that the customer experiences. Customer satisfaction typically involves two factors: preconsumption expectations and postconsumption perceptions of the degree to which the service(s) met and exceeded those expectations. Deviation in performance from expectations results in two outcomes: positive satisfaction when expectations are exceeded and dissatisfaction when expectations are not met.

When expectations are met, no one notices. If customers expect employees to be courteous and they are, the fact is accepted. If patients expect a hospital to be clean, and it is, that is accepted as standard. It is only when expectations are not met—or when they are exceeded—that customers notice. What are the primary expectations of your customers?

DEFINING YOUR CUSTOMERS

Before answering that question, it is important to define just who your customers are. In the broadest sense of the word, customers are those persons who either currently use your product or who may be in the market for your product in the future. Defined this way, hospitals have many customers, ranging from physicians to patients, family members, visitors, volunteers, payers, and even vendors. Anyone who is in a position to learn about or observe your service and, thus, to contemplate using your hospital if he or she requires medical care should be identified as a potential customer.

In addition, within the internal hospital structure, departments are customers of other departments. Housekeeping employees are dependent upon the linen department to deliver sheets and towels to the floors in a timely manner so that rooms can be ready when patients are admitted. The billing department staff is dependent upon the unit clerks to make entries into the computer so that bills can be issued quickly and accurately, even before the patient is ready to go home. Radiology personnel are dependent upon outpatient registration clerks to check patients in quickly, so that schedules can be maintained and patients are not kept waiting.

Every department produces and delivers a service (or an array of services) that is of value to a primary customer group. Departments have three *primary* customers: patients, physicians, and other departments. The primary customers of the operating room are the physicians. Although it is true that surgical nurses perform services that benefit patients, their most direct customers are the physicians. The primary customers of the emergency department are patients. The primary customers of the materiel management department are other departments. (The primary customers of the business office are the payers. That constitutes an exception to the three customer groups listed above. There are other isolated instances in which similar exceptions can be made, but for the most part, each department can identify one of these three customer groups as its primary user.)

Every department serves the end user—the patient. If employees are not serving the patient directly, they are serving someone who is.

Customer groups can be segmented in numerous ways, one of which is by characteristics of the predominant users. For example, some units serve diagnostic segments. The customers of those who work in maternity units are women who are, on average, between the ages of 18 and 35. These customers can be characterized as having different expectations than customers of gerontology units who are older, less ambulatory, and hold more traditional values. This distinction is important when you consider that the values held by the customer influence his or her expectations. The patient on a maternity unit may not be at all surprised to find that nurses wear pastel-colored uniforms, whereas the older patient becomes aggravated because the nurses no longer wear caps.

Researchers will often use what is called psychographic research to identify basic motivations that underlie human behavior. They can identify what values are important to a person that may influence his or her behavior. For example, convenience may be of great importance to someone who is managing the demands of a career and family. A service that is more convenient, albeit more expensive, may be what that person buys.

In segmenting your customer populations and conducting research to identify what characteristics of service they value, you can more strategically design the service package to conform to needs and expectations. What is important to one group may not be as important to another. Scandinavian Airline Systems targeted the business travelers and invested in services and developed standards that were vastly different from what they would have been if vacation travelers had been targeted. People Express, by contrast, floundered when it tried to capture two widely differing market segments with essentially the same service. The airline's famous No Frills strategy was what budget travelers sought. Operating revenues soared from $139 million to $978 million in 1985. When People Express tried to appeal to business travelers with its No Frills strategy, it failed. In 1986, Texas Air picked up the troubled airline.[2]

EXPECTATIONS ARE KEY

One goal of service management is to deliver services that will *exceed* the customer's expectations. For the most part, this is challenging to do because his or her expectations are high for several reasons:

- Patients, for the most part, are inexperienced in their role and do not know what to expect. They are invited into a foreign world and expected to assimilate their environment quickly. Because of their relative lack of experience, they formulate assumptions that may be unrealistic. Often, the hospital does little to help them shape expectations, and as a result, they develop unrealistic expectations that are more difficult to meet.
- The cost of medical care has created a public mindset, ''If it costs this much, it had better be good.''
- The media portrayal of medical care and facilities—the Marcus Welby syndrome—has shaped expectations (if not demands) for instant restoration to full and complete function.
- Moreover, a long-standing perception persists that a hospital's sole mission is to be benevolent, charitable, and personally attentive. To these expectations are added the natural tendencies of sick people to perceive that theirs are the only relevant problems and that, regardless of other circumstances, they are entitled to immediate, personalized attention.

What are patients' most basic expectations of your hospital? First and foremost, the patient expects that you will deliver competent, quality medical care. Because the patient does not possess the needed information to evaluate whether you indeed provide quality care, it is important to look deeper at those expectations of service that will influence his or her perception of quality.

The patient uses three primary dimensions to evaluate the quality of service: information, courtesy, and responsiveness. Other factors, such as the taste and temperature of food, the cleanliness of the room, and the appearance of the surrounding facilities, will also influence the overall perception, but these three characteristics override other less significant factors.

Information

A high correlation exists between the degree of predictability of time and events and the degree of satisfaction that will be experienced. When you help the patient determine realistic expectations and thereby enable him or her to predict more accurately what will take place, the level of satisfaction experienced is increased. Ideally, the process of shaping expectations should begin before the patient's arrival and continue after discharge. Once he or she has arrived, everyone in the hospital should then assume some role in defining and clarifying expectations for the patient and family members. Physicians should offer explanations of diagnoses, treatment modalities, and outcomes. Employees should state the purpose of their visit to the patient's room, explain procedures, and offer information that will help the patient anticipate what is likely to occur.

This process of shaping expectations is supposed to take place, but often it does not. The repetitive disclosure of important information becomes so routine that many employees hurry through it. Then they conclude their cursory explanation with a nonverbal expression that conveys the message: "You *don't* have any questions, *do you*?" Although nurses and other employees are instructed to explain routine information to the newly admitted patient, there are few controls to ensure that they do so in an effective manner that will assure consistency.

The only way to achieve quality control on the clarity and content of information is to standardize the message and broadcast it over media that can be controlled. The patient handbook has become the most common method of disseminating this information, but it is still an imperfect one because there are no assurances that the patient will read the handbook. You cannot guarantee a patient's comprehension any more than you can force someone to listen if he or she is unwilling to do so. However, you can increase the probability that the message will be understood if you stimulate several of the intended receiver's senses in the process. For this reason, it is advantageous to support verbal messages with written material and written material with verbal communication.

One of the best ways to do so is to routinely educate patients from the beginning of their stay in the hospital. By producing an educational videotape to be broadcast over a closed-circuit television channel, you can ensure that all patients will receive the same information and that it is presented in such a way as to shape more realistic expectations.

Anticipating needs and providing information can help increase the levels of satisfaction experienced by patients.

Courtesy

The expectation of being treated with courtesy and respect is not one held solely by patients. Everyone has a basic need to be respected, held in esteem, and treated with consideration. When individuals are hospitalized, however, their increased vulnerability causes their need for courtesy and respect to be more pronounced.

The attitude of employees and the care and courtesy they demonstrate in their actions are viewed as essential elements of quality care. In one study, 4,000 consumers, 1,600 physicians, and 1,600 employers were interviewed. Of the attributes associated with high-quality care, patient relations and employees' caring attitudes were mentioned by 52 percent of the consumers. Some 64 percent of employers cited patient relations and employees' caring attitudes as an important attribute of quality. Physicians identified these factors 39 percent of the time.[3]

Caring attitudes are most often demonstrated by courteous expressions. In the minds of many patients, ''high touch'' characteristics of care are just as important as the ''high tech'' capabilities when it comes to defining quality. Quality of interaction is a dimension used frequently to evaluate a hospitalization experience.

Responsiveness

One of the most flagrant violations of this basic expectation of responsiveness occurs when patients cool their heels (literally)—barely clothed—for long periods of time waiting on gurneys or exam tables for procedures to begin. It happens over and over again. The service delivery system breaks down, and patients encounter unnecessary and prolonged delays that are graphic indications that the hospital's systems are not designed to meet the basic expectations of customers.

It is not unrealistic for patients to expect that their needs will be responded to within a reasonable amount of time while they are hospitalized. Yet, breakdowns do occur, and it is therefore necessary to help patients understand why the delay has occurred and what they can expect. Almost every patient believes that response to *his* or *her* needs should be the employees' first concern; it is difficult to explain that the employees have other demands that may compete with the patient's need for immediate attention. Although patients will never have an easy time understanding or tolerating delay, you are more likely to extend their thresholds of tolerance if you are responsive in providing information. From the time of admission, let them know that you will do everything you can to respond promptly but that delays do sometimes occur.

Research has shown that intangible benefits result from attempts to keep patients informed. A patient's willingness to return to a particular emergency room is more strongly related to being kept informed than to the absence of irritating delays. In one specific example, 40 percent of patients said that they had waited more than 30 minutes to be seen, but 90 percent said they would return to that emergency room. The reason: two-thirds of the patients felt that they were kept informed while waiting for treatment.[4]

Responsiveness is also one criterion that affects repeat purchase probability when a customer has a complaint. For health care providers this probability is difficult to quantify because health care services offered by hospitals are not designed for consumption at will. Nonetheless, research done by TARP to correlate market behavior with complaint handling reveals interesting conclusions that illustrate how responsiveness can affect satisfaction. TARP found:[5]

- Those who complain are ultimately more loyal than those who do not complain.

- Those who complain but are dissatisfied with the response are ultimately more loyal than those who do not complain.
- Those who complain and are satisfied with the response are ultimately more loyal than those who complain but receive a dissatisfactory response.
- Those who complain and receive a satisfactory response *quickly* are more loyal than those who complain and receive a satisfactory response.

Specifically, TARP found that 37 percent of customers with major complaints (over $100 losses) who did not complain would purchase from the company again. If the customer complained, even though the problem was not resolved, the probability of repurchase increased to 46 percent. Seventy percent of those who complained and whose complaint was resolved to their satisfaction would purchase again. The most astonishing result of the research was the discovery that the probability of repeat purchase jumped to 95 percent if the complaint was resolved *quickly*. Thus, responsiveness is a key dimension that shapes satisfaction.

Although this discussion of expectations has centered around the patient, one can assume that other customer groups hold similar expectations. Physicians want to be treated with courtesy and respect. Departments expect responsive performance from the other departments on which they depend. Employees want to be informed about what is going on.

EMPLOYEES AS CUSTOMERS

In one of Disney's management handbooks is found a simple statement: "We fully believe that our guests will only receive the quality of treatment and have the experience we want them to have when the members of our cast (employees) receive the same quality of care and attention from the management of this organization."[6]

Disney's statement suggests that an organization should view its employees as customers. Those who are willing to do so realize that the organization exists to serve the needs of those who are serving the customers. Many of the supportive and caring initiatives that employees are encouraged to display in their interactions with customers are similar to those that managers should extend to their employees. Those who are devoted to creating and maintaining a motivated and satisfied staff who vigorously contribute to service excellence must treat employees as they expect them to treat customers.

ARE CUSTOMERS SATISFIED?

When the Conference Board, a national research firm, asked consumers to look at 19 services they purchase and indicate those that gave them their money's worth, only two were cited: electricity and airfare. What is even more revealing is how consumers clustered those services and products from which they did not receive a fair dollar's return. Doctor's fees, dentist's fees, health insurance, hospital charges, and used cars were all lumped together![7] Although consumers may be dissatisfied with the high costs of health care and the perceived *value* of the services, one would hope that the industry's image and the health care consumer's trust have not fallen so low as to be compared with used car dealers!

Actually, other more encouraging studies indicate that consumer satisfaction is on the rise. The decreasing number of "not satisfied" responses from patients in recent studies suggests that the growing emphasis on customer satisfaction and guest relations has had an impact. These findings below were derived from recent research that compared annual increases and decreases in patient satisfaction.[8]

- *Nursing care:* Nearly 81 percent of respondents were "very satisfied" with the nursing care they received, as compared with 73.4 percent the year before. Fewer than 4 percent of respondents said they were not satisfied.

- *Physicians:* Physicians are becoming more attuned to patients' needs. A total of 82.4 percent of the respondents were very satisfied with their treatment by physicians. Only 4.6 percent were not.

- *Attitudes of employees:* The number of patients who were "very satisfied" with the attitudes of hospital employees grew over 1 year's time from 77.7 percent to 79.8 percent. Only 1 percent of the respondents said they were not satisfied.

- *Billing procedures:* There is still much room for improvement, but overall satisfaction with billing procedures has increased. A 5.8 percent climb in satisfaction levels over the year before was reported, with 68.6 percent of patients indicating that they were satisfied.

- *Food:* Satisfaction with food quality lags behind, and yet this is the area that has shown the greatest improvement, with 54.7 percent very satisfied—up from 45.6 percent the year before.

- *Room:* Hospitals in the western part of the United States appear to have the greatest eye for design. These hospitals experienced an overwhelming 92.7 percent satisfaction rating from patients, as contrasted with the national standard of 82 percent.

Although satisfaction on every dimension is improving, some patients still remain displeased. What specific reasons are cited by dissatisfied patients?

Those who commented on nursing care cited the following factors: discourteous nurses (35.7 percent), not enough nursing personnel (20 percent), lack of prompt response (25.6 percent), and lack of personalized care (9.1 percent).

Dissatisfaction with attitudes of hospital staff was caused primarily by discourteousness (66.8 percent) and lack of explanations (12.5 percent).

The quality of food was determined to be poor when it had no taste (49 percent), the choices were limited (25.6 percent), and it was poorly prepared (25.3 percent).

Billing procedures could be improved if patients could better understand their statements (24.3 percent). Also cited as contributing to dissatisfaction with billing procedures were high charges (23.4 percent), incorrect information (22 percent), and collection procedures (13.6 percent).

Finally, the appearance of the room was rated to be unsatisfactory when the furniture was old and worn (28.5 percent); the decor was not cheerful (15.8 percent); there was no privacy (7.9 percent); and the room was dirty (29.8 percent), crowded (6.4 percent), noisy (6.4 percent), and too small (5.2 percent).

SUMMARY

A commitment to quality starts with the customer. Hospitals and other health care organizations that want to succeed in service delivery must be aware of and responsive to the needs and expectations of patients and their family members, physicians, payers, and employees. Indifference will drive customers to seek other service providers who will satisfy their expectations. There is no better example of this phenomenon than in Detroit, where for years American automotive manufacturers ignored marketplace needs. The recent success of several American-made car models is due in great part to a revision of the product design process. An integrative approach that considered the needs of the user, as well as those of manufacturing, assembly, and service caused a shift from a superficial approach to styling to an in-depth design that focused on the driver and passengers.

It is only through understanding your customers' needs and expectations that you will be able to design and deliver services that ultimately will result in satisfaction.

NOTES

1. Bob Greene, "Why Must a Jerk Always Be Right?" *Chicago Tribune,* 13 March, 1984.

2. Bro Uttal, "Companies That Serve You Best," *Fortune* (December 7, 1987): 112–113.

3. Michael D. Hays, "Consumers Base Quality Perceptions on Patient Relations, Staff Qualifications," *Modern Healthcare,* (February 27, 1987): 33.

4. Lynn Cunningham and Karen Ross, "Aggressive Hospitality," *Southern Hospitals* (January/February 1986): 30–32.

5. "Customers Mean Business. . . . Surveys Show You Have More Dissatisfied Customers Than You Think," (Washington, D.C.: Direct Selling Education Foundation, 1982).

6. Ron Zemke, "The Service Challenge, Executive Forum 1987." (Speech delivered to the American College of Healthcare Executives, Chicago, Il., February 1987).

7. Ibid.

8. Suzanne Powills, "Marketing: Consumer Gripes About Hospital Services Drop," *Hospitals* (April 5, 1986): 60.

Chapter 5

Service Strategy: Transforming Vision into Action

The patient is greeted on admission by a clerk wearing a "We Care" button, but must wait in an uncomfortable area for more than an hour before being taken to her room. She arrives in her room and reads the message from the CEO that is featured inside the patient booklet. In essence, the message says, "You are our guest and we are committed to making your experience as comfortable as possible." Yet, the room is dark and stark, with its only amenity being an out-of-tune television for which she pays extra. She notices a questionnaire resting on the bedside table that states, "Your opinion is important to us." Yet no one comes by to say, "How are you doing?", "How are we doing?", or "May I do anything to make you more comfortable?" She acts on the suggestion printed on a tent card and calls the noted telephone extension to report an upsetting problem. A recorded message informs her, "Your call is important to us. The department is closed. Please leave a message and I will call you in the morning."

At this point, the moments of truth have invalidated the message that the hospital tried so hard to convey. Cognitive dissonance—the conflict between what is said and what is observed or experienced—occurs when a patient who has been influenced by the promotional message, "We Care," actually confronts the hospital's systems and its people to discover that those are empty words.

When a hospital does not deliver on its promise or intent, it is usually a sign that it has a weak service strategy. The hospital may have done everything "by the book" when it implemented the guest relations program. That program has little worth, however, if the hospital does not have a plan to overcome the obstacles that stand in the way of customer satisfaction.

Your hospital's image is the perception in the customer's mind of the way you do business. This needs to be a managed perception. The message to be conveyed is that all attentions and energies are devoted to delivering quality care and superior service.

Now compare the above example with a different scenario, thinking, in the process, of the implied or real promises you make to your patients. Start with the same patient, the same "We Care" buttons, the same messages in booklets and on questionnaires. This time, however, the admission process is swift, comfortable, and personable. The assigned room is well decorated with interesting art. A radio and television are provided free of charge, comfortable seating is available for visitors, and the hospital's patient representative stops by to introduce herself. She leaves information with the patient about how to get in touch with someone, 24 hours a day, to make a request or report a problem.

In the latter example, the professed value is validated by the environment, the services, the systems, and the expressed attitude of the employee. There is evidence that a strong service strategy is in place.

DEVELOPING THE SERVICE STRATEGY

To create an environment in which service is distinctive and visible—an environment in which you can honestly lay claim to your messages—you need a service strategy. Such a strategy is a formula for delivering service keyed to a benefit premise. This premise says to the marketplace: "This is what we are, this is what we believe, and this is what we do."

Given today's increased competitiveness, the first step in developing a service strategy must be to acquire a customer orientation. From this vantage point, you can look at your hospital and the services you provide in a different light.

The service strategy is tied to the overall mission of the hospital. If you have ever participated in a strategic planning process, you know that drafting a mission statement can be a painstaking process. Although the end result may be a few simple sentences, an organization must first thoughtfully explore the following issues:

- What business are we in?
- What business should we be in?
- Who are our customers?
- Who should our customers be?
- What do/will our customers want and expect?
- How do we want our customers to know us?
- How will we achieve our goals?

What Business Are We In?

Effective strategies start with a clear business definition, one that is stated in terms of results produced for customers.

Herb Dorsett, president of Southwest Florida Regional Medical Center in Fort Meyers, Florida, once responded to the question, "What business are you in?" by saying simply, "We are in the business of sending people home."

His statement captured the essence of what patients want and expect from the services that a hospital provides. When employees understand that that is the business they are in, there is real cause for celebration every time a patient is discharged.

Is SAS in the airline business? Jan Carlzon did not think so. He decided that SAS was in the business of transporting people from one place to another in the safest and most efficient way possible. He believed that if you are oriented toward your customers, you view your business as providing them with a service, in addition to the "hardware" itself.[1]

You may be in the hospital business and provide health care services, but are you not also in the business of *caring* for patients so that you can ultimately send them home? Which of these two definitions gives you a greater sense of the mission and purpose of your business?

Adopting a mission statement that is consumer oriented will create new role dimensions for the employees of the hospital and of individual departments. Maintenance engineers provide comfort, housekeepers reduce the risk of infection, dietary employees satisfy one of the most basic care needs in providing nutrition, and medical records clerks manage important information. These roles are quite different from calibrating thermostats, scrubbing walls, serving food, and transcribing dictation.

In defining your business purpose, do not ignore other customers. Your business purpose is also influenced by other customers' needs and what they expect you to provide. Physicians also want to send patients home, and the hospital can extend its efforts and energies to make sure that physicians are supported in achieving that goal. Employers want to manage benefit costs and reduce losses that result when employees are not able to work because of illness and hospitalization. In this sense, hospitals are not only in the business of sending patients home but in sending patients back to work.

Theodore Levitt, one of the most respected experts in the field of service marketing and management, stated in his book, *The Marketing Imagination,* that the purpose of any business is to "get and keep customers."[2] This is true of a hospital business, although few hospitals want to keep patients longer than they have to! Certainly physicians are important customers whose loyalties hospitals want to retain. Relationships with third party payers and contractual arrangements with other entities that feed business to the hospital must also be invited and managed for a hospital to achieve its goals.

Defining what business you are in may be a more protracted exercise than simply coming up with general statements, such as the ones mentioned in this section. Challenge yourself and those around you to think of your business in terms of the benefits your customers receive when they select you as their provider. That perspective will keep you on the right track.

Who Are Our Customers?

As was discussed in the previous chapter, your customers will be identified differently depending on your vantage point. If you are a hospital administrator, you will probably identify physicians, patients, payers, and employers as your primary customers. Employees and volunteers may also be included in that definition.

If you are a department manager, you will identify your primary customers as patients, physicians, and/or other departments. Depending on which departments you represent, you may also include family members, insurers, emergency medical technicians, physicians' employees, nursing home administrators, and others as secondary customers.

It is important to identify who your primary customers are so that you can then ask the next question: What do these customers expect?

What Do Customers Want and Expect?

It is essential to understand your customers' needs, wants, and expectations. How you think your customers perceive your hospital and how they really perceive it can be very different. What you think your customers want and what they actually desire can be very different as well.

Years ago, successful marketing-driven organizations discovered that they could no longer design products solely on the hope that people would buy them. That is when they turned to insightful, customer-focused market research. Although market research can be expensive, it is also very costly to try to guess what people want and what they will pay for. If you do not adapt to the needs of your customers, they will not be satisfied. Patients and physicians, in particular, are very self-centered because they have their own needs to fulfill. They are not concerned with the day-to-day problems of running the business. They want basic things: quality, value, and service.

Hospitals that have introduced product lines have already learned how valuable consumer preference research can be in designing their service products. Determining what patients or physicians expect and what characteristics or elements of service will exceed their expectations is very useful in packaging services to respond to customers' stated preferences. This point can be illustrated by the number of hospitals that have designed birthing rooms, relaxed policies on child visitation, encouraged families to participate at the birth, employed midwives, instituted special dinners, and introduced numerous other customer-satisfying procedures and amenities for obstetrical patients.

The Keckley Group in Nashville, Tennessee, has documented, through research, other elements of care that are important to obstetrical patients. Their findings provide clues as to how employees can approach, care for, and interact with these patients and their immediate family members:[3]

- policies and procedures allowing the husband to be involved in the delivery
- a room that allows plenty of rest after delivery
- a physician willing to answer questions about the condition of the baby
- amenities for family members during the predelivery waiting period
- a conscientious effort on the part of physicians and nurses to preserve the dignity of the mother during labor and delivery, including securing her privacy
- the staff's willingness to provide information and assurances during birth

As has been demonstrated by the changes over the past decade in attitudes about childbirth and the parents' preferences for certain amenities, services, and care, customer needs and expectations also change over time. These changing needs, expectations, and perceptions underscore how important it is to conduct regular research and listen to your customers. This research will also help you and the departments within your hospitals identify what services and characteristics of service will be important to a patient.

Patients are not the only customer segment that has definite ideas of what services and amenities are of value. It is also important to conduct regular research to determine your physicians' needs and expectations. Physician surveys will reveal far-reaching needs—from preferences for more efficient scheduling procedures in the operating room to better parking in the garage. If designed appropriately, they will also tell you how the administration is perceived in the eyes of the physicians, and how your physician-employee relations measure up. After determining what physicians want, some hospitals now sample physician opinions annually as a benchmark to learn if the steps they have taken to respond have been noticed and appreciated.

Many physicians welcome the opportunity to share their ideas, especially on service-related issues. Physicians are a strong referral source, and their opinions and suggestions should be solicited. In Chapter 16, some alternative methods for capturing this feedback will be explored.

Opening up the channels of communication between management and employees and asking employees for their input, reactions, and suggestions can also provide useful information and help shape future service development. Because front-line employees are the ones who, on a consistent basis, observe and interact with customers, they are in a position to understand customer likes and dislikes.

The research you initiate does not have to be costly. When designing new product lines, it is a good investment to sponsor research that is conducted by trained and experienced researchers. If, however, you are looking for new insight and ideas into how to enhance your existing services and to be more customer-directed, you can design and administer a simple survey, conduct personal or telephone interviews, or use focus groups.

After you have conducted research among your important customer groups, it is incumbent on you to respond to the needs identified. Nothing disgruntles physicians and employees more than to be asked for input and then to have it ignored. Consumers will also let you know if you have not responded to their needs and desires: they will simply choose another hospital.

Who Do We Want Our Customers To Be?

Years ago, many hoteliers recognized the growing numbers of professional women who were traveling and targeted this group as a specific segment of the business traveler market. Eager to appeal to these women, they called in their interior designers to decorate a certain number of rooms to have a feminine decor. Locating these rooms in safer areas near elevators and on the ground floor, they equipped them with hair dryers, irons, ironing boards, and other items identified as important by professional women who participated in focus groups. Conducting these focus groups and other qualitative research was necessary for the hotels to make adequate and appropriate improvements in their services.

Whereas hospitals used to be comfortable being "all things to all people," many are now targeting segments of markets of which they desire to capture a greater share. Macrosegmentation—the division of a customer base into demographic segments, such as women, the elderly, or adolescents—has resulted in some interesting changes.

Many hospitals are showing keen interest in the female market—and with good reason. Research indicates that women wield significant clout in the medical marketplace. Overall, women select providers 58 percent of the time, and are four times more likely than men to select a health care provider to treat a child.[4] Although these statistics relate specifically to the selection of physicians as health care providers, the attitudes held and behaviors demonstrated by women have caused hospitals to direct their attention to this particular segment of the market. Providers seek insight into their needs, preferences, and values and then design and deliver services that appeal to them. Those hospitals that are successful cultivate an institutional attitude that reflects their understanding and appreciation of the special needs and concerns of women.

For example, the First Lady Suites at the Medical Center of Bowling Green in Bowling Green, Kentucky, were specifically designed with a feminine touch. Sixteen private rooms and two suites are reserved for female patients other than OB patients. (Obstetrics was excluded because the nursery is located on another floor, and babies could not be transported by elevators.) Each private room is furnished with a brass bed, printed bedspreads, carpeting, china-top vanities, and brass accessories. The colors of mauve and green are used throughout the unit. The two larger suites have the same amenities plus a Jacuzzi and a sitting room with enough space for family members to stay overnight. Special lighting creates a pleasant atmosphere in the unit, as do 42 works of art by local women artists. Some of the extra amenities provided to patients include gourmet meals, a rose on admission, personal toiletries imprinted with the First Lady logo, and thick terry-cloth robes for use during their stays. The unit enjoys an 85 to 90 percent occupancy rate. Private rooms are $12.50 more than a regular private room, and suites are $32 more than a regular private room.

The design of facilities, systems, and services with the specific intent of appealing to a particular customer group, such as women, insured patients, elders or whomever, is a useful strategy to achieve market share.

How Do We Want Our Customers To Know Us?

How do you want to be known? Do you want to be known as the most profitable hospital in your community? As the best heart center within a 200-mile radius? As the hospital that has captured the greatest market share? The goals you define will determine the strategies you will employ. A strategy for achieving profitability may be to cut staffing to the lowest levels possible without compromising quality standards. Recruiting a renowned heart specialist may be a strategy for achieving distinction in open-heart surgical procedures. Ambitious marketing and product line development may be the strategies for gaining the greatest market share.

Service can be the strategy that enables a hospital to achieve market share, a distinguished reputation as a center of excellence, and even profit. With so many hospitals retrenching in the aftermath of DRGs, it may be difficult to view service as a strategy to achieve profitability and manage costs. The perception is that service is an expense. Yet, many successful organizations have received a hefty return on investment by making customer satisfaction a top priority. Nordstrom, a retail chain based in Seattle, has carved its niche in retailing by putting the customer first. It would be hard to find a retail organization that is more obsessively dedicated to service. And there have been big payoffs. From 1978 to 1984, the chain more than doubled sales while tripling its earnings. That translated into annual average sales increases of about 20 percent and average annual earnings growth of 18.5 percent. Nordstrom has employed many strategies to achieve success, but foremost has been its emphasis on customer service.[5]

Nordstrom's growth has been stellar. It is difficult to retrieve more recent statistics on its performance and, specifically, greater insight into its service strategies, because the company is tight-lipped. At a convention, you will likely not hear Nordstrom executives deliver boastful, after-dinner speeches. Recently, when asked to send someone to speak at a conference on service, the company's public relations representative politely declined saying that Nordstrom preferred to deliver service than to talk about it. Given the fact that everybody is talking about service, but few are doing it, this attitude is refreshing.

Nordstrom is not the only example of success through service. The Strategic Planning Institute of Cambridge, Massachusetts, has analyzed the performance of approximately 2,600 businesses over the past 15 years. Its profit impact of market strategy (PIMS) research shows that financial performance is tied directly to the perceived quality of a company's goods and services. According to the PIMS study, among the most powerful tools for shaping perceptions of overall quality is customer service.[6]

A mission statement that embraces quality service as a fundamental value can provide a conceptual premise from which strategies can be developed to enable your hospital to achieve its goals.

Of course, the mission can include other prevailing priorities and values. Some religious hospitals have integrated into their mission statements their long-standing commitment to provide services to indigent patients who otherwise might not have access to the care they need. Investor-owned hospitals recognize that they have an obligation to shareholders who have made financial investments in their operations. The basic premise for any of these hospitals is attainment of a healthy bottom line. A strong service strategy can help hospitals achieve that goal.

NCR Corporation in Dayton, Ohio, has produced a series of print advertisements that clearly define the company's overall mission and the company's attitudes about the constituencies it serves. The statement is simple. "NCR's Mission: Create Value for Our Stakeholders." Of these stakeholders, NCR states, "We believe in building mutually beneficial and enduring relationships with all of our stakeholders, based on conducting business activities with integrity and respect." Each ad in the series identifies one of the stakeholders and relates the company's essential values in relation to them.

Of customers, NCR states, "We take customer satisfaction personally; we are committed to providing superior value in our products and services on a continuing basis."

Of suppliers, NCR states, "We think of our suppliers as partners who share our goal of achieving the highest quality standards and the most consistent level of service."

Of the community, NCR states, "We are committed to being caring and supportive corporate citizens within the worldwide communities in which we operate."

Of shareholders, NCR states, "We are dedicated to creating value for our shareholders and financial communities by performing in a manner that will enhance returns on investments."

Of employees, NCR states, "We respect the individuality of each employee and foster an environment in which employees' creativity and productivity are encouraged, recognized, valued, and rewarded."

NCR's mission and value statements define that which the company stands for. This is precisely what a hospital must do in terms of its service strategy. Relationships must be defined and the values that will enable the hospital to achieve its goals should be articulated and integrated into the mission.

How Will We Achieve Our Goals?

Targeting market segments, understanding the customers' needs and expectations, and creating value-added service will not do the job of creating customer satisfaction. You must influence the delivery of your services and the performance of your people to make a service strategy work. It is at this point that the hospital, and every department, should scrutinize the values that drive the delivery of service and determine if it has positioned itself to deal with the changing marketplace.

Think of values as pilings driven into bedrock to provide a stable, sound foundation for the building that rises above. For the health care organization, the analogy is very apt. The strength of an organization is the direct result of the strength of the foundation on which its culture is built. At the cornerstone of every culture are the driving values that identify what the leaders believe in. These eventually prescribe "how we do things around here" and predict the organization's future success.

Normative behaviors are outgrowths of underlying values, but you cannot always identify an organization's values by what its leaders *say* are its values. Instead, a more accurate interpretation can be made by observing and analyzing the following indicators:

- who is recognized and why
- how decisions are made (criteria used)
- what is celebrated and why (rites and rituals)
- who is promoted and why

The values cannot be ambiguous. The degree to which the implied values resemble the professed values will determine whether the culture is dysfunctional culture or harmonious and purposeful.

Analyze the rites and rituals of the organization. If a hospital sponsors annual award dinners and the ceremony centers around awards for longevity, it is clear that the organization values length of service. Observe how "situational heroes" are recognized. If an academic medical center continually recognizes and promotes (through publicity, promotions, salary, etc.) research breakthroughs and those responsible for them, to the virtual exclusion of those who have gone out of their way to make the hospital experience better for patients, it is clearly a sign that the medical center values research more than patient care.

The concept of dissonance was introduced at the beginning of this chapter. It is appropriate to mention it again in relation to values because, when implied values do not support the professed values, dissonance occurs. Patients are not the only observers of conflicting values. Hospitals articulate their values, yet countless times employees are confused about what is really valued by the organization. Consider the following examples:

- Hospital leaders profess to care about employees. Yet, they fail to inform employees of important information affecting the institution or the industry. The result is that employees are left to speculate about the implications of management actions.
- Hospital leaders say they are committed to guest relations. They put all employees through a 4-hour training program; however, key members from administration never attend because they are "too busy."
- Hospital leaders continually stress courtesy. Yet, management tolerates the rude, negative, and indifferent behavior of some employees.
- Hospital leaders stress innovation and employee involvement. Yet, suggestions for improving patient care may be solicited but never acted on. Employees never learn why their suggestions were not implemented.

When situations such as these occur, symptoms of dissonance appear, the most prevalent of which are poor employee morale and lack of loyalty and commitment. Everyone working for the hospital or health care organization must become responsible for the values that they together cherish. All employees, from those who manage to those who carry out the organization's daily work, must assume the responsibility of acting on the principles that guide the organization.

Before introducing their guest relations program, Newton Wellesley Hospital in Newton, Massachusetts, developed a statement of values. Each of the values, shown in Exhibit 5-1, is intended to express not only what the organization believes but also to be a springboard from which the hospital can be guided in its management practices, policies, and decision making.

Exhibit 5-1 Newton-Wellesley Hospital Organizational Values

1. We believe our patients deserve the best care possible and that the skill, dedication, cooperation and loyalty of our employees are what make the difference.
2. As a teaching institution, we value the role of all employees in educating the health care workers of tomorrow.
3. We believe in providing services of consistently high quality that are cost effective.
4. We believe in excellence through teamwork.
5. We value courteous and friendly behavior on the part of all employees.
6. We believe if our managers treat employees fairly, our employees will treat each other and everyone with whom they have contact fairly.
7. We value the growth and development of our employees.
8. We value the clean and attractive appearance of our facility.
9. We take pride in the work performed by employees and volunteers and recognize their achievements and contributions.
10. We value the long term employment of productive people.

Source: Courtesy of Newton-Wellesley Hospital, Newton, Massachusetts.

Baptist Medical Center in Oklahoma City, Oklahoma, has drafted specific belief statements that summarize its attitudes toward patients, the patients' families and friends, and employees. These statements, shown in Exhibit 5-2, communicate important fundamental underlying values.

Value-driven organizations have strong cultures. These values must be periodically reviewed and modified. Will the traditional values continue to serve the organization in the future?

The strength of a culture can sometimes inhibit rather than facilitate change. A strong sense of who we are and what we are all about can be very beneficial, but it can also present some problems if the fundamental values on which the mission is built change. This occurred in religious hospitals, most noticeably in Catholic hospitals that, for decades, have recognized the intrinsic dignity and infinite value of every person—both of those they serve and of those who serve. What evolved was a strong sense of ''maternal protectionism'' which fostered the attitude that, no matter how bad the fiscal situation, the hospital would not lay off employees. When layoffs in these institutions eventually occurred, employees perceived that the basic values had been violated. This had a much more sobering impact on the cultures of the mission-driven religious hospitals than on those with weaker value orientations. Adjusting the culture to blend bottom-line fiscal considerations with the mission of caring does not necessarily weaken the caring orientation. The task merely becomes one of clearly articulating values in light of today's cost-driven and customer-driven climate. The leaders of health care organizations must identify and articulate values and assess whether those values will continue to help

Exhibit 5-2 Baptist Medical Center—Our Commitment to Care

Baptist Medical Center exists to improve the quality of life by promoting wellness and advancing the fight against human illness. We, the people who make up Baptist Medical Center, are committed to maintaining our medical center as a superior health care facility, and we want you—our customer—to know that we are working to do the things that make this a reality. We believe that by dedicating our total resources to this purpose, everyone benefits: our patients, their families and friends, our physicians, our employees and our volunteers.

To Our Patients, Their Families, and Friends	We believe that you should be treated as we would want members of our own families to be treated.
	We believe you deserve to be listened to and to be given information about the care you are receiving.
	We believe your care should be provided in a professional and personal manner.
	We believe in providing you quality medical technology.
	We believe in providing your care at an appropriate and reasonable cost.
	We pledge to pursue these goals with respect and courtesy.
To Our Employees	We believe in the dignity of each employee, and we pledge to be fair and professional in all our dealings with you.
	We believe in hiring and retaining excellent people who are willing to work toward these common goals and who are proud of this medical center.
	We seek to develop our employees by recognizing training and rewarding those of you who wish to share our tradition of excellence.
	We believe you should be listened to and kept informed. We seek to encourage your participation in decisions which directly affect your work.

Source: Courtesy of Baptist Medical Center, Oklahoma City, Oklahoma.

---

them achieve their goals in the future. Every decision must be weighed against those values.

Yet, it is not enough to identify and then simply articulate to employees what the values are. Values, as the foundation of a service strategy, must be continually reinforced through every channel of communication available. There are three ways in which values are communicated:

1. *Verbal communication:* A CEO who addresses a department management meeting and begins by reading a letter praising the action of an employee or department is certainly indicating that first and foremost he or she recognizes and appreciates value-driven, customer-oriented service. Those who hear the words hear that message. Although storytelling is interpretative and anecdotal, it is a suitable method of verbal communication.
2. *Written communication:* It is very interesting to note the various communication organs within the hospital and assess the degree to which they convey what is important to the organization. Memos and other internal correspondence can enhance or diminish the clarity of values as well.
3. *Behavioral communication:* It is not so much what leaders say but what they do that indicates the organization's true values. How decisions are made, what decisions are made, and nonverbal indicators of values are very revealing. Managers and executives should spend a great deal of time wandering throughout the organization. Management by Wandering Around (MBWA), a major tenet and fundamental practice of Hewlett Packard, was publicly introduced by Tom Peters and Bob Waterman in their book, *In Search of Excellence*. According to the MBWA concept, managers who are out there among the troops are better leaders because they gain information, interact with customers, and can listen and see. Through this regular exercise, they can make important observations as to what is important to customers. More importantly, they are close to their employees. They work alongside and with them; they support, listen, and observe what is meaningful and important to employees. As managers wander, they can demonstrate what is important by such obvious actions as stooping down to pick up a piece of paper, noting what is clean or dirty, giving an employee positive feedback, or making suggestions about how a situation could have been handled differently for a more positive outcome. Visible managers and executives who have a commitment to values understand the axiom: "Actions speak louder than words."

SUMMARY

Service quality and consistency do not happen by accident. A service strategy can provide managers and employees with a common focus. It is the vision of what the organization is trying to become in the customer's eyes. It should be sufficiently differentiating so as to distinguish the hospital's services from that of its competitors. The service strategy is built on the mission that defines the purpose of the business. The actions to achieve its vision are influenced by what the organization values. Derived from an understanding of the customer's needs, the service strategy is the framework that describes the services the organization is offering to satisfy customer needs and expectation.

It is important for an organization to communicate its service strategy to both employees and customers. Defining and communicating the service strategy are important for orienting employees and managers to the common goals, developing delivery systems, and measuring organizational performance.

NOTES

1. Jan Carlzon, *Moments of Truth* (Cambridge, Mass.: Ballinger Publishing Co., 1987), 43.

2. Theodore Levitt, *The Marketing Imagination* (New York: The Free Press, 1983), 5.

3. Paul Keckley, *The Keckley Report* (February 16, 1987).

4. Joyce Jensen, ''Women Pick the Providers Who Treat Their Illnesses, Those of Their Children,'' *Modern Healthcare* (May 9, 1986): 66.

5. Nancy Yoshiharo, ''Nordstrom—Chain Sets Itself Apart With an Old-Fashioned Service Policy,'' *Los Angeles Times* (September 30, 1984): Section V.

6. Bro Uttal, ''Companies that Serve You Best,'' *Fortune* (December 7, 1987): 98.

Chapter 6

Service Systems: Fluid and Flexible Design

Although very much in an embryonic stage, the emphasis on care of the customer is changing the ways in which service is conceptualized, operationalized, and delivered in hospitals. One such example can be found in San Francisco where Planetree, a 13-bed medical-surgical unit located in Pacific Presbyterian Medical Center, was conceived. Born of a vision one woman had after her nightmarish confrontation with the traditional health care delivery system in 1977, Planetree is an impressive and innovative project that illustrates how service strategies and operational strategies can be integrated.

In Planetree the service delivery system supports the philosophy of its unique mission—to encourage maximum patient and family involvement in the healing process. The creation of an optimal healing environment was the cornerstone of the Planetree concept.

The architect designed the unit to encourage patient and family involvement. The nurses' station is open and has no counters that separate the nurses from patients and their families. This design naturally encourages interaction between patients and staff. All of the patient rooms have large windows and built-in shelves for patients' personal belongings and plants. Rooms feature bulletin boards, printed sheets, and cubicle curtains. The extensive use of wood and soft lighting creates a home-like rather than institutional feeling.

The primary nursing model was put in place because it was felt to be consistent with the philosophy of promoting patient and family involvement. Each nurse is assigned a small caseload of patients for whom they are responsible for providing total care. This approach is believed to (1) provide greater coordination of patient care, (2) reduce the likelihood of complications developing because a nurse is caring for the patient from a holistic perspective, and (3) facilitate better patient education and preparation for discharge.[1]

Planetree encourages family participation in the education, care, and emotional support of patients. There are no visiting hours or age limits imposed on visitation.

Patients have access to their charts, and they are encouraged to read them and to ask questions of their doctors when they do not understand their disease and treatment. Patients also have access to The Planetree Health Resource Center, a library that contains resource materials and files of current medical research. A book cart is circulated through the units so that patients may read about their diagnoses. Nutritional counseling and education are also emphasized. Patients' personal food preferences are honored as much as possible. When they arrive on the unit, they are asked what foods they especially like or dislike. An effort is made to stock these favorite foods in the unit's kitchen, and patients and family members are encouraged to cook their own meals.

A VCR and a library of videocassette tapes are available in the lounge. Every Wednesday patients are invited to the lounge to view movies together. Relaxation tapes are used frequently to help patients rest before and after surgery. Sony Walkmans are available on request to any patient.

Studies are being conducted to compare the effects of placement on the Planetree unit to placement on a traditional hospital medical-surgical unit. The impact on health status, patient satisfaction, and cost are being evaluated. If the comparative analysis indicates that patients do recover faster and experience higher levels of satisfaction, the Planetree approach could very well become a model that other hospitals around the country emulate.[2]

Planetree's services are *designed* to be consistent with its mission and values. Thoughtful consideration to the basic needs and expectations of its patients is reflected in its service delivery system.

SERVICE PACKAGE

Every customer has a set of needs and expectations. If the service package is designed to meet these needs and expectations, customers will not only be satisfied but also a reputation for delivering quality service will prevail.

A service package has two components. The first is the *primary* service package. It comprises the core services, such as the diagnostic procedure, the clinical care, and the technical expertise. The services in the primary package respond to customers' *needs* that motivate their consumption of the service. The *secondary* service package contains the service features that respond to what people *value* and *expect*. These most often relate to care, comfort, and convenience factors. The features of the secondary package are what customers most often use to evaluate the quality of the service.

If a patient has a heart attack, he or she will seek relief from the discomfort and prevention of future attacks. The primary service components that respond to these needs are diagnostic procedures, medications, and perhaps surgery. In addition, counseling about diet planning and exercise regimens may be included. The secondary service package contains the attributes that are designed to fulfill the expectations the patient has while he or she is hospitalized. The patient may expect prompt response to calls for a nurse, information about his or her condition that is explained in understandable terms, easy passage through the medical assembly line, courtesy, and comfort. To meet these expectations, the responsive hospital will fine tune its systems to prevent or minimize recurring delays, analyze staffing patterns, train employees to respond appropriately with respect and regard for the patient's needs, and establish standards against which the service delivery effectiveness will be measured. In addition, the hospital may undertake focused research to identify what special services would be valued. Closed-circuit televised programming of open-heart surgery and gourmet (low-cholesterol) meals are just two examples of special services that might be added for heart patients. Other more generalized services, such as valet parking or a patient "hotline," may be added to convince the patient that the hospital is serious about exceeding his or her expectations.

BALANCING CONFLICTING GOALS

A hospital, not unlike most service businesses, is forced to balance conflicting goals—satisfying operational needs while also satisfying customer needs. The design of the service delivery system is of paramount importance if a hospital is to achieve its service goals. Service must be fully integrated into operations.

In his book, *Managing in the Service Economy,* author James Heskett writes:

> Systems that deliver successfully consist of well-thought-out jobs for people with the capabilities and attitudes necessary for their successful performance: equipment, facilities and layouts for effective customer and work flow; and carefully developed procedures aimed at a common set of clearly defined objectives. They provide sufficient capacity (neither too little nor too much) to meet most commonly experienced levels of demand efficiently. They can help to reduce customers' perceptions of risk. And the delivery systems themselves often help insure that the standards for service quality are met, that services perceived by customers are differentiated from the competition, and that barriers to competitive entry are built.[3]

SERVICE DELIVERY SYSTEM

A hospital's service delivery system is exceedingly complex. Some services are delivered to the patient at the bedside, whereas others necessitate that he or she be transported to another location. Procedures and policies, too numerous even to estimate how many, regulate the delivery of service. Sometimes the system's capacity is sufficient to respond to demand; at other times demand exceeds the system's capacity. The greater the scope of services, the more complex the system.

Hospitals have constructed sophisticated systems to manage and coordinate the delivery of services from the time the patient arrives until the time of discharge, and, in some instances, after discharge, as in hospital-sponsored home care programs. The service delivery system shown in Figure 6-1 is made up of many entities composed of various departments. These entities are described by the services they deliver:

- *Entry:* The two most common points of entry into the system are the admitting department and the emergency department.
- *Transport:* This system moves patients from one point of service delivery to another. It is facilitated by transporters, volunteers, and employees using wheelchairs and gurneys.
- *Diagnostic:* Lab, imaging, and radiology departments are found within the diagnostic system.
- *Clinical:* Clinical services are performed at the patient's bedside by nursing staff, physicians, and other allied health professionals.
- *Ancillary:* Cardiopulmonary and physical therapy are two examples of ancillary services.

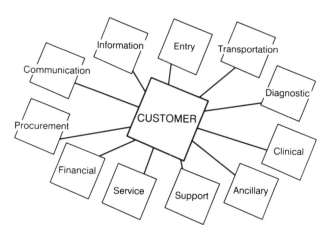

Figure 6-1 Service Delivery System

- *Support:* This system supports the execution of business. Education and training and patient relations are two such departments.
- *Service:* Food service, housekeeping, maintenance, laundry, and security are service departments. Services performed by social workers and discharge planners also belong within this category.
- *Communications:* The communication system relays information over telephones, computers, and pneumatic systems.
- *Financial:* The financial systems are created to ensure payment for services rendered.
- *Information:* Information pertaining to the patient, his or her diagnosis, and treatment is managed by the medical records department.
- *Procurement:* The central supply, pharmacy, and materiel management departments are part of the system that acquires the supplies needed to perform services for customers and support the staff in the execution of their jobs.

As shown in the figure, the customer is at the hub. Every service delivered by every entity is designed, either directly or indirectly, to support the care of the patient.

In the service delivery system, hundreds of services are performed, from conducting an upper GI series to serving dinner, fixing a broken compressor to repairing a broken leg. Within each department, other smaller services, such as preregistering the patient, completing paperwork, verifying insurance information, confirming the schedule for surgery, greeting the patient, notifying the unit of the patient's arrival, and arranging for the patient to be delivered to the floor, are carried out. Scheduling systems, procedures, policies, equipment, facility capacity and design, staffing patterns, and the like are all systems that make up the larger delivery system.

Industrial engineers have developed sophisticated methods to analyze whether a system's capacity, design, and staffing can adequately meet demand, control costs, and optimize efficiency. Traditionally, such analyses have not considered the effect of operational changes on customer satisfaction. Yet, just as they must take into account the randomness with which patients arrive, interruptions in the normal work flow, and the effect of machine outage or downtime, so customer expectations should not be ignored.

A department that wants to improve service delivery must balance operational needs and service expectations. Service standards cannot be established in a vacuum but must be based on extensive data and information gathered from (1) interviews with department management and personnel; (2) a review of department policies, procedures, and statistics; and (3) an analysis of patient arrival patterns, volume, mix, and acuity, ancillary services necessary to perform the service, the physical facility and layout, job functions, and staffing mix and levels. The system should be designed to be fluid and flexible so that a department can handle the demand for service in a manner that is consistent with the expectations the patient holds.

SYSTEM BREAKDOWNS

If a hospital is really serious about managing service delivery, little will be left to chance. The hospital and departments will analyze the system to identify where and under what circumstances breakdowns occur. Delays are the most prevalent symptoms of system breakdowns. The delays can be brought on by unanticipated demand, inadequate communication, equipment malfunction, faulty scheduling, nonconformance to procedures, or inadequate supplies, equipment, staffing, or facilities.

Once a system breaks down, it is almost impossible to get it back on line. Although some of the delays that occur in hospitals are due to uncontrollable circumstances, many others can be prevented or minimized if a hospital will take the time to analyze chronic and systemic problems within its delivery system.

It is important to take a look at what functions of the service delivery system may adversely affect efficiency, performance, or customer satisfaction. For example, patients often do not understand why they receive two bills for a radiology procedure. Even though the registration clerks routinely alert patients of this fact, many do not remember it, and the billing causes confusion and complaints. One solution is to change the billing system. A change of this sort requires careful analysis that weighs the benefits for the patient against any consequences the hospital might suffer financially by imposing an additional collection burden or by delaying reimbursement to physicians. Nonetheless, any frequent or repetitive complaint signals a need for system modification.

If the system cannot be modified, there are other ways to approach the problem. Patients' experiences in the emergency room serve as useful illustrations of this point. No one who comes into the emergency room thinks that his or her emergency is unimportant. Immediate attention is expected. Those with minor emergencies expect that their treatment will take a short time. Actually, the inverse is true. The service delivery system within an emergency room is designed for trauma. It can accommodate minor situations when other, more immediate emergencies do not compete for the attention of staff, facilities, and equipment. In the real world of emergency medicine, there are few times when the demand is entirely consistent with the system's capacity. So, in the case of minor emergencies, people wait. The minutes tick by. They become disgruntled. They observe others who came in after them being taken to the treatment rooms and do not understand why they are not being seen. If no one is keeping them apprised of the situation, the waiting finally becomes more than they can bear. The patient (or family member interceding as advocate for the patient) approaches an employee and makes a fuss. The employee does not necessarily mean to respond rudely. It is just that it has been a terribly busy day, this is a bothersome interruption that is diverting her attentions from those who really need care, and it is the last thing she wants to hear.

Analyze the situation. Is the guest's expectation realistic or unrealistic? It is *not* unrealistic for a patient to expect treatment within a reasonable amount of time. The challenge is to resolve the seeming disparity between the patient's reasonable expectation for prompt treatment and the staff's legitimate need to respond to more serious emergencies.

Many hospitals have done so by structuring delivery of the service to minimize future complaints. Recognizing that many people complain because they do not understand what is going on, special attention is paid to those waiting by volunteers or patient representatives who circulate within the room and keep waiting patients and the family members of other patients apprised of the situation. Another solution has been to set up a system whereby all patients entering the emergency room, regardless of the severity of their condition, are triaged by a physician or nurse within a couple of minutes of their arrival. Explaining to patients the staff is aware of their presence and condition and keeping patients and other family members comfortable while they wait are virtually all that can be done in this situation. If the employees are not sensitized to patients' expectations and the systems are not modified to respond, one of the most important networks on which the hospital depends to feed admissions through the system becomes a liability.

Diagnostic tools can be used to identify system breakdowns. Data from patient surveys can target sources of dissatisfaction caused by faulty systems. Employees can also identify elements of ineffective systems because they confront obstacles daily that stand in their way of delivering superior service. By asking employees to engage in discussions to identify system problems and improvements, you tap a ready and willing resource. The following questions can be used to initiate the discussions, identify the problems, and uncover potential solutions.

What Questions Are Frequently Asked by Guests?

Questions are expressions of needs for information. When a department receives repeated questions about the same issue, this should signal that on a consistent basis guests have needs for information that are not being satisfied. In response, you should ask: What can we do to meet the informational needs of guests more effectively? Can we improve signage? Should we develop written information or rewrite existing instructions or information that is unclear? Do we need to volunteer information before the guest has to ask?

What Complaints Are Frequently Expressed by Guests?

A complaint is simply an expression of dissatisfaction when expectations are not met. Repetitive complaints should signal that, on a consistent basis, expectations are not being met. To rectify this problem, first identify whether the guest's expectations are realistic or unrealistic. If they are unrealistic, you then have the responsibility to educate the guest as to what he or she can and should rightfully expect. If the guest's expectations are realistic, however, you need to look at ways in which you can prevent the complaint or minimize the consequences of unmet expectations.

What Policies and Procedures Are Difficult for Guests To Understand?

Policies and procedures are the rules and guidelines that often prescribe how services are delivered. Policies are established to ensure the well-being of the people who are in the hospital. Yet, many policies serve the needs of the provider, rather than the needs of the guest. Many policies, even when they exist for legitimate and purposeful reasons, can be frustrating for the guest.

Hospitals have many seemingly senseless policies and procedures. People who feel perfectly well and can walk are placed in wheelchairs. Why? Because if they slip and fall, the hospital is responsible. Yet, if you have ever been forced to sit in a wheelchair when you really did not want to do so, you probably found it maddening when someone explained the reason by saying, "It's hospital policy." People remark constantly that they think it is crazy to be wakened at all hours of the night, sometimes just to be given a sleeping pill. Again, it is the routine that governs. Patients are told when to eat, when to bathe, and when to get up. The delivery system and schedule are thrown awry when patients do not conform to the schedules. Although these scheduling systems are necessary to some degree to keep the hospital operating efficiently, minor changes can be made without throwing the system into chaos.

By analyzing those policies that are difficult for the guests to understand or that create frustration, you can identify ways to explain them so that you will gain cooperation. You might also be able to identify some policies that can be relaxed without compromising the reason underlying them. If you cannot relax or eliminate the policy, you might then work to sensitize the staff on how they can explain the policy better.

What Information About Our Procedures Do We Perceive Other Departments Do Not Understand?

There is a corollary question to the one posed above: What information about other departments' operations do we not understand?

The interrelationships and mutual dependencies among departments demand cooperation among employees. When a significant number of employees within a department do not conform to the standard procedures that have been established by another department, operational effectiveness is minimized.

By encouraging employees to identify what they perceive other departments do not understand about their operations and what they do not fully understand about other departments' operations, you can identify information needs and facilitate an exchange of information that will build greater interdepartmental teamwork.

QUALITY CIRCLES

A quality circle is a group of employees working in the same department who meet on a regular basis to identify, analyze, and solve problems that affect their work performance. Many industrial and manufacturing companies adopted the concept of quality circles from the Japanese in the early 1970s. The popularity of this approach to managing quality, productivity, and costs soon spread to the health care industry.

Quality circles can be used to solve system problems internally. When employees are given the latitude to identify, discuss, and solve problems, their participation fosters a sense of greater investment in their work unit. Managers who ignore this vital need for belonging cannot hope to solve performance or system problems relating to service delivery.

To implement effectively a quality circle program in your hospital, careful planning and analysis should take place to determine the structure and methodology to be used. Someone who is knowledgeable about group process techniques and who can structure the process should be recruited to function as the circle leader.

STANDARDS AND REWARDS

By establishing service standards each department can fine-tune its operational systems to create a more customer responsive operation. Service standards are similar to performance standards and quality assurance standards, and are criteria against which the operational and service performance of a department can be measured. Service standards will be discussed in greater detail in Chapter 9.

The methods used to measure and reward both employee and departmental performance are part of the management systems that influence the delivery of service. These methods will be discussed in greater detail in Chapter 7.

Establishing service standards is one way for individual departments to develop systems that create a more customer-responsive environment. The process of creating these standards is in itself beneficial because it focuses the attention of employees and their managers on how they deliver services.

SUMMARY

The systems enable the people to deliver service. The delivery systems include physical facilities, policies, procedures, methods, and communication processes service people must have at their disposal to meet the customer's needs.

Customer-friendly systems will enable your employees to be more customer-friendly. When employees are frustrated by rigid policies, inefficient systems, and inadequate information, the ability to perform optimally in behalf of the customer is inhibited. Service also suffers when employees are not given the freedom to override the systems when it is in the best interest of the customer.

When defining, designing, and developing service delivery systems, service goals and operational goals must be balanced. An effective service delivery system that facilitates the flow of patients, the delivery of services, and the interactions between people can result in satisfied customers, a more efficient operation, and a more productive work force.

NOTES

1. Judith K. Jenna, "Toward the Patient Driven Hospital," *Healthcare Forum* (May/June 1986): 8–18.

2. Judith K. Jenna, "Toward the Patient Driven Hospital," *Healthcare Forum* (July/August 1986): 55–59.

3. James L. Heskett, *Managing in the Service Economy* (Boston: Harvard Business School Press, 1986), 20.

Chapter 7

Service-Oriented People: Achieving Optimal Performance

A story is told about a hotel shopper who checked into a hotel, went up to her room, unpacked her suitcase, and placed the towels in her empty luggage. An hour later, she and her husband went down to the restaurant for dinner. Engaging the waitress in small talk, they mentioned that they were impressed with the hotel, but found it curious that their room had no towels. After dinner, they returned to the room to see if the towels had been delivered. New towels were already hanging on the rack.

The hotel shopper had purposely packed the towels away and had then mentioned that they were missing because she wanted to see if the waitress would respond. In this hotel, the employees were trained so that even those working in the restaurant knew to report dissatisfaction immediately to the appropriate person.

Managers can talk until they are blue in the face about the importance of meeting and exceeding expectations, but how does one motivate someone to act? This waitress understood that it was her job to see that the guests had towels when they returned. It did not matter that the housekeeper was sure that she had put towels out earlier. No questions were asked. The towels were not there so they were replaced.

TRANSLATING EXPECTATIONS INTO ACTIONS

What motivates employees? The answers to that question are very different from what they were several decades ago. Just as organizational values change, so do the individual values of employees. Recall the employees of several decades ago. They generally had a high degree of commitment to their employers, they did as they were told, and they accepted decisions without much disagreement. They valued job security, pay, and benefits.

Modern-day employees are quite different. They focus less on the future. They still value job security, but to a much lesser degree. They are most likely to place their own interests before the organization's, and few will stay in a job if it does not fulfill basic quality of life requirements.

The Public Agenda Foundation's 1983 study identified the ten most important qualities that people want in a job today:[1]

1. working with people who treat me with respect
2. interesting work
3. recognition of good work
4. chance to develop skills
5. working for people who listen if I have ideas about how to do things better
6. a chance to think for myself, rather than just carry out instructions
7. seeing the end results of my work
8. working with efficient managers
9. a job that is not too easy
10. feeling well-informed about what is going on

In this particular study, job security, high pay, and good benefits were not among the top ten qualities; however, these findings should not diminish the importance of rewarding employees with commensurate pay, providing competitive benefits, and ensuring a modicum of security. One needs only to take a look at how productivity and customer service are affected by a major reduction in work force or benefits to recognize fully the consequences of job insecurity and the importance of rewards. The point is clear, however: Money alone will not motivate employees. Providing opportunities that enable employees to fulfill these basic motivations will create a more productive work force that has a greater commitment to contribute.

Employees become personally invested in the mission when they understand the scope and definition of their job. They need to know what is expected of them, and then they need clear and frequent feedback on how well they are doing. When people feel more secure, they shift their inward preoccupation to concern for the status of the department. They begin to define their work and that of co-workers in terms of the overall goals of the hospital. Employees then look to reach beyond the perimeters of their jobs to help the hospital succeed. If they understand that the hospital's success is their own success and they can see and understand how their personal investments will benefit them, they will *act* on the messages that are sent from above.

There is no magic formula for translating expectations into actions. It starts with a strong service strategy and a culture that fosters the enthusiastic, grassroots participation of your employees. It is built on the premise that you care, truly care about those whom you employ. Finally, it concerns the messages that are sent to employees and how those messages are then translated into the employees' relations with the customer.

These messages are vitally important to the strength of the organization's response to the customers. How messages are conveyed and translated was explored by Robert L. Desatnick in his book, *Managing to Keep the Customer*.[2] Five fundamental themes are shown in Table 7-1.

Customer relations mirror employee relations. Taking care of human relations is equivalent to taking care of the business. Organizational studies indicate that there is a strong correlation between customer and employee views of service quality and the internal climate for service. When employees view favorably an organization's human resource policies, customers view favorably the quality of the service they receive.[3]

You do not have to be a linguist to translate the message, "We care," to employees so that the expectations you hold for performance will be translated into actions that serve the customer. Sound human resource practices will demonstrate your concern for their well-being and fulfillment.

Educate Employees

Education is the process of expanding employees' horizons by keeping them apprised of changes taking place in the industry that affect the future of the

---

Table 7-1 Managing To Keep the Customer

Management to Employee	Employee to Customer
1. What are your problems and how can I help solve them?	1. How may I be of assistance to you?
2. We want you to know what is happening in our organization, so here is what is going on.	2. I am capable of helping you because I am in the know.
3. Each of us is the company, so we all share accountability for what happens around here.	3. I am empowered to help you and take pride in my ability to do so.
4. We treat each other with professional respect.	4. I have respect for you as the individual you are.
5. We stand behind each other's decisions and support each other.	5. You can count on me and my company to deliver on our promises.

Source: Reprinted from *Managing To Keep the Customer* by R.L. Desatnick, p. 20, with permission of Jossey-Bass, Inc., Publishers, © 1987.

hospital. Employees do not typically have the information and resources at their fingertips that managers and executives have. For this reason, employees often do not have a full grasp and comprehension of issues that affect internal decision making.

The new age of competition has created confusion for many employees. When they see the groundbreaking of a new MRI facility concurrent with a staff layoff, their naive and uninformed perspective leaves them questioning the judgment of management. They may also question the introduction of guest relations programs. You are likely to hear, "With staffing situations like we have here, we don't need charm school. We need more people!" To those employees, the money that is spent on advertising, facility improvement, and service programs is not a wise investment. It is an expense that is made at their expense.

Employees' need to feel informed is not the only reason why you should educate them about the needs of the organization. On more than one occasion, employees have been overheard saying such things as "We don't need to make a profit, because we're a not-for-profit hospital." This statement implies that customer satisfaction and marketing are not nearly as important to not-for-profit hospitals as they are to their for-profit counterparts. They do not understand that their jobs, their pay, and their futures depend on how well the customers are satisfied because the organization's financial solvency (profit or not-for-profit alike) is dependent on generating income in excess of expenses. Regular education contributes to a more unified sense of organizational direction and purpose and helps allay fear and insecurity.

Train Employees

Excelling in guest relations requires that you provide employees with the training and development to help them do their jobs.

Proficiency in the skill of interacting with others is second nature for some, but not all employees. Workshops and seminars that teach communication skills, telephone courtesy, and complaint resolution skills, as well as stress reduction and other coping techniques, can improve employees' interactions with others, build their confidence, and make them more productive members of the health care delivery team. Training contributes to job enrichment and personal investment. Employees experience greater satisfaction and fulfillment on the job when they recognize that their employer willingly invests in their professional growth and development and supports them in attaining levels of performance to meet the expectations. Support systems that teach and reinforce the expected behaviors are essential to good management.

Historically, hospitals have invested in training and education because of the technical nature of the work that is performed and the need to keep employees and physicians apprised of new developments and proficient in new techniques or procedures that can improve the quality of care. Yet, the budget appropriations for training in the areas of personal growth and professional development in non-clinical areas have been meager. Hospitals are not the only service business guilty of this poor investment in customer-contact training. Despite the furor over the poor quality of service, American corporations are spending only $2.58 per employee to improve their dealings with the public. Most of that money goes to train workers to sell more or to calm complaining customers.[4]

There are exceptions. Emery Air Freight is launching a service training program that will cost $1,000 per worker. Although this level of investment is not financially feasible for most hospitals, executives should take a hard look at quality training programs that will equip employees to deal with the public.

The success of a guest relations program, or any training program for that matter, relies in large measure on how managers and supervisors communicate and reinforce management's expectations. Supervisors and managers play important roles in making certain that the skills acquired through training are used successfully and consistently in the workplace.

Communicate Expectations

You cannot leave employees to second guess what you expect from them in their performance. Employees need a clear definition of what is expected of them and periodic progress reviews to let them know how well they are doing.

Informed people are happier, less confused, and more aware of benefits and opportunities. If managers want to achieve superior service, they must place communication as a top priority. Expressing expectations of performance, providing regular feedback, and keeping employees informed of their standing are essential dimensions.

Job Descriptions and Performance Evaluations

Job descriptions and performance evaluations should address standards of service behavior. Performance expectations can be defined in several ways. One method is to examine general expectations and to identify specific actions relating to each expectation. For example, it's not enough to say, "Be nice to the guest" or "Demonstrate respect." Demonstrating respect means acknowledging the patient's need for privacy by knocking before entering the room or pulling the privacy curtain during the patient's bath or treatments, addressing the patient by surname, avoiding endearing names, and controlling noise at the unit stations. Expectations should be interpreted in specific terms.

Albany Medical Center in Albany, New York, incorporated performance expectations into their criteria-based performance evaluation system. Eight general factors were used in the overall evaluation: knowledge of work, quality of work, productivity, initiative, dependability, interpersonal relations, adaptability, and judgment. The specific performance expectations that are included in the job descriptions for the factor "Interpersonal Relations" are shown in Exhibit 7-1.

Anderson Memorial Hospital in Anderson, South Carolina, incorporated similar standards into its performance review system. The evaluation form that is used during the review with employees is shown in Exhibit 7-2.

Once you adopt the standards to be used, you must assign importance to them. Unfortunately, service performance standards rarely have been weighted greater than 10 percent in the overall evaluation. More hospitals should follow the example of St. Joseph's Hospital and Medical Center in Paterson, New Jersey. One-third of the overall performance evaluation is focused on the employee's guest relations performance. With these standards weighted 33 percent, employees realize that their service performance is integral to their success at the medical center.

Compensable factors in the performance evaluation that best reflect the unique values of your organization are vitally important if you want to achieve superior service. If the standards relate to what is necessary for effective job performance, are clearly defined and communicated to employees, and if the hospital provides the training and support to enable the employee to meet the expectations of service performance, legal requirements for fairness and objectivity are upheld.

Obviously, a front-line employee will be expected to utilize customer-contact skills to a greater degree and with greater proficiency than will a data entry clerk in your computer room. Job analysis to determine which positions have the greatest interaction with the customers should be used to define the weighting of the compensable factors.

Scripting

Another way to communicate explicit expectations of performance is to develop specific protocols for various procedures. Repetitive, predictable interactions with guests are handled by employees in a variety of ways. "Scripts" can be developed to identify statements, gestures, and activities that will create positive impressions.

Scripting is not new. It has made playwrights and actors alike rich and famous. Creatively worded scripts have delighted millions of audiences. Chances are that, the last time you checked into a hotel the bellman used a "script" when he relieved you of your luggage, gave you a verbal grand tour of the hotel, and checked out the thermostat, television, and light bulbs before he left your room. Scripting is relatively easy if you analyze the tasks and identify those key phrases and gestures

Exhibit 7-1 Criteria-Based Assessment Factors

FACTOR 6
INTERPERSONAL RELATIONS

PART I: The Following Factor(s) Must Be Contained on Each Criteria-Based Assessment as Stated:

1. Presents a professional image daily; follows the departmental professional appearance standards.

2. Exhibits commitment and pride through personal example by speaking positively about the Center, the department, employees, and guests.

3. Contributes to teamwork and creates harmonious, effective and positive working relationship with others by:

   - Responding to requests in a cooperative and responsive manner
   - Speaking respectfully of/to other employees and guests by minimizing criticism and adversarial attitudes
   - Assuming responsibility without making excuses, offering assistance whenever possible without being asked.

4. Respects, understands, and responds with sensitivity to employees and guests by:

   - Knocking before entering an occupied room
   - Introducing self by name and job function
   - Addressing others by proper name and avoiding endearing terms
   - Treating others as one would wish to be treated.

5. Resolves conflicts and problem-solves by:

   - Remaining calm when confronted
   - Listening carefully
   - Acknowledging that the problem is valid to the other person's perception
   - Attempting to identify solutions and/or referring person to the appropriate authority or control
   - Attempting to deliver more than is expected.

6. Anticipates and responds to the needs of guests and employees for information by:

   - Maintaining eye contact and full attention
   - Using clear "language" which can be understood, avoid hospital, academic or technical "jargon"
   - Offering an explanation for the purposes of policies, procedures, and interactions when appropriate.

Exhibit 7-1 continued

7. Exhibits telephone courtesy by:

   • Answering within 3 rings with proper name and department/unit
   • Speaking with a pleasant tone while focusing attention to caller
   • Transferring calls correctly and promptly
   • Attending to calls on hold in a timely manner.

8. Maintains confidentiality by:

   • Discouraging gossip
   • Using discretion when discussing patient, work or Center-related information with others.

   Source: Courtesy of Albany Medical Center, Albany, New York.

that make the patient feel that he or she is special. It is not enough to say to employees, ''Admit a patient courteously.'' Although most employees do understand the concept of courtesy, their execution of the task may not communicate the level of consideration and respect that you desire.[5]

When developing scripts, identify the purpose of the interaction, the content of the message, the information that should be shared with the patient, the approaches/techniques used to meet patient needs, and the extra measures of service to exceed patient expectations. Anticipate patients' questions, special needs, and sources of dissatisfaction.

For example, a clerk who admits a patient can use the following format in scripting:

1. Acknowledge arrival   Eye contact
                          Nod
2. Extend greeting   Good morning
3. Introduce self   My name is _____
4. Establish rapport   Eye contact
                          Smile
                          Call patient by name
5. Extend empathy   ''I realize that you are probably anxious to get settled but I will need to ask you a few questions. . . .''
6. Anticipate needs   ''Are you comfortable?''
                          ''Do you have any questions?''

Exhibit 7-2 Guest Relations Performance Standards—Job Specific

Position _____   Department _____
Employee _____   Review Date _____

Critical	Exceedable?	Standards of Performance Guest Relations Standards	Consistently Exceeds Standards	Consistently meets standards	Needs Improvement To Meet Standards	Not Applicable
		1. Personalizes interactions with guests by introducing one's self to guest on first meeting, maintaining eye contact, smiling, calling guests by name, and extending a few words of concern.				
		2. Demonstrates a caring attitude and responsiveness to guests' needs and problems by, first, listening with understanding and, when action is called for, acting in a quick, tactful, and nondefensive manner.				
		3. Communicates procedures, directions, and helpful information to guests.				
		4. Promotes positive telephone etiquette by identifying one's self and department/work area, by sounding pleasant and enthusiastic, and by being courteous and helpful.				
		5. Maintains a professional atmosphere by keeping noise levels to a minimum and work areas neat and uncluttered.				

Source: Courtesy of Anderson Memorial Hospital, Anderson, South Carolina.

7. Deliver service   Ask questions
                                         Display facial expressions
                                         Use patient's name

8. Communicate expectations   "Thank you for your patience. I will have Mrs. Tiernan, one of our escort volunteers, take you to your room."

9. Closure   "Thank you, Mrs. Hernandez. Please let any of us know if we can respond to any other questions or needs while you are here."

Yet, an admitting manager might exclaim, "My clerk has worked at the hospital for over 16 years and has admitted thousands of patients. I'm not about to insult her by suggesting that she develop a script!"

The script development process need not be perceived as an insult to employees. If you instead enlist their knowledge and experience in helping you develop a script under the guise that it will be useful to new employees, you can later adopt it as the standard for the entire group. The very activity of defining the script will result in a greater awareness of the small gestures, the content and the delivery of information, and the "little" things that shape larger impressions.

Telephone Protocols

The professional courtesy and conduct exhibited by employees over the telephone can have a decided impact on a customer's overall impression of a hospital. Telephone standards should be drafted for use hospital-wide. The telephone standards that were developed and publicized by Michael Reese Hospital in Chicago are included in Exhibit 7-3.

Professional Appearance Standards

Banks and other large corporations that are interested in preserving a certain image do not let personal style and taste dictate the appearance of their employees. They tell their employees how they are expected to dress.

A hospital should be no less interested in and concerned about its public image, and yet most hospitals have been reluctant to clarify expectations of what image an employee should project or to enforce dress codes.

It is important to keep in mind that a patient's expectation of what a health care professional should look like has been shaped, to the greatest degree, by actors and actresses. If you have ever watched the daytime soap operas, you know that Nurse Jessie still dresses like the consummate professional she is. She wears a starched white dress. It is never wrinkled or spotted with stains, nor does the neck plunge or the buttons bulge. Her shoes are polished white (not that you ever see them, but you just know they are). Her hose do not run or wrinkle at the ankles. She wears

Exhibit 7-3 Telephone Standards

Telephone Protocol

Answer calls promptly.

Identify yourself and your department.

Transfer calls properly. Let the caller know you are transferring the call and give him the extension number in case the line is disconnected.

Be prepared to take a message and have the Medical Center's telephone directory close at hand.

Take clear and concise messages; include the name of the caller, the date and time, and any message. Repeat messages back to the caller for accuracy.

Ask first before putting a caller on hold. Do not leave the line open; background noises can be disturbing to a caller.

Periodically check back with a caller who is on hold to reassure him that the needed information is being obtained or the person he is waiting for will be with him shortly.

Notify your peers when you leave the work area as well as when you return.

And most important, put a smile on your voice.

I.O.U. *A program for all of us to make life better at Michael Reese*

Source: Copyright © 1987. Michael Reese Hospital and Medical Center, Chicago, Illinois. Reprinted by permission.

her cap and sometimes dons her cape. Is it any wonder that patients exclaim, "I haven't seen a nurse in 3 days!" (They have, but they did not recognize him or her.)

Dress codes can be found in almost every hospital, although in many, the pages on which they are written are yellowed with age. To influence the overall image of your hospital, you must have *specific* standards of professional appearance that are *enforced*.

Jewish Hospital in Louisville, Kentucky, has drafted standards of professional appearance and conduct that specify acceptable and unacceptable clothing, jewelry, shoes, grooming, and behaviors such as chewing gum, eating, and smoking. These standards were incorporated into a full-color brochure to reinforce to existing employees and to communicate to prospective employees what is expected of professionalism. Anderson Memorial Hospital in Anderson, South Carolina, engaged in a similar activity to define professional standards. To communicate its importance, the hospital designed a humorous brochure featuring N.E.R.D.s (non-users of employee-required dress) depicting unacceptable appearances. Both hospitals have done excellent jobs in defining and communicating expectation levels and it is apparent in their employees' professionalism.

Provide Feedback

Employees need frequent feedback on their performance. Guidelines for providing feedback are offered by Mediatec, a La Canada, California-based training and consulting firm that works with hospitals, as well as retail stores and financial service institutions, to improve service delivery and customer satisfaction. Guidelines on performance feedback are provided in their training program called "The Competitive Edge."[6] These include:

- *Observe employees' performance personally:* Supervisors and managers should try to schedule regular times to observe staff members interacting with patients/guests. First-hand observation will give them the most immediate and accurate feedback and will provide valuable opportunities for intervening, when required. If staff members are not performing as expected, then supervisors and managers should do something about it promptly.
- *Give prompt feedback:* After observing the performance of their staff members, supervisors and managers should immediately share whatever information they have. If an action requires correction, the situation is still fresh in everyone's minds. Feedback can be given immediately following the performance or at the time the performance is being observed. However, great care should be taken by supervisors in the latter case. Staff members do not

want to be embarrassed in front of their patients or co-workers. Any intervention on the part of supervisors should be made with tact and care.

- *Be descriptive, rather than evaluative:* Supervisors should describe to their employees what they are doing and how effective their performances are in improving patient satisfaction. Supervisors should also attempt to be completely objective, describing only what they themselves have seen staff members say or do. The best approach is to avoid judgmental or evaluative language, which will only make people react defensively.

- *Begin with positive feedback:* So many times, people find it difficult to accept critical feedback, so it is important for supervisors and managers to create an atmosphere that does not upset the employee. Feedback that balances negative and positive information is much more effective than merely negative feedback. And starting with a positive statement will put staff members in a better frame of mind to receive any criticism.

To reinforce desired performance, the following tips are offered:

- *Provide the most available and reusable reinforcers.* Showing appreciation and remembering to compliment staff members on jobs well done are rewards that can be used anywhere and anytime. If this verbal praise can be said within earshot of co-workers, so much the better. Just knowing that they will be recognized when they do something satisfactorily is reinforcing of good performance. All employees enjoy recognition and praise, and a sign of appreciation from supervisors and managers is very satisfying. Staff members will feel that what they are doing is important and that they are making important contributions. By using the most available and reusable reinforcers, supervisors and managers can reward their employees for efforts that lead to accomplishment—immediately and often. This kind of reinforcement will encourage staff to continue using the service skills as effectively as they can.

- *Be specific.* When giving praise and showing recognition for jobs well done, supervisors must be specific about what actions are being rewarded. Employees should be told what was done well and why they are being complimented. Just telling them to "keep up the good work" is meaningless. If a particular action is to be reinforced, then supervisors' praise must be specific. Vague praise may lead employees to draw wrong conclusions and think that they are being praised for an incorrect reason.

- *Schedule positive reinforcement periodically.* Once supervisors observe improvement in performance, it is critical that they continue to strengthen and reinforce those behaviors by intermittently giving praise and demonstrating their enthusiasm about the higher level of patient satisfaction that has resulted. Some staff members will require praise at more frequent intervals than others. In these instances, if recognition is no longer forthcoming, performance will surely decline as well. It is not necessary for supervisors to reinforce performance each time they observe a job well done, but by periodically showing recognition, they will continue to reinforce desired behaviors. This praise will maintain those behaviors until they become routine.

Reward and Recognize Employees

What do you do for those employees who contribute and achieve the expectations of performance? They should be rewarded and recognized. If you have been giving all employees the standard 3 percent cost-of-living increases and other pay adjustments without tying service performance standards to your compensation and incentive system, you are reducing the efficacy of your service management program. Yet, money by itself is not a sufficient stimulator. Employee recognition programs should run constantly. The employees who excel in customer service should be acknowledged as "situational heroes." Word of their efforts should be publicized.

Employees who are cited in patient questionnaires or in letters that are written by discharged patients or family members should be recognized. Posting letters on a bulletin board, publishing comments in the employee newsletter, or recognizing employees during staff meetings are ways employees can receive public acknowledgment for their contributions.

You can stimulate employee recognition by asking patients to specifically identify employees who have gone out of their way to make their hospital stay more pleasant and satisfying. Inviting patients to identify employees by including a special place on the questionnaire is one method of encouragement. You might also consider printing special nomination ballots that can be distributed on patient food trays or by the patient representative, placing tent cards on the bedside table instructing patients to phone the patient hotline with complaints or compliments, and suggesting that your physicians nominate employees through the physician dictation system.

Hospitals throughout the country have developed specific recognition programs to honor those employees who contribute to customer satisfaction. A "caught in the act program" provides on-the-spot unexpected recognition. Individuals who are instructed to "wander" throughout the hospital observe interactions for which a previously identified employee can be recognized. The awards given to these employees do not need to be expensive. A voucher for a free meal in the cafeteria or a button that says, "I Was Caught in the Act" can be given.

A program that promotes recognition of employees and volunteers who consistently demonstrate commitment to customer satisfaction can also be instituted. This type of special recognition program should be geared to honoring those employees who personify the values of service, commitment, and loyalty. A program of this type should be distinguished from an Employee of the Month program. Most hospitals recognize many employees every quarter and induct them into a special club, such as the Ambassador Club.

Recognition is a symbolic act. Programs that celebrate the heroes of the organization are excellent ways to promote the "hoopla" that is characteristic of healthy cultures. It is important not to forget the silent heroes—those employees who are loyal, dedicated, and supportive, but who may not be engaging or outgoing. It is also important to include those who may not be as visible given the secluded nature of their work.

Organizations with strong cultures believe in rituals and ceremonies because they reinforce the values that are the cornerstone of the organization's mission. Consider the Mary Kay Cosmetic Company. To thousands of Mary Kay cosmetic sales representatives, a pink Cadillac has become a symbol of professional achievement. Who, in their right minds, would select pink as a color for a luxury car? Those who work for this company do and this very fact demonstrates just how important these symbols and rewards are in motivating employees to excel and achieve.

Provide Fair Warning

Finally, you have to be prepared to dismiss those employees who do not meet your expectations. Employees who do not contribute pull the organization down, rather than propel it forward. To summarize:

- Communicate expectations . . . and be specific.
- Coach those who do not meet the expectations.
- Reward and recognize those who contribute.
- Dismiss those who have not responded to counseling, coaching, and fair warnings.
- At all times, be a role model!

HIRE THE RIGHT PEOPLE

One major factor in implementing a service strategy is whom you hire and promote. For this reason, it is important to hire the right people—those who have values similar to yours. During the screening process, you must assess the degree to which the values that they hold are similar to organizational values. You cannot train someone to care. Caring is an inherent trait; people either care or they do not. If you are selecting and hiring those individuals who have an inherent desire to assume the customer-first orientation, you will have a more unified service organization.

Accurately predicting which candidates will be a "good fit" is no easy task. The problems that most managers encounter in selecting the right employees who have both the technical competence and the predisposition to service can be attributed, to a significant degree, to the inadequacy of the screening and interviewing processes. The technique of behavioral interviewing can be effectively used to improve the probability of a good match.

Behavioral interviewing is highly structured in format. It is based on the axiom that the best predictor of future behavior is past behavior. Candidates are asked a set of predetermined questions that are designed to elicit specific examples of behavioral responses that they made in previous jobs. For example, asking candidates to cite an example of a difficult situation in their previous job that involved a dissatisfied patient and to describe how they handled it can provide insight into their aptitude and ability to assess a situation, prioritize the patient's needs, solve problems, and act in behalf of the customer.

It is also important to let people know from the outset what you stand for and what you expect. Organizational values should be shared in the screening process. The Whitehall North, an excellent long-term care facility in Deerfield, Illinois, expects every nurse to wear a cap and pin. This expectation is conveyed to job applicants over the telephone and in person when candidates inquire about positions. The Whitehall North's staff attitude is that if candidates do not like this rule, they do not have to work there. Pure and simple.

If you have a large organization and a fair amount of turnover, you may have a difficult time recruiting nurses if you require them to wear caps and pins. The illustration makes an important point, however. You have to communicate what is important to you and what you feel will help you achieve your goals. The Whitehall's approach is not unlike that of the Disney organization. If you have ever wondered how it is that all of the employees at Disney World look so clean and fresh, it is because Disney takes an almost militaristic approach to how its people should look. The organization spells out standards of appearance, including acceptable hair styles, makeup, jewelry, and clothing. And it enforces them. This degree of specificity creates uniform standards, and these standards produce the uniform impressions that have made Disney successful.

Communication of expectations continues when a new employee begins the job. Think back on your first day at the hospital. Did you feel welcome? Did you sense that the new job would provide stimulating opportunities? Were you left with the impression that you would assume an important role? Did you sense what was important to your new employer?

Starting off on the right foot is very important. Orientation should be a welcoming celebration. Yet, for most hospitals, it is an obligatory period of variable duration, set aside to educate employees about the organization's policies and procedures. Few hospitals provide strong orientation to the organization's culture, traditions, and values. New employee orientation can most certainly be an investment that will reap future paybacks in employee and customer satisfaction.

Again, the industry example that best illustrates what new employee orientation should be like is from the Disney organization. Disney requires every new employee to participate in a comprehensive orientation. A part-time ticket taker does not receive an abbreviated course; he attends the entire orientation course. Graduation from "Traditions 1," a full day devoted to culture, values, history, and traditions is mandatory before employees can advance to specialized or technical training. Disney University is a multilevel educational institution from which every employee, regardless of status or level, must matriculate before spending time on the job.[7]

How can you extend a more hearty welcome to new employees and more clearly communicate what you expect? Consider these suggestions:

- Reserve time to educate employees about the goals and mission of the hospital; to explain past traditions, to introduce your heroes, and to share your rites and rituals. There is no better time than during orientation to let employees know that you have made a commitment to creating guest satisfaction and that they were hired because you perceived that they would assume a constructive role in making it happen.

- Take new employees on a grand tour. Afterwards, corral them into a special dining room for a free lunch with members of administration. If this is not feasible, offer a reception in the afternoon and invite department heads. Whatever you can do to provide the new employees with exposure to people, places, and information will be appreciated.

- At the conclusion of orientation, distribute special buttons to be worn for a period of 2-3 weeks. A button that says, "I am a new member of the General Hospital team," will be a signal to other employees that this is a person to greet and offer assistance. It also helps guests understand and tolerate delays that may be created by a lack of proficiency in yet-to-be-acquired skills.

Byron Bullard, president of Presbyterian Hospital in Charlotte, North Carolina, spends 1 hour with new employees on their first day. He introduces these employees to the values and the traditions of this 566-bed hospital. He also gives every employee a homework assignment at the conclusion of his talk. He asks them to read the book, *How To Win Friends and Influence People,* by Dale Carnegie, and to complete a short book report for his review.

You may feel that you do not have the time to devote to new employee orientation nor the inclination to ask new employees to complete a book report. The methods do not particularly matter as long as they convey the implicit message of hospital values and expectations.

LEADERSHIP IS VITAL

Socioenvironmental explanations of motivation appear in scores of popular business management books. Decreased productivity, poor profits, employee turnover, and a number of other business afflictions are purported to be caused by the lack of strong values and value-driven leadership. Leadership, therefore, is the motivating force. Without the "champions" to promote the values, to articulate the visions, and to untie the bonds that limit human potential, the organization is without purpose and direction.

The responsibility does not fall on the shoulders of one person, nor is it the exclusive domain of a few people at the top of the organizational chart. Although the health care industry is filled with managers, consultants, planners, and analysts, it has a dearth of the single most vital force: leaders. Perhaps this advertisement published by United Technologies in *The Wall Street Journal* says it best:

**Let's Get
Rid of
Management**

People
don't want
to be
managed.
They want
to be led.
Whoever heard
of a world
manager?
World leader,
yes.
Educational leader.
Political leader.
Religious leader.
Scout leader.
Community leader.
Labor leader.
Business leader.
They lead.
They don't manage.
The carrot

always wins
over the stick.
Ask your horse.
You can *lead* your
horse to water,
but you can't
manage him
to drink.
If you want to
manage somebody,
manage yourself.
Do that well
and you'll
be ready to
stop managing.
And start
leading.*

Leaders convey a vision of the future. They are continually interpreting today's events in terms of tomorrow's opportunities. They are not living in the past and seldom, if ever, bemoan the fact that "things aren't the way they used to be." Tomorrow represents a vision of new opportunity for leaders, one that has limitless opportunity for change, improvement, and excellence.

Leaders encourage people to think and act for themselves because they view their own role as one of providing advice, encouragement and direction. They are role models and realize that they cannot expect of their employees what they themselves do not demonstrate.

Leaders are change agents and social architects. They are called to manage relationships and restructure their organizations to meet the needs and demands of the marketplace. It is also management's responsibility to ensure that employees have the capabilities and resources to implement a service approach. Eliminating unnecessary roles, policies, and other hindrances will go a long way to make it easier for employees to serve the customers.

SUMMARY

Expectations are translated into actions when employees clearly understand what is expected of them and can recognize how their participation will benefit them. Leaders create an awareness of corporate and personal values through their words and their behaviors. They have a special talent for identifying with emotional issues that appeal to their employees and cause employees to enlist in causes

---

*Reprinted with permission of United Technologies Corporation, Hartford, Connecticut, © 1986.

that give purpose to their work and lives. The degree to which employees "buy in" to the mission is determined by their perception of the sincerity of the messages.

NOTES

1. James C. Shaffer, "Seven Emerging Trends in Organizational Communication." *IABC Communication World* (February 1986): 36–37.

2. Robert L. Desatnick, *Managing to Keep the Customer* (San Francisco: Jossey-Bass Publishers, 1987), 20.

3. Ibid., 20.

4. *The Wall Street Journal* (March 17, 1987): 1.

5. Kristine E. Peterson, "Internal Marketing—Closing the Loop." In *Reaching Women*, by Barbara B. Alpern (Chicago: Pluribus Press, Inc., 1987): 122–123.

6. *The Competitive Edge: Achieving New Levels of Patient Satisfaction*, Transfer of Training Module (workbook), Mediatec, Inc., 1984.

7. N.W. (Red) Pope, "Mickey Mouse Marketing," *American Banker*, (July 25, 1979).

Chapter 8

Guest Relations Program Pitfalls

Although few health care executives would describe their guest relations programs as total failures, many are disheartened by the fleeting effects of their efforts. Most programs are perceived to lack staying power. In one survey of nursing executives, of those who indicated that they had guest relations programs in their hospitals, only 5 percent believed that their current efforts would be affecting hospital operations in 18 months.[1]

Why are the predictions for the future viability of guest relations programs so dismal? Why are the net returns so low? Are the initial expectations too high? What can be done to increase the likelihood that a program will be successful? Clearly, there are no easy answers or simple solutions because the degree of success or failure achieved can be influenced by many factors. But just as success is never a matter of pure luck, failure is rarely the result of circumstances beyond one's control. Failure may not be attributable to a program's content, but rather to the design, or lack thereof, of the implementation process.

In some instances, failure is inevitable because of the nature of the individual hospital. The internal culture simply cannot or will not accept guest relations. If I have come to appreciate one fact during my years of consulting, it is that, although all hospitals share similar characteristics, each has a unique culture. Over the past 9 years, I have observed essentially four different types of hospitals:

1. *Bold hospitals:* These are a joy to work with because they already have very healthy cultures. They are sincere in their commitment to guest relations and aware of what it will cost in terms of time and resources. They have visible and involved leaders. They have their share of internal problems, but also a sense of purposeful direction. They are always poised for action and move forward from the start, overcoming obstacles with relative ease. Although they are eager to learn what others are doing, they do not rely on this information because their own innovations are plentiful and creative. They

tend to be very fluid, with decentralized structures of authority and few controls. They make their consultants look good when, in fact, these consultants can take little of the credit.

2. *Strong hospitals:* These are perhaps the most common, although they vary vastly in size and scope. They move forward at a determined pace and do not deviate frequently from the prescribed structures and schedules. They have relatively strong leaders who are involved and committed, although not always to the optimal extent. Through the process of designing and implementing guest relations, they learn to be more innovative; however, they tend to rely on borrowed ideas as the springboard for new ideas. Strong organizations are enjoyable to work with, and their programs survive and prosper long after the training programs are over.

3. *Confused hospitals:* These are organizations with confused identities. Their values are ill-defined and ambiguous. They have their share of problems as well, which tend to emanate from poor employee morale. They have competent managers and administrators who collectively lack a little guest relations gusto. They say they are committed to it, but they are reluctant to invest the necessary resources to make their efforts succeed. They tend to quantify everything and view the time that employees spend away from their jobs for guest relations activities as a sacrifice, rather than an investment. Progress is slow, often because confused hospitals tend to be large and cumbersome organizations; yet they show little interest in breaking down the larger organization into smaller, more productive, and innovative centers.

4. *ERA hospitals (also known as Everything to Resist Action):* These organizations spend most of their time dreaming up reasons why it won't work and excuses for why it doesn't work. I regret to say that I can often identify these hospitals before ever stepping foot in the front door. They call to say, "We need a proposal so that our committee of 30 can review it by Friday (3 days away). Be sure to send it Federal Express because we are meeting at 10:30 A.M. and have to make a recommendation to administration by Monday." With ERA hospitals, it is always "hurry up and wait." Everyone is afraid to make decisions without appropriate approval. Their leaders are totally dependent on ideas from others. Individuals within the organization think, but never reach a collective meeting of the minds. The general lacks leadership, the colonels are powerless, and the lieutenants waste much time fighting turf battles. These hospitals are an effort to work with, not a challenge.

Unless a guest relations program is designed to identify and analyze characteristics of the culture that will support or inhibit the emphasis on guest satisfaction, the program's effectiveness will be minimal.

FACTORS THAT LIMIT SUCCESS

By determining why guest relations programs fail, we can learn how to help them succeed. The following common factors dilute a health care organization's opportunities for success in guest relations. By identifying these factors, we have the opportunity to correct similar problems, or, from the outset, to design programs that take them into account.

Lack of a Defined Service Strategy

A service strategy is the heart of a service program. The achievement of a sustainable initiative is only possible when the hospital has a strategy for service that provides managers and employees with a common focus. It is characterized by a mission that people can understand. The strategy is built on fundamental values that declare customer satisfaction and quality service to be of utmost importance, and these values become the guiding principles for the guest relations program. If hospital leaders have not clearly defined organizational values, they will find it difficult to create the sense of purposeful direction needed to sustain the effort.

A service strategy should be developed for the corporate body. Each department or service entity within the organization should also have one. The driving forces behind a strong guest relations program are the commitment that is made and the strategies that are developed to transform the culture to become more service-driven and customer-responsive.

Premature Introduction

Ignoring the fact that successful service management is based on a thorough analysis of many dimensions of operational and managerial practices, hospitals often begin training programs without investing the time to make certain that their strategies and systems for achieving superior service are defined and finely tuned. Doing so inevitably hinders the fulfillment of the following needs:

- *Need for planning:* What sense does it make to begin a journey without knowing your destination? The fact is, if you do not know where you are going or how to get there, you will probably never arrive there. It is necessary to think strategically and to develop an action plan that will outline the objectives and chart the course to reach them.

- *Need for organizational assessment:* It is beneficial to identify existing conditions that will favorably or negatively affect guest relations efforts. By recognizing your organization's strengths and acknowledging its weaknesses, you increase the probability of success of service management. It is far better to have a strategy of crisis *prevention* than one of crisis *intervention.*

- *Need for commitment from the top:* The necessary support should be generated from top management; however, executives do not shoulder the entire weight. Middle managers play crucial roles in making guest relations successful. All too often, managers are given subtle ultimatums that imply, "You will support guest relations or else . . ." If managers do not understand how a service strategy can benefit their own department's operations and their employees, their commitment will be weak. It is necessary to spend time educating managers and soliciting their input and involvement.

- *Need for baseline data:* It is difficult to measure success without baseline data. An effort to define the measures and monitor the process of implementing a service strategy will help justify its expenditures. Accountability is an important characteristic of results-oriented organizations.

- *Need to generate grassroots support:* Just as lukewarm commitment from the top will inhibit success, so also will guest relations be weakened if people within the organization do not understand why the hospital is undertaking the process. The power that emanates from shared commitment will propel the organization to be more consumer-driven. This energy cannot be generated without early support-building efforts directed at all segments of the hospital population.

Weak and Invisible Leadership

Champions of guest relations are leaders who assume prominent roles in articulating the visions and values that will enlist the support of employees. Leaders, through their words and actions, can infuse great energy into a program. Because enormous commitment is required to make a guest relations program successful, visible support of the process must be extended. Success in instilling values derives from an obvious and sincere commitment to those values. Although it is always more effective if the lead champion is the chief executive officer, it is not absolutely necessary. Delegating leadership to the right representative who has influence and the credibility to communicate administration's support will signal top management's sincerity and depth of commitment.

Leaders who "wander" realize that Management by Walking Around (MBWA) is more than just a popular gimmick promoted by excellent companies. If leaders are to be close to their customers, they must be physically close to them, which requires that significant time be spent walking and listening. If you try this approach, you will discover what your customers are saying about you and the service that you provide. You will find out more from informal interviews with patients and family members than you will from surveys and questionnaires. By wandering, leaders can also learn much about and from their employees, and they can reinforce core guest relations values. Providing directions to a lost guest and chatting with a group of employees on a nursing unit are tangible expressions of a sincere belief that "I can make the difference." In addition, by being accessible and approachable, leaders can stay in touch. One of the worst facility planning decisions an organization makes is to locate the corporate offices off campus. This loss of proximity naturally discourages wandering. And when the organization's leaders make decisions in the confines of their offices, they frequently lose touch with the reality of hospital life. They begin to respond to numbers, rather than people.

Excessive Reductions in Staffing

All good business executives are sensitive to overhead costs; however, the leader committed to delivering superior service recognizes the cost of doing business in a customer-driven marketplace. In a competitive arena where discriminating customers value quality service, the provider must allocate the resources to deliver that service. Weak cultures, poor morale, and dissatisfied customers are characteristics of hospitals obsessively concerned with productivity measures and staffing formulas. They cut their staffing levels to the bare minimum and then expect quality service. Cost controls and efficiency, over the long run, will be achieved by an emphasis on quality and service. The revenue line comes first, but cost control and quality service can be parallel goals. Neither is achievable if employees withhold their personal investment in the mission of the hospital. If employees do not perceive that the hospital really cares about and supports them, they will put in their hours, but they will not invest their hearts. They will perform at levels below their capacities.

Lack of Accountability

It is discouraging to witness the number of institutions that tolerate inferior performance while they hotly pursue the goal of superior service. If you admire Disney World or the Marriott Corporation, then consider for what length of time they would tolerate an individual who sabotages their corporate culture with contemptible behavior. How do you think employees feel when they work hard to contribute, yet witness managers consistently overlooking the poor performances of others? Successful hospitals create cultures that reward those who contribute to guest relations and dismiss those who are hopelessly negative, rude to guests, unsupportive of management, and uncooperative with others.

What do you really value if, in response to a reduction in force, you lay off employees who exhibit excellent guest contact skills and attitudes, but retain tenured employees who are rude and negative? You value length of service, not guest relations.

Accountability extends to departmental operations as well. How are managers held accountable? Every department is responsible for service delivery. To hold managers accountable for superior service, measures by which to evaluate departmental performance must be defined. Performance bonuses should be based on dimensions of customer satisfaction, as well as profitability and competency.

Absence of an Infrastructure

Measurement of customer satisfaction and feedback are principal themes of effective service organizations. Without these elements an organization has no mechanism for monitoring customer satisfaction or stimulating action that will result in service or performance improvements. An infrastructure comprises satisfaction feedback mechanisms that regularly measure satisfaction levels of patients, physicians, departments, and employees. By its very design, an infrastructure will force ongoing change and evolution. Every effort to identify satisfaction will reveal areas of unmet expectations or needs to which the hospital can respond. Surveys, telephone interviews, personal interviews, focus groups, open forums, and other methods used to gather feedback and to monitor satisfaction will generate ideas for improvement. They will also provide the innovators with opportunities to translate needs into the new programs, services, and "extra touches" that will create greater satisfaction among patients, visitors, physicians, and employees.

Once the hospital creates the information loop, people must respond to the sources of satisfaction and dissatisfaction. Just as you cannot assign total responsibility for the budget to the financial officer, you cannot assign total responsibility for guest relations to the personnel department or the marketing director or the patient representative. A structure that involves individuals from all levels and corporate divisions on committees and task forces will promote widespread ownership of the guest relations program. The effort will not receive the necessary support if you do not have representatives who can voice their opinions, contribute their energies, and recruit their peers to buy into it. Devote the people, devote the resources, devote the time.

Weak Employee/Patient Relations

Two departments within a hospital can have a measurable impact on the overall success of a guest relations program: the patient representative department and the personnel department. How powerful or powerless are your patient representative and your personnel director? What levels of credibility do they maintain? What influence do they assert?

Too many hospitals view the patient representative as a hostess whose two-fold mission is to spread goodwill and to put out fires. Rather, the patient representative should be a risk manager whose mission is to assist management constructively in preventing litigation and maintaining customer satisfaction. The patient representative should be an educator of patients, physicians, and employees. He or she should have the authority to act on grievances. The patient representative or director should have the political savvy to function as an intermediary between patients, family members, physicians, departments, divisions, administration, management, and employees; the credibility to win the trust of physicians; and the ability to earn the trust and respect of employees so that they will refer significant problems to them.

In essence, the patient representative should be a strong leader who is given the autonomy and control to exercise good judgment on behalf of the patients and the hospital. The patient relations department can be viewed as the hospital's equivalent of the consumer affairs department found in many established businesses. Patient representatives should be given responsibility to participate visibly in activities and interventions that will improve customer satisfaction.

As hospitals recognize the importance of their personnel and the impact that they have on the future success of the hospital, they place greater emphasis on the role of the personnel director, commonly known today as the director or vice president of human resources. Hospital administrators who do not recognize the powerful role of human resource development and who view the personnel department as only having the responsibility to execute hire and fire decisions are contributing significantly to the inevitable erosion of employee relations. This, in turn, can have a severe impact on the hospital's customer relations. The human resource and organizational development functions should be executed by an individual who has the resources and tools to recruit, select, and retain top quality leaders and innovators. The mission of this department should be to improve the quality of work life in the organization. A health care system under constant change demands that high-caliber managers and employees be hired, developed, and retained.

Exclusion of Critical Audiences

Take a look at your organization. As a hospital, you have the following segments: trustees, executives, managers, employees, volunteers, and physicians. All too often, a guest relations program is sponsored by management for employees, but three important audiences are left out: the trustees, volunteers, and physicians.

If an organization's culture is influenced from the top, you cannot go higher, in an organizational sense, than the board of trustees. These leaders should be knowledgeable about and involved in the guest relations effort. In addition to their interest in protecting the mission of the hospital, many may also have a keen interest in the hospital's program as a model for their own businesses.

With the increasing incidence of staff layoffs, hospitals are relying to a greater extent on volunteers. Most volunteers hold very visible front-line positions, such as at the front desk, the surgical waiting rooms, and the gift shop. They deliver newspapers and hospitality items to patient rooms. They transport patients and deliver work orders to departments.

Because the volunteers play important roles in shaping patients' and family members' impressions of the hospital, they should be viewed as unpaid employees. Your expectations of them should be no lower than those of your employees who receive a paycheck. The fact that volunteers donate their time should not compromise your standards or expectations. Ask volunteers to participate in training programs with employees. Do not exclude them from recognition. Their involvement helps improve volunteer/employee relations which are strained in many hospitals, with employees viewing volunteers as threats to their job security. Likewise, because volunteers are not rewarded monetarily, they are made to feel that their roles are insignificant. This prevailing attitude emphasizes the need to bolster the image of the volunteer roles and to demonstrate appreciation for the services they provide. Expressions of appreciation fuel volunteers' motivations to provide quality service.

Physicians may be independent practitioners, but in the eyes of the patients they are members of the hospital's team. The approach you take to involve them will differ from that taken with employees, but physicians should not be excluded from the guest relations program. Mandatory participation in a guest relations training program is not recommended, nor is it realistic. Instead, share the program goals and strategies and offer physicians an abbreviated and modified version of the program. Strategies for doing so are set forth in Chapter 16. Academic medical centers should not ignore physicians from patient care, education, and research divisions.

Lack of a Systems Approach

The service delivery system delivers the service. Each time the customer confronts each of these points of service delivery, a moment of truth occurs within your organization. Systems evolve to guide service delivery. Whether the procedures are developed for evaluating employee performance or for transporting a patient from point A to point B, there is a need to monitor constantly the effectiveness of those procedures and systems. You must analyze how your systems work independently and how they work together. You must also ask, "Do our systems exist to serve our needs or those of our customers?"

Health care providers are extremely adept at perpetuating policies under the guise of what is best for the patient. Ask a hospital to remove visiting restrictions and you will find that those who fight to the end for the patient's best interest are really trying to preserve some control over bothersome visitors who get in the way. Likewise, the hospital admitting system usually focuses on payment, rather than on customer comfort. And if you have ever visited the emergency room for what you considered a real emergency, and then had to suffer through an insurance verification process conducted with total disregard for your discomfort and pain, you can understand why hospitals now take the brunt of the consumer's revolt. Is there a better way? More and more hospitals are asking that question. Certainly, there are ways to deliver health care services that do not compromise the patient's needs for control, dignity, and comfort or the hospital's needs for quality and efficiency. Those hospitals that choose to ignore these vital patient needs may find some consolation in discovering that they will have fewer and fewer patients to get in the way in the future.

A guest relations program designed to diagnose system problems and to encourage service delivery improvements adds essential depth and substance to the overall effort.

Poverty of Spirit

When employees' needs and expectations are not fulfilled by their organization, morale plunges and productivity declines. It takes more than a guest relations program to overcome the fundamental deficiencies of a weak culture that is characterized by underutilized, underrecognized, and understimulated employees. In far too many hospitals in this country, a poverty of spirit prevails, creating insuperable barriers to guest relations success. Without a spirit of service, guest relations fails.

WHERE DO WE GO FROM HERE?

If you have already implemented a guest relations program and have wondered, "Where do we go from here?," it is time to assess your current situation and identify the strategies that will help you get back on track.

The Einstein Consulting Group, affiliated with Albert Einstein Medical Center in Philadelphia, has worked with numerous hospitals throughout the country to implement their "Hospitality" guest relations program. The "Guest Relations Follow Through Needs Inventory" was developed by the Einstein Consulting Group to help hospitals diagnose needs for guest relations program expansion.

The instrument used in this diagnostic survey is found in Appendix 8-A. To complete the inventory, answer each statement with a "yes" or "no." It is important to choose an answer, even though you may prefer to answer "somewhat" or "maybe" on some questions.

Once you have completed the inventory, count the number of "yes" answers for each section and write the total for each at the end of that section. Then transfer the totals for each section to the scoring sheet provided in Appendix 8-B. Multiply each total by the factor next to it and write the number in the score column.

The numbers in the circles indicate your degree of success in each category. The highest score possible for each category is 36. The higher the number, the more successful the program. Lower numbers reflect gaps or weaknesses. To learn from these weaknesses, go back and analyze the items that decreased your score, because these reveal promising directions for follow-up.

The following descriptions of each category are provided to help you recognize what you have accomplished and to what areas you should devote further attention.

Success Indicators (A): This score indicates how much success you feel your guest relations program has already achieved. Those with higher scores in this category should feel proud and accomplished! For the future, the challenge to you is how to maintain and even strengthen the gains you have made.

If your score is low here, you are probably dissatisfied with the results you have achieved. The items with lower scores suggest possible areas for follow-up.

Awareness (B): The lower the score, the more you need to reconsider strategies for raising employee awareness of guest relations, for assessing what your hospital stands to gain from excellence, and for determining what every employee can do (and must do) to help. Consider these options:

- Make your guest relations values and behaviors much more explicit in your culture, policies, and procedures.
- Steep your management team and supervisors in a customer-oriented management philosophy and skills.

- Institute periodic refresher programs for all employees.
- Strengthen visual campaigns that call people's attention to guest relations themes, behaviors, and success.

Accountability (C): Does your guest relations approach have "teeth?" Lower scores here indicate that the program has a weak foundation. Employees might be very aware of the value your organization places on guest relations, but without accountability mechanisms, you cannot expect lasting results. Consider these options:

- State mandatory guest relations job requirements in behavioral terms. Build these into policies, job descriptions, employee orientation, hiring practices, and the performance appraisal process.
- Arrange for focused training of administrators, middle managers, and supervisors on their role in achieving guest relations excellence, including the manager as role model, setting and communicating job-specific expectations, reinforcing and enforcing high standards, managing the rude or indifferent employee, and other topics.

System for Evaluation, Problem Solving, and Communications (D): To sustain motivation and energy for guest relations, an organization must have systems for *ongoing* evaluation, problem solving, and communication. Otherwise, employees become disillusioned and frustrated. Lower scores here need to be taken very seriously, because they indicate an undercurrent of employee feeling that interferes with their ability to extend themselves to patients, visitors, physicians, and co-workers. Consider these options:

- Stay close to your customers and the people who make your organization tick. Institute ongoing methods for evaluating patient, visitor, physician, and employee satisfaction. Share the results with every person in your system who should be influenced by them, such as managers and all employees. Develop a system for follow-up.
- Strengthen systems for inviting employee complaints and suggestions.
- Strengthen systems for solving problems, including interdepartmental problems, making sure to institute prompt action on problems that decrease guest satisfaction and employee motivation.
- Revamp systems for systematic downward communication that inform employees, physicians, and patients when actions will be taken in response to their complaints and suggestions or why no actions will be taken.
- Institute *explicit* downward communication vehicles, such as truthful newsletters and periodic rap sessions.

- Examine your methods of handling complaints, from beginning to end. Improve your system so that people are invited to complain, their complaints land in the hands of people with the power to act, resolutions are found and communicated to the complainer in a timely fashion, and complaints are monitored as a key indicator of trends, problems, and needs for intervention.
- Train managers and supervisors in team building, participatory management, and group problem solving. Develop a squad of facilitators who convene key people and help them tackle difficult problems.

Systems and Amenities (E): People skills are not enough! Employees can only apologize so many times for patient discomfort, inconvenience, and cumbersome systems. Lower scores in this category suggest that systemic problems and insufficient amenities or extras for guests interfere with your achieving the goal of service excellence. Consider these options:

- Bring in an expert with "new eyes" to audit your key services and amenities, such as dietary, housekeeping, transport, admissions, discharge planning, and others. Invite his or her recommendations and develop implementation plans.
- Develop a "user-friendly committee" of employees and/or community members to look at your organization and suggest ways to make it more user-friendly.
- Hold contests and campaigns that invite employees to suggest ways to improve frustrating systems and improve patient comfort and convenience.

Skill Development Strategies (F): The people skills that constitute excellent guest relations are not easy to acquire. It is hard not to be good, but it is very hard to be excellent—to impress your guests with your compassionate, responsive, and respectful treatment. Doing so takes skills! Lower scores in this area suggest the need for skill-building programs and other employee development strategies. Consider these options:

- Offer skill-building programs targeted to specific job clusters.
- Develop job instruction guides, as do hotels, with optional "scripts" for handling typical situations.
- Offer training to the important people who use the phone extensively.
- Offer "professional renewal" programs that revive people's energy for their jobs (so they give you their best!)
- Teach your entire work force to invite and handle complaints well.

Physician Involvement (G): If physicians are not involved in your guest relations strategy, then your employees are probably angry! Also, physicians are caregivers and part of the team, so how can you ignore them? Lower scores in this area indicate a need to develop or strengthen your physician strategy. The shape of this strategy depends on the role and structure of your physician groups, e.g., voluntary, full-time staff, residents, students, or a combination. Consider these options:

- Hold physician focus groups to identify issues and decide how best to reach the physicians.
- Schedule briefings for physicians about your overall guest relations strategy and how physicians can help.
- Initiate a serious effort to improve opportunities for input, problem solving, and communication so the physicians feel respected, listened to, and cared about.
- Develop a physician-to-physician strategy.

Effective Plan (H): To make your strategy an enduring one, you need a long-range strategic guest relations plan. Lower scores in this section indicate a weakness in your blueprint and inadequate support for your guest relations leadership. Consider these options:

- Devote time to determining whether guest relations was meant to be a passing fad or an enduring cultural thrust.
- Bring in an outside expert to help.
- Devote time to developing a strategic guest relations plan.
- Re-examine who in your organization is responsible for guest relations. Is the responsibility too concentrated on one person and thus involvement and investment are too narrow?
- Regroup.

SUMMARY

If you previously implemented a guest relations program that failed to achieve spectacular results, do not despair. You can resurrect the program and get back on track. Identifying factors that cause guest relations programs to fail can be instructional in helping you implement future strategies that will succeed. Subsequent chapters will describe specific guest relations approaches that can be adapted to meet your organization's needs.

NOTE

1. Rita Fritz, "Developing a Consumer-Driven Hospital—Four Fatal Flaws" *Healthcare Forum* (May/June 1986): 39–40.

Appendix 8-A

Guest Relations Follow Through Needs Inventory

A. *HOW GREAT IS YOUR NEED FOR FOLLOW THROUGH?*

	Y	N
1. Patients hardly ever complain about employee attitudes and behavior.		
2. Our organization's atmosphere is generally seen as very friendly.		
3. Physicians are generally satisfied with the cooperation they get from staff.		
4. Physicians are generally satisfied with staff behavior toward their patients.		
5. Our employees speak positively about our organization to outsiders.		
6. Our physicians are generally seen as hospitable toward staff.		
7. Our physicians are generally seen as hospitable toward patients and their visitors.		
8. If a visitor looks lost or confused, our employees typically help them find their way.		
9. Our employees are friendly toward visitors, patients, physicians and one another in public areas.		
10. Our organization has a reputation in the community for being a friendly place.		
11. Generally, we have a spirit of teamwork and cooperation among our employees.		
12. Generally, we have a spirit of teamwork and cooperation between our employees and physicians.		
A. TOTAL # YES		

Source: Reprinted with permission of The Einstein Consulting Group, Philadelphia, Pennsylvania.

B. *AWARENESS HIGH?*

	Y	N
1. Most of our employees can explain the importance of patient satisfaction to our organization's mission and health, and to their own job security.		
2. Most of our employees can explain the importance of visitor satisfaction to our organization's mission and health, and to their own job security.		
3. Most of our employees can explain the importance of physician satisfaction to our organization's health and to their own job security.		
4. Most of our employees can explain the importance of co-worker cooperation to our organization's mission and health and to their own job security.		
5. Our employees at all levels are informed about our hospital's financial situation and competitive position.		
6. Our employees at all levels are generally aware of the new challenges that hospitals face and the strategies underway at our hospital to tackle these challenges.		
7. Our employees are generally aware of their importance in attracting patients.		
8. In our hospital's written materials (eg., annual report, employee and patient handbooks, etc.), our high priority on guest satisfaction is stated and restated . . . to reinforce its importance in our organization's culture.		
9. We generate periodic visual reminders that reinforce guest relations messages (eg., posters, T-shirts, buttons, etc.)		
10. Our house publications carry features on guest relations issues, events, and accomplishments.		
11. Administrators frequently refer to guest relations and patient satisfaction as driving forces in our culture.		

	Y	N
12. We have a system for updating our employees on the economic challenges ahead for our organization, so they know how we're doing and what we're doing to succeed.		
B. TOTAL # YES		

C. *ARE PEOPLE ACCOUNTABLE?*

	Y	N
1. Courteous, respectful, and compassionate behavior toward patients and other guests is a requirement in our organization, not an option.		
2. For our employees, we've instituted clear, written behavioral expectations that describe guest relations behavior in specific terms.		
3. Managers and supervisors hold employees accountable for their behavior toward hospital guests, confronting problem employees when such employees darken the hospital's image.		
4. At our hospital, we are encouraged to coach, discipline and eventually terminate employees who persist in their failure to meet high guest relations standards.		
5. Department heads and supervisors who are technically competent, but negative in their interpersonal skills toward employees and hospital guests are under pressure to meet guest relations standards.		
6. Generally, our top administrators show courtesy, friendliness, and a caring attitude toward patients and visitors.		
7. Generally, our top administrators show courtesy, friendliness, and a caring attitude toward employees.		

	Y	N
8. Managers and supervisors are under pressure to be role models of positive guest relations.		
9. The atmosphere in my organization makes it impossible any longer for rude and belligerent employees to remain secure employees and accepted year after year.		
10. Our department heads and supervisors have established and communicated clear, job-specific expectations to the people they supervise.		
11. Our administrators have communicated clear expectations to the people they supervise.		
12. Specific guest relations responsibilities are built into job descriptions.		
13. Our hiring practices include specific techniques for screening applicants for guest relations instincts and skills.		
14. Guest relations behavior has a prominent place in our performance appraisal process.		
15. Employees who show excellent guest relations receive appreciation and praise for their efforts.		
16. The quality of one's behavior toward hospital guests affects employee pay increases and promotions.		
17. Our New Employee Orientation emphasizes the importance we place on guest satisfaction and communicates the specific behavior expected of every employee to achieve guest satisfaction.		
18. Our hospital has systems for recognizing employees who are wonderful to guests.		
C. TOTAL # YES		

D. *DO YOU HAVE SYSTEMS FOR EVALUATION,*
   PROBLEM SOLVING, AND COMMUNICATION?

	Y	N
1. We have systems in place to assess visitor satisfaction with our staff and services.		
2. We have strategies in place to assess patient satisfaction with our staff and services.		
3. We have strategies in place to monitor physician satisfaction with our staff and services.		
4. We have strategies in place to monitor employee satisfaction with their co-workers, managers, our work environment, and hospital systems.		
5. Generally, our staff welcome and invite guest complaints, since complaints give us a chance to show our concern and responsiveness.		
6. Generally, people here are apologetic and concerned when patients are not satisfied; staff bend over backwards to resolve complaints.		
7. When patients have a complaint or concern, they know whom to call.		
8. We have a clear system for handling patient complaints and needs.		
9. We have a system for communicating to patients any actions taken as a result of their complaints or requests.		
10. When employees have complaints or suggestions, they know specific channels for expressing them.		
11. Our administration and middle managers generally respond to employee complaints and concerns, even if they don't act on them.		
12. Our administration is generally perceived as open to employee complaints and suggestions.		
D. TOTAL # YES		

E. *ARE SYSTEMS AND AMENITIES COMFORTING, EASY TO USE, AND CONVENIENT?*

	Y	N
1. We examine our systems periodically to see if we can make them more "user-friendly."		
2. Generally, evaluations of food and food services are positive in our organization.		
3. Generally, evaluations of cleanliness are positive in our organization.		
4. Generally, people can get from place to place in our organization without getting too frustrated.		
5. Generally, the admissions process runs smoothly without long waits.		
6. Generally, the discharge process runs smoothly from the patient's point of view, without undue confusion or unexpected waits.		
7. Generally, in-house transport services run smoothly, without unexplainable patient waits or equipment shortages that cause undue delays.		
8. Our employees generally are tolerant of systems problems in our hospital, because they're aware of management's commitment to making things run more smoothly.		
9. We have effective ways to tackle systems problems that involve many departments simultaneously.		
10. Generally, systems in our hospital work smoothly enough that employees don't have to apologize endlessly for systems problems and breakdowns.		
11. We periodically examine those services with the greatest effect on consumer satisfaction to see if we can improve them.		
12. We look at the amenities or extras we offer periodically to see if we can increase patient comfort and satisfaction.		
E. TOTAL # YES		

F. *DO YOU HAVE SYSTEMS FOR IMPROVING EMPLOYEE SKILLS?*

	Y	N
1. Our organization offers training programs periodically to upgrade the guest relations skills of all employees.		
2. Our organization offers training programs to upgrade the job-specific guest relations skills among: Parking attendants Security Information desk staff Admissions staff Nurses Medical/Unit Secretaries Radiology techs Housekeepers Tray delivery personnel Maintenance staff Billing/Cashiers Ambulatory care personnel Supervisors Emergency Unit staff Others as needed . . .		
3. We train our people with the most telephone contact in telephone skills.		
4. We offer training in handling complaints, so that complaints are seen as giving us another chance to satisfy our guests.		
5. We offer professional renewal programs to help our nurses and others handle the stress, pressure, and burnout felt by many these days.		
6. We have strategies for team building, so that problems within groups and between groups are not ignored.		
F. TOTAL # YES		

G. *ARE YOUR PHYSICIANS INVOLVED?*

	Y	N
1. Physicians are aware of our organization's priority on guest relations.		
2. Physicians see themselves as an important part of our guest relations strategy.		
3. We've made physicians aware of the specific behavior expectations that constitute positive guest relations.		
4. When a physician violates our guest relations standards, that physician is confronted in a constructive way.		
5. When doctors have a complaint, they know whom to call.		
6. We have a clear system for responding to physician complaints and needs.		
G. TOTAL # YES		

H. *A CLEAR, EFFECTIVE GUEST RELATIONS STRATEGY?*

1. Our guest relations strategy is clear for the coming year.		
2. A variety of people share clear responsibilities for our guest relations strategy.		
3. We have one person who is seen as primarily responsible for coordinating our guest relations strategy.		
4. Key people in our organization realize that guest relations can't be a program that ends, but instead needs to be a long-range, far-reaching strategy.		
5. Our in-house coordinator experiences support and cooperation within our organization.		
6. Administrators view guest relations as an organizational priority, not the job of a particular person or department.		
H. TOTAL # YES		

Appendix 8-B

Scoring Sheet

How To Score

1. Make sure you've responded to every item.
2. Count the number of "Yes" answers for each section and write the total for each at the end of that section.
3. Now, transfer the totals for each section to the corresponding section below TOTAL column.
4. Now multiply each TOTAL above by the factor next to it, and write the answer in the circle in the score column.

	Section	*Total*	$\times$	*Factor*	$=$	*Score* *0 to 36*
Success Indicators	A		$\times$	3	$=$	$\bigcirc$
Awareness	B		$\times$	3	$=$	$\bigcirc$
Accountability	C		$\times$	2	$=$	$\bigcirc$
Systems for Evaluation, Problem Solving, and Communication	D		$\times$	3	$=$	$\bigcirc$
Systems and Amenities	E		$\times$	3	$=$	$\bigcirc$
Skill Development Strategies	F		$\times$	6	$=$	$\bigcirc$
Physician Involvement	G		$\times$	6	$=$	$\bigcirc$
Effective Plan	H		$\times$	6	$=$	$\bigcirc$

Source: Reprinted with permission of The Einstein Consulting Group, Philadelphia, Pennsylvania.

Chapter 9

Accountability: Expect, Empower, Enforce

The goal of service management is to create exceptional satisfaction from external customers (patients, physicians) and internal providers (departments, employees, and volunteers). To attain that goal, you must have an accountability system in place.

Quality service and customer satisfaction should be an expressed expectation of every department and person. If you recognize that the hospital is made up of many small service delivery entities, then you will find useful the concept that department directors or managers are leaders of their own small "In Search of Excellence" companies. Following this model, it becomes imperative that hospital administrators decentralize hospital operations and hold department directors and managers accountable for quality service. Therefore, the focus of accountability should be on the managerial level.

Many hospitals that have implemented guest relations programs have focused on individual accountability by developing performance standards and incorporating them into the *employee* performance evaluation system. Although it is certainly important to hold employees accountable for service performance, it is significantly more important to hold managers accountable for creating customer satisfaction. If managers are not held accountable, regardless of whether their primary customer is the physician, patient, or another department, the system fails. Departmental accountability will then demand employee performance accountability.

To hold departments and their managers accountable, you must have satisfaction monitoring systems in place. One of the reasons why the Marriott Corporation is so successful in achieving guest satisfaction is that it elicits, analyzes, and responds to very sophisticated guest satisfaction survey data.

Marriott Corporation's Office of Consumer Affairs receives over 15,000 questionnaires a week. Data are entered, and the satisfaction levels for each of the hotel sites are monitored. When the satisfaction level deviates from the norm, regional operations officers and hotel general managers are notified. And they are expected to make changes to correct the situation.

Accountability requires a sturdy infrastructure. An infrastructure is the foundation on which a program should be built. The structural support of a program is provided by systems that enable you to monitor satisfaction, diagnose problems, and implement solutions. The infrastructure should be designed to identify those systemic problems that stand in the way of delivering superior service and achieving superior performance. When satisfaction feedback is measured against standards that describe desirable levels of service quality and people are empowered to make changes that will resolve root sources of customer and employee dissatisfaction, everyone benefits.

THE INFRASTRUCTURE

The presence of an infrastructure can mean the difference between having to initiate redundant training programs as a feeble attempt to achieve guest relations greatness, and moving forward to eliminate the obstacles that prevent guests from experiencing less than 100 percent satisfaction. The infrastructure is, in essence, an accountability mechanism that will prevent complacency and force improvements.

The infrastructure comprises the following elements:

- a monitoring system that continually provides you with feedback on customer/guest satisfaction and identifies areas in which improvements should be contemplated and made
- service and performance standards against which departmental and individual performance can be evaluated
- a structure of committees that involve a wide representation of people who initiate activities and respond to needs

The satisfaction monitoring system provides both quantitative and qualitative feedback about customer/employee satisfaction. If designed well, this system will target sources of dissatisfaction and feed ideas as to how to develop service improvements. The standards against which departmental and employee performance is measured will give you the ability to isolate performance problems. You must continually collect, analyze and *act* upon this feedback.

PATIENT SATISFACTION FEEDBACK SYSTEM

Feedback from patients can be solicited in a variety of different ways.

Patient Satisfaction Surveys

A survey is the easiest and least expensive way to solicit feedback from the patient. It is a quantitative research tool designed to: (1) measure patients' overall satisfaction, (2) obtain diagnostic data that explain their satisfaction ratings, and (3) track levels of patient satisfaction over time.

Taking a benchmark measurement of overall satisfaction tells you how well you are doing presently and provides the basis for setting short-term and long-term goals for the levels of satisfaction you want to achieve. The diagnostic data help you identify opportunities and develop strategies to reach your goals. Tracking satisfaction levels will enable you to determine the effectiveness of the actions you have taken and the progress you have made toward achieving your customer satisfaction goals.

To be effective, a survey must be diagnostic. It must ask the questions that isolate performance or procedural problems. Survey data may not be conclusive and further investigation may be necessary to validate the seriousness of a perceived problem. If the survey is not designed appropriately, however, you may waste considerable time as insufficient or inaccurate data will prevent you from knowing where to target improvements. For more information on designing and implementing a patient survey, see Chapter 12.

Complaint Tracking

Repetitive complaints signal recurring dissatisfaction with particular services. A good system of tracking and analyzing complaints will provide much useful information. More information on this subject is found in Chapter 11.

Telephone Surveys

If conducted by qualified personnel, telephone surveys can provide revealing information about patient satisfaction. Interviewers ask discharged patients a series of predetermined questions. One of the advantages of the telephone survey is the ability to probe deeper when the patient identifies dissatisfaction. By encouraging the respondent to be more specific, the interviewer can isolate factors that contributed to his or her overall dissatisfaction with the service.

Focus Groups

The focus group is a form of qualitative research that is used to satisfy a variety of needs: to identify sources of satisfaction and dissatisfaction, to stimulate ideas from the users that will increase satisfaction in the future, to define expectations that will assist the hospital in designing quantitative measurement tools, to measure reactions to a proposed product or service, and to define more specifically the characteristics that the user would value in a new product/service. There are many advantages to inviting former patients to participate in focus groups. The interaction between people who share a common experience (hospitalization) will often stimulate new ideas and insights. Participants feel more open to disclose opinions, ideas, and feelings in the group interaction.

Discussions do not necessarily have to be conducted as formal focus groups. Some hospitals are discovering that good responsiveness and participation can be elicited by informal group discussions. Kettering Medical Center, located in Kettering, Ohio, has instituted a "Dinner with the Administrator" program as a forum for patients and their family members to offer feedback, both positive and negative, about their hospital stays. Groups of approximately 20 persons are selected on a monthly basis; these include a mix of former inpatients, outpatients, and emergency room patients. Their input and comments not only help hospital administrators identify sources of satisfaction and dissatisfaction, but also generate new ideas for services. The patients receive a gift at the conclusion of the session and a subsequent follow-up report. You can be sure that this initiative prompts some positive word-of-mouth advertising.[1]

Personal Interviews

Conducted while the patient is in the hospital, these personal interviews can help identify patient satisfaction with the overall experience or a specific aspect of service. For example, on a regular basis, a manager may conduct interviews with patients to identify their degree of satisfaction with the particular service delivered by the department. Personal interviews are particularly helpful in allowing managers to become close to their customers. One disadvantage, however, is the unwillingness of many patients to be candid and open while they are still in the hospital. Fearful of retaliation, these patients may withhold their true feelings and opinions.

Referral Information

Some staff members who have frequent contact with patients can collect and refer patient satisfaction information. These people include patient representatives, chaplains, administrators, physicians, and physicians' employees. However, because their perceptions are influenced by their own interpretations of situations, this is not an accurate method of satisfaction measurement.

PHYSICIAN SATISFACTION FEEDBACK SYSTEM

Physicians are important customers. Depending on the location of the hospital and its competition and referral patterns, physicians are directly responsible for anywhere between 40 percent to 90 percent of the direct admissions.

Physicians encounter, on a routine basis, a few nursing units and other interface departments, such as medical records, admitting, patient accounting, emergency room, radiology, lab, and the cafeteria. It is, therefore, a good idea to have physicians evaluate those departments with which they frequently interact.

Evaluating the critical encounters that occur on a frequent or routine basis between physicians and employees gives the hospital an opportunity to enhance its relationships with physicians. A critical customer encounter is defined as a one-on-one interaction that either enhances or detracts from the physicians' (1) overall impression of the organization, (2) ability to handle rounds quickly and in an effective manner, and (3) ability of their office staffs to work effectively with the hospital.

Corporate Systems and Images, Inc. (CSI), a consulting firm with headquarters in South Bend, Indiana, that specializes in customer-oriented management, provides insight into methods to use in a physician satisfaction feedback system. The information contained in the sections on focus groups and surveys was contributed by the firm.

Focus Groups

Focus groups can be used to gather information and suggestions, to identify physicians' expectations, and to determine what critical service components are important to physicians. For example, the focus group moderator might ask, "What service components make you want to admit your patients to a particular hospital?" or "What causes you to avoid admitting your patients to a particular hospital?" In addition to these general questions, specific questions that relate directly to the personal services that physicians value can help define what is important to them. For instance, the following question could be used, "What specific services do you expect from personnel on a nursing unit?"

CSI reports that physicians often respond by saying that they expect and value:

- walking onto a unit and being greeted by the personnel
- having charts readily available when they need them for rounds or to write orders
- having supplies readily available when they need to perform procedures
- having assistance when needed to care for the patient

An often-used approach in the survey development process is to conduct focus groups to determine on which dimensions a quantitative survey instrument should be focused. Doing so will enable you to measure satisfaction on those dimensions that are used by customers to evaluate your services.

Physician Surveys

CSI suggests the following steps for developing physician surveys:

1. Identify those departments that have a high degree of physician interaction.
2. Identify the four or five issues for each of the high-interaction departments that either enhance or detract from physician relationships with that department in the hospital.
3. Develop a statement that can be evaluated concerning the issue identified.
4. Prepare a simple survey on which the physicians can evaluate (on a continuum, i.e., excellent to poor or strongly agree to strongly disagree) the excellence of the services.

It is important to keep the survey simple. Physicians are less likely to fill it out if they perceive that it will take a long time to complete. You may also find that surveys mailed to physicians' offices are not always returned promptly or frequently. Asking the physicians to complete the surveys at a medical staff meeting or another similar gathering will produce a better response rate. The survey can also be administered by a department head (for services delivered by that department only) or by a physician liaison during a regularly scheduled visit.

A sample survey designed by CSI is shown in Exhibit 9-1.

Other Methods of Collecting Feedback

Interviews: An interview is a qualitative research method designed specifically to generate useful information that will identify potential service improvements, rather than to measure levels of satisfaction. The interview questions outlined in Chapter 16 solicit useful feedback, opinions, suggestions, and ideas from physicians.

Physician attitude studies: An outside marketing firm can be retained to implement a physician attitude survey. This is generally a costly alternative, but it can be a valuable investment, especially if it is designed to measure systematically and accurately the attitudes of all physicians on your medical staff. Because a person outside the system administers the surveys, physicians are often willing to be more

Exhibit 9-1 Physician Survey

Please identify your department:

☐ Allergy   ☐ Anesthesia
☐ Cardiology   ☐ General Surgery
☐ Dermatology   ☐ Neurosurgery
☐ Internal Medicine ☐ OB/GYN
☐ Neurology   ☐ Ophthalmology

	Strongly Agree	Agree	Undecided	Disagree	Strongly Disagree	Not Applicable
Medical Records						
A. Staff is courteous and helpful.	5	4	3	2	1	0
B. Records of previous visits are readily available.	5	4	3	2	1	0
C. Dictation is placed on patients' charts in a timely fashion.	5	4	3	2	1	0
D. Quality of typewritten reports is acceptable (spelling, format).	5	4	3	2	1	0
E. The staff is appropriately trained and qualified.	5	4	3	2	1	0
Comments: _____						
Regarding the _____ (fill in the blank) nursing unit:						
A. The personnel are courteous and helpful.	5	4	3	2	1	0
B. The unit is well organized.	5	4	3	2	1	0
C. Supplies and charts are readily available.	5	4	3	2	1	0
D. When I'm called, the calls are appropriate and the personnel are organized.	5	4	3	2	1	0
E. The staff is appropriately trained and qualified.	5	4	3	2	1	0
Comments: _____						
Regarding the Emergency Room:						
A. The personnel are courteous and helpful.	5	4	3	2	1	0
B. The unit is well organized.	5	4	3	2	1	0
C. Supplies and charts are readily available.	5	4	3	2	1	0
D. When I'm called, the calls are appropriate and the personnel are organized.	5	4	3	2	1	0
E. The staff is appropriately trained and qualified.	5	4	3	2	1	0
Comments: _____						

Exhibit 9-1 continued

I find the services of the following departments to be satisfactory:						
a. Utilization Review	5	4	3	2	1	0
b. Laboratory Technologists	5	4	3	2	1	0
c. Health Education	5	4	3	2	1	0
d. Medical Education	5	4	3	2	1	0
e. Housekeeping	5	4	3	2	1	0
f. Radiology Technologists	5	4	3	2	1	0
g. Business office	5	4	3	2	1	0

candid in their responses. Issues identified through the study are typically referred to the administrative/trustee level.

Physician liaison programs: As explained in Chapter 16, a physician liaison program can enable the hospital to become closer to the physician customer.

President's relationship: Obviously, the relationship between the president of the hospital and the president of the medical staff is designed to bring the hospital and physicians closer together. Sources of satisfaction and dissatisfaction are frequently referred to administration by the medical staff president or members of the medical staff executive committee. These are informal but very important sources of information that enable administrators to manage hospital-physician relationships.

When you provide quality care and service to patients and when employees exhibit cooperation, respect, and courtesy to the physicians, two of the physicians' strong expectations are satisfied. How well you are succeeding in meeting these expectations is measured by the physicians' assessment. Ask for feedback on a regular basis.

DEPARTMENTAL SATISFACTION

Every department produces and delivers a service to at least one customer group. Although some departments have other departments as their primary customer group, *every* department supports one or more other departments in the delivery of service. On a regular and routine basis, departments should be surveyed to identify their levels of satisfaction with the services performed by other departments.

The People to People process, developed by Memorial Health System, Inc., in South Bend, Indiana, has been implemented in hospitals and other health care organizations throughout the country as a strategy to enhance health care service. The Departmental Services Survey is a key component of the People to People process, emphasizing quality of internal service delivery. It is a mechanism to evaluate other departments' satisfaction with services. The survey process is conducted over a 3-4 month period, allowing enough time for effective planning, administration, interpretation, and response development. Although the Departmental Services Survey is tailored to meet the specific needs of each client, the design of every survey incorporates the following features (Exhibit 9-2):

- Subjectivity is not discouraged. After all, to the customer, perception is reality.
- Feedback is anonymous. The department directors and managers who are instructed to complete the survey are not identified by name or department.
- Feedback is confidential. The survey results for each department are seen only by that department and appropriate executive staff.
- Before completing the survey, managers are asked to solicit and include feedback from their own staff.
- Raters (department heads and managers) are given carefully constructed guidelines for providing written feedback in order to ensure that it is as specific and concrete as possible. Written feedback is generally requested in terms of compliments/strengths and suggestions for improvement.
- Raters evaluate a limited number of departments with which they have frequent interaction.

The People to People survey is analyzed by an impressive computer tabulation methodology that produces general and dimension-specific profiles. Sample profiles for a *hypothetical* department of nursing service are illustrated in Figures 9-1 and 9-2. Figure 9-1 is a summary profile providing overall results, whereas Figure 9-2 shows a comparison between the department's performance on each dimension and the overall results for the medical center on the same dimension. Four rater groups assessed each dimension.

To preserve the anonymity of the responses, departmental raters are grouped into several related areas, with responses reported by rater groups. Written comments are also compiled and provided to each department. The feedback process is critical to the effective use of the survey results. The Departmental Services Survey uses a "cascade" approach to feedback that includes coaching for management and a strategy to ensure that the results lead to action planning. By including this dimension, you increase the organization's awareness that other departments are customers.

Exhibit 9-2 Services Survey

Department _____

	Excellent	Good	Avg.	Fair	Poor
1. How well does the department perform with regard to **Courtesy**?					
2. How well does the department perform with regard to **Professionalism**?					
3. How well does the department perform with regard to **Timeliness**?					
4. How well does the department perform with regard to **Quality**?					
5. How well does the department perform with regard to **Problem Solving**?					

6. Praise and suggestions (Use reverse side if additional space is needed): Please provide at least one praise and one suggestion for each department you are rating.

NOTE: If a department you have chosen has a subsection that you wish to write praise or suggestions for, please indicate that subsection (e.g., if you have chosen the laboratory department and wish to be specific about the outpatient lab, please indicate outpatient lab).

Source: Courtesy of Memorial Health System, Inc., South Bend, Indiana, © 1987.

Such a mechanism as this survey provides an internal measure of accountability for departmental performance. It can be used as a factor in performance-based pay plans for executives and managers and to reward entire departments or specific employees. There is no question that, in the context of leadership commitment to the service ethic, the Departmental Services Survey is a powerful intervention that supports the development of a more service-oriented health care culture.

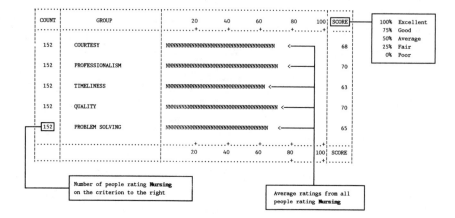

Figure 9-1 Medical Center Perception of Nursing Services: Summary Profile—All Criteria. *Source:* Courtesy of Memorial Health Systems, Inc., South Bend, Indiana, © 1987.

Louis A. Weiss Memorial Hospital in Chicago, Illinois, is one of the most innovative hospitals in guest relations. The hospital actively encourages its managers to take the initiative to implement ideas and improvements that will enhance the quality of service delivered by departments. The hospital's security and safety department designs and regularly distributes a survey enabling employees to rate the responsiveness of the department and attitude of its employees. The survey, shown in Exhibit 9-3, is an excellent feedback tool and provides an example of how other departmental surveys can be structured to rate the quality of guest relations.

EMPLOYEE SATISFACTION FEEDBACK

Employees' willingness to contribute to guest relations is influenced by the degree to which they feel good about:

- who they are (self esteem)
- where they work (pride)
- what they do (purpose)

It is important to monitor employee satisfaction regularly. In addition, it is necessary to keep the channels of communication open and to encourage employee-management-administration interaction.

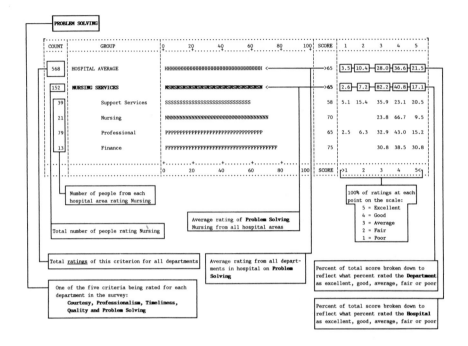

Figure 9-2 Medical Center Perception of Nursing Services: Comparison with Hospital. *Source:* Courtesy of Memorial Health System Inc., South Bend, Indiana, © 1987.

Measuring employee satisfaction can be done in a number of ways:

- *Internal surveys:* A survey designed to measure employees' opinions and perceptions on dimensions that relate directly to guest relations and service is found in Chapter 14. Used on an ongoing basis, it will identify fluctuations in employee attitudes, as well as areas of perceived change resulting from the emphasis on guest relations.
- *Employee satisfaction (attitude) surveys:* Most hospitals periodically conduct employee attitude studies that are designed to measure employee perceptions. However, once the results are reported, many hospitals are puzzled about what the data mean and how they can use the information. For any research study of this scope (regardless of the audience to whom it is directed), be sure to work with a reputable firm that knows how to interpret the data and guide development of strategies that will respond to key areas of need. The information is useless unless you are ready to do something with it. This

Exhibit 9-3 Departmental Satisfaction Survey

Guest Relations Feedback Survey

We hope our security and safety department has interacted well with you. We would appreciate a few minutes of your time to elicit feedback on the quality of our guest relations.

On a scale of 5 to 1, please rate the following statements about our department. A score of "5" indicates the highest degree of satisfaction, while a score of "1" shows the least amount of satisfaction.

Please rate:	Greatest		Satisfaction		Least
1. Security's ability to keep commitments made to you.	5	4	3	2	1
2. Security's accessibility to you.	5	4	3	2	1
3. Security's willingness to get involved and go the extra mile for you when the need arises.	5	4	3	2	1
4. The way the phones in security administration (7th floor) are answered. (extensions 4400, 4441, 4446)	5	4	3	2	1
5. The way the phones in security's Emergency Room office are answered. (extension 4444)	5	4	3	2	1
6. The ability of the security staff to listen and empathize with your situation and/or concerns.	5	4	3	2	1
7. Security's promptness in responding to your requests for information or service.	5	4	3	2	1
8. Security's ability to direct you to the appropriate resource if they were unable to help you.	5	4	3	2	1
9. Overall quality of guest relations in security and safety.	5	4	3	2	1
10. Please circle the shift which you normally work.	DAYS	PM'S	NIGHTS		
11. Comments:					

_____

_____

_____

(If you need additional space for comments, please use the reverse side.)

Please return this survey to Mike Cohen, chairperson of the guest relations committee. The results of each department's survey will be forwarded confidentially to that department. Thank you for your assistance.

Source: Courtesy of Louis A. Weiss Memorial Hospital, Chicago, Illinois.

---

method is limited in providing ongoing feedback because of the infrequency of its use.

- *Employee focus groups:* Focus groups can be used to elicit employee concerns and ideas for making the hospital a better place in which to work. Focus groups are particularly useful when management would like to obtain more specific information about particular concerns and problems.

- *Interviews:* Random interviews can be scheduled to generate employee feedback, but it is difficult to guarantee objectivity by this method. Unless the sample size is significant enough to obtain a representative cross-section of employee feedback, it is not a desirable method. It is also difficult to convince employees that their comments are confidential, and therefore, it is difficult to interpret the degree to which employees are providing valid information and feedback. Exit interviews, conducted when employees voluntarily or involuntarily separate from the hospital, are appropriate forums to solicit and interpret information that can be used to target sources of dissatisfaction and improvement areas.

- *Communication forums:* Regular meetings between employees and administrators can be effective in soliciting feedback from employees. These meetings also give administration a chance to communicate information to employees. Whether these forums are structured as weekly coffees, monthly lunches with the administrator, or as "town meetings" held round the clock on a quarterly basis, they provide informal feedback and are helpful in keeping administrators in touch with the important members of their service delivery team. These forums must generate two-way communication to be effective. The less formal the structure, the more likely the employees will be to participate.

As you monitor satisfaction quantitatively over time, you should remain sensitive to factors that may dramatically affect the levels of customer and employee satisfaction. A reduction in force, an announcement that the hospital will not offer raises above the cost of living, or a reduction in benefits will be certain to affect employee morale negatively. As a result, patient perceptions of the hospital experience may be negatively affected for a time as well. The hospital may implement an unpopular program or policy that is viewed by some physicians as a threat. If not handled well, this can diminish the physicians' loyalty and willingness to contribute ideas and suggestions.

The satisfaction feedback systems identified in this chapter will help generate new ideas for service improvements and isolate areas in which service performance is not meeting the expectations of customers. The quantitative measures of satisfaction, such as patient, physician, and employee questionnaires, provide measures of accountability. The qualitative measures of satisfaction—narrative forms of feedback—are more useful in generating ideas. There is one other method of research that can be used to identify the degree to which departments are meeting the expectations of service: observational research (see Chapter 10).

ACCOUNTABILITY STANDARDS

If you are aware of the dimensions that customers use to evaluate service, you will be able to formulate corresponding service and performance standards.

Service Standards

Hospitals can manage service quality by establishing service standards that can then be tailored to each department. Hospitals have a solid foundation on which to develop service standards because they already have quality assurance standards.

A service standard is a measure of quality from the customer's perspective. American Airlines has developed service standards that guide the delivery of service to meet the expectations of customers. These standards are constructed to achieve certain levels of performance efficiency and effectiveness at a rate that is deemed appropriate. Examples of American Airlines service standards include:[2]

- Passengers will wait in line no more than 15 minutes (85 percent of the time).
- Reservations phones will be answered within 20 seconds.
- Airplane doors will be opened within 70 seconds.
- Airplanes will arrive within 15 minutes of scheduled arrival time (85 percent of the time).

American Airlines uses these standards to determine the staffing levels at various operating stations. If the airline knows that peak times for phone reservations are Monday mornings and Friday afternoons, for example, the department is staffed with more reservation agents at those times. The service standards are also used to evaluate manager performance. Performance bonuses are tied to the service standards.

The service standards must be customer driven. American Express is acknowledged to have one of the most sophisticated systems for tracking service quality. In the early 1970s, the company experienced a surge of complaints as its card operation expanded quickly overseas. The twelve departments responsible for card operations were asked to develop standards for their own performance and to measure their achievement as a remedy for growing customer disenchantment with service. This was done but the system did not work. After an analysis, it was discovered that each department was doing well according to its own standards but service was not improving. Instead of controlling quality department by department, American Express decided to measure the impact of all the departments' actions on customers. With the help of McKinsey & Company, American Express devised a service tracking system to measure the card operation's success in processing new applications within 15 days, replacing lost or stolen cards in one day, sending out bills that are completely accurate, and performing over 100 other tasks. These standards were scrutinized on a monthly basis to determine how well operations in all parts of the world were performing.[3]

The examples of service standards developed by American Airlines and American Express point out why so few hospitals have been successful at making great strides in service delivery improvement. Few hospitals are bold enough to make commitments and then to devise the systems to monitor performance against the standards on an ongoing basis.

Standards should be developed after a detailed analysis of current practices. Service standards must be realistic, achievable, and responsive to customer expectations. Here again, you have to balance customer expectations with what is achievable given the available resources. You may desire to process and treat admissions to the emergency room within one hour, recognizing that responsiveness in treatment is a primary expectation of customers. If you do not have sufficient treatment suites, physicians, or staff to adequately respond to the demand however, frustration and failure will result.

American Airlines realizes that it cannot expect to achieve the stated standard 100 percent of the time and for that reason, the service standards are expressed as desired standards with tolerable exception rates. Establishing and adhering to service standards does produce results. In the fall of 1987, American Airlines was able to advertise its success in meeting customer expectations. The print advertisement headline read, "When you put the customer first, two things happen." The copy went on to read that the Department of Transportation reported American Airlines #1 for on-time dependability based on data filed for September 1987 with the U.S. Department of Transportation by the fourteen largest United States airlines. It should come as no surprise that the "other thing that happened" was that North American frequent fliers selected American Airlines #1 in the world based on an independent survey of 28,000 frequent fliers conducted by the International Foundation of Airline Passenger Associations.

Are you ready, willing, and able to determine that your nurses will respond to call lights within five minutes as Eastwood Hospital in Memphis, Tennessee, did several years ago? Will your admitting clerks commit to the standard of escorting pre-registered guests to their rooms within ten minutes of their arrival? Is the outpatient radiology department willing to give a patient the opportunity to reschedule his/her appointment if he or she will have to wait longer than 30 minutes? These are difficult issues, but hospitals that are willing to make such commitments may soon be able to advertise that their hospital was rated the #1 hospital in the service area.

It is necessary to have feedback mechanisms that identify whether the service standards are indeed being achieved. If admitting department personnel determine that they will admit a patient within 10 minutes of arrival, they will need to develop methods by which to assess the frequency of their success and diagnose problems or obstacles that prevent them from achieving that goal. A somewhat subjective method is to include a question on the patient survey relating to the promptness of service delivery in the admitting department. If this question is monitored monthly, department members will know if they have achieved their goal, based on patients' perceptions of efficiency and promptness. They will not know whether they have admitted 85 percent of their patients within 10 minutes, but they will have a good indication of the degree of patient satisfaction. The other method is to use a time clock to track patients from arrival in the admitting area through dismissal to the rooms. This is a much more exact method that requires additional record keeping but provides useful information.

Employee Performance Standards

Every person employed by the hospital contributes, directly or indirectly, to the delivery of the services that are ultimately valued by your customers. Achieving a high level of customer service requires dedication to acquiring and preserving high standards of service performance.

Employees need to be aware of what they are accountable for and against what standards their performance will be measured. Performance standards must be measurable and obtainable so that employees have an idea of how to reach a level of service performance that will satisfy management's expectations. Expectations of performance for managers should be no less specific or stringent. Employees and managers should also know, in explicit terms, what rewards are triggered by meeting or exceeding the expectations and what consequences result from not conforming to expectations.

A job description describes the scope of responsibility for a position. It also serves as a tool for setting expectations, establishing standards, coaching performance, and conducting performance reviews.

The degree to which expectations of employees' service performance were met can be monitored by the quantitative feedback received from customers. If patient surveys are designed to measure levels of satisfaction on dimensions relating to courtesy, respect, and willingness to provide information, the data can be sorted to indicate the degree to which various departments delivered on the expectations.

COMMITTEES

The last thing we need at this hospital is another committee! How often have you heard or felt that? Participation on committees is time consuming. It can also be frustrating, because collective efforts are not as productive as the individual efforts of those who have the authority and autonomy to act swiftly and decisively. Yet, committees are important because ownership is shared and decisions are weighed against the needs or interests of many, rather than a few.

Committees are also critically important to the development of a strong infrastructure for a guest relations program. They will guide the initial implementation of a guest relations program and will then provide strong, ongoing vehicles through which your service systems are monitored, changed, and/or fine tuned.

This chapter presents a brief overview of how the committees can be structured and their general responsibilities. More information is provided in Chapter 14.

Steering Committee

Composed of a diverse cross-section of administrators, managers, and employees, the steering committee oversees the implementation of a service management program, reports and makes recommendations to executives, initiates responses to needs that are identified by the monitoring systems, and directs the activities of subcommittees and task forces.

Subcommittees

How you use subcommittees will significantly affect the role of the steering committee. You may decide to keep most of the responsibility and control at the steering committee level. Or the subcommittees can report to the steering committee and carry out a variety of activities, thereby reducing the need to have steering committee members involved in operational details.

An education and training subcommittee, for example, can respond to the targeted training needs required by various departments or individuals. These needs may be identified through feedback solicited from patients, physicians, managers, and employees. If patient questionnaires indicate dissatisfaction with procedures in the billing office, for example, a course in complaint resolution for billing clerks could be implemented to enhance the effectiveness of those responsible for collections. If employee surveys indicate that employees do not feel they are kept apprised of what is going on in the hospital, the education and training subcommittee might respond by scheduling "Quarterly Update" educational forums. These forums would be conducted by administrators to share important information about the strategic direction of the hospital and changes in the industry that are affecting operations.

Task Forces

The steering committee is responsible for naming task forces it deems appropriate to focus attention on a specific need. For example, responses from physician satisfaction surveys and interviews may identify the need to focus attention on physician relations. A task force on physician relations can be named if it does not conflict with the scope of an existing committee or the role of the physician liaison. This task force must be sanctioned by the chief executive officer and should be chaired by a member of the administrative staff or co-chaired by a member of the medical staff. It would be composed of other physicians, staff and nurse managers, and key individuals who have frequent interaction with physicians and their office staffs, such as members of the admitting, lab, and radiology departments. The task force would investigate further the needs and perceptions of physicians *and* employees and examine how more productive, cooperative, and supportive working relationships could be fostered.

Individuals

Individuals or individual departments may be given responsibility for some aspect of the program. The director or vice president of human resources may be asked by the steering committee (and in all probability will serve on the committee, as well) to (1) incorporate guest relations standards into performance criteria, (2) institute a merit program to reward employees and managers for service performance, (3) investigate behavioral interviewing programs to offer to managers to sharpen their candidate selection skills, (4) develop a new employee orientation program, or (5) administer an employee opinion survey.

SUMMARY

A hospital should expect to receive a return on its investment in a service program. Without standards to determine levels of desired performance, directed both at employees *and* departments, the results will be weak. The infrastructure described in this chapter provides an impetus for action and a measure of accountability. Hospitals that ask the question, ''Where do we go from here?'' lack the important feedback that can guide their direction and decisions. It is only by monitoring the satisfaction of external customers and internal service providers, establishing realistic, achievable, customer-oriented performance and service standards to which incentives are tied, and empowering people to make changes that will measurably improve service quality that a health care organization can hope to achieve a payback.

NOTES

1. "Dinner with the Administrator at Kettering Medical Center," *Hospital Guest Relations Report* (January 1987): 10–11.

2. James Heskett, *Managing in the Service Economy* (Boston: Harvard Business School Press, 1986), 95.

3. Bro Uttal, "Companies that Serve You Best," *Fortune* (December 7, 1987): 99.

Chapter 10

Observational Research: Informed Insights

Imagine a job that called for you to check into a hotel, steal light bulbs, walk into washrooms clearly marked for the opposite sex, and eat in every single food outlet of the hotel. That is what a professional hotel shopper does. Shopper programs are a popular derivative of observational research.

HOTEL SHOPPER PROGRAMS

To a hotel, the professional shopper program is an important management tool. A professional shopper is carefully trained to observe specific details as he or she visits, writes, or telephones the intended organization. A professional shopper can monitor specific attitudes, practices, and skills of employees; evaluate employees' efficiency and productivity; and pinpoint and corroborate particular sources of dissatisfaction identified through survey research.

Based on the comprehensive list of standards and practices used by the hotel to define service excellence and the criteria used by guests to evaluate hotel services, the professional shopper assesses the hotel's delivery of service. During his or her stay, the shopper will make careful notes that will later be incorporated into a full report to management on the delivery of service.

The professional hotel shopper is likely to wake up and be down at the front desk by 6:30 A.M. to observe the efficiency and friendliness of the employees at the front desk while they check guests out of the hotel. Afterward, he or she will proceed to the hotel's breakfast buffet and evaluate the helpfulness of the staff, the supply of silverware and plates, and the temperature and appearance of the food. The shopper may go back up to the room and order breakfast from room service, counting the number of times the telephone rings before the room service representative answers. Does the person on the other end of the line tell the shopper how long to expect to wait for the delivery of food? Does that person also call him or her by name? The shopper may use a stopwatch to note the length of time it takes for food to be delivered. He or she will taste the eggs and sample the other foods once the tray arrives to check their temperature and taste. The shopper will note whether the server was well mannered.

He or she will walk every hall in the hotel, looking for tears, burns, or stains in the carpet. During the tour, the professional shopper will check to see if the maids have pulled their carts in front of the open doors to block potential thieves from ducking in while the maid is working in the bathroom. Later, he or she may use a stopwatch to time the housekeeping inspector who is checking the guest rooms once they have been cleaned by the maids. The shopper knows that, if the inspection is completed in less than 90 seconds, the inspector is not paying close enough attention to every detail that is supposed to be checked.

The role of the professional shopper is not to trick the hotel staff. He or she may, however, initiate requests or actions that will gauge the attentiveness and responsiveness of the staff to concerns that might routinely come up and annoy a guest or a prospective customer. For instance, the shopper may unscrew a lightbulb from a lamp in the room to see if the maid notices and replaces it. He or she may place a deliberately confusing order with room service. The shopper may drop a toothpick on the floor of the public restroom to see if the housekeeper has picked it up by the time she comes through again in a couple of hours. Another tactic is to call the front desk with a problem to see how it is handled. Or, the shopper may call the hotel's marketing department and pose as a corporate meeting planner in order to evaluate how well the salesman sells the hotel's amenities and ascertains the needs of the fictitious company.[1]

In the report, the professional shopper will name names, identifying the waiter who smiles and the desk clerk who does paperwork while he or she stood waiting for service. The goal is not to get anyone in trouble or point out a particular individual's deficiencies, but rather to correct the behavior of someone who may not be giving a guest satisfactory service.

CLEVELAND CLINIC'S SHOPPER PROGRAM

There are few professional shopper programs currently in operation in hospitals and clinics. However, one of the most notable such programs in the health care industry was developed by the Cleveland Clinic Foundation in Cleveland, Ohio. It created, pilot tested, and evaluated a professional shopping program to improve the organization's ability to identify and monitor areas where patient satisfaction is of particular concern. Before instituting the program, the clinic foundation evaluated its survey research techniques and noted that, although telephone surveys and mail questionnaires were helpful in monitoring patient satisfaction, they had some inherent limitations. Survey questionnaires administered during or immediately after a patient's visit were thought to be biased by the patient's anxiety and stress. Responses to those interviews or questionnaires that were conducted days or even weeks after the visit were affected by some patients' poor recall of their experiences. But perhaps the most important limitation is the very fact that a patient is often unable to identify specific determinants of his or her generalized perceptions of satisfaction or dissatisfaction. Because the Cleveland Clinic Foundation felt that certain indirect or unobservable aspects of the patient's experience have a significant impact on the patient's satisfaction, they initially developed two distinct programs. One used trained researchers as simulated patients; the other involved mail or telephone shopping.[2]

The selected shoppers received training in the general principles of observational research. Then they were oriented to the procedures and services provided by the laboratory, which was the site of the first shopping expedition. They were instructed on what questions to ask and what areas to observe. They were told to report good, neutral, and negative observations, as well as the feelings associated with each experience. After their observations, shoppers reported their findings, both in a narrative report and by filling out a form.

The professional shoppers conducted their research in the blood drawing area. They recorded specific information about the amount of time they spent waiting, the courtesy extended to them by the receptionists, the degree to which blood drawing policies were followed, and what information was routinely shared with them. These data were documented and reviewed to assess the extent to which routine procedures were followed and to identify areas of improvement.

Although a professional patient-shopper program can be a very useful evaluation tool, it has a potential disadvantage that can present serious problems. If employees are made to feel that the program is being implemented because the hospital lacks confidence and trust in their abilities to perform, it can be very demoralizing. Additionally, some managers may feel threatened by someone "looking over their shoulders." If employees and managers alike do not feel that the professional shopper program is a constructive and positive means to achieve a common goal, it can evoke resentful feelings and slow progress toward that goal.

For that reason, the Cleveland Clinic Foundation (CCF) conducted a survey of its employees before initiating the professional shopper program in an effort to identify employee receptivity to the program. They found that the employees would support the program, as shown in Table 10-1.

To shape employees' perceptions about a professional shopper program, you should be open and candid with them from the beginning. Explain the program in terms of the benefits that can be achieved by it. Let employees know that it will not be a "Sting" operation, nor will the shopper initiate absurd "Candid Camera"-type episodes. Never ask a professional shopper to start a fight although a sequence of events may eventually turn into a legitimate problem about which the shopper can complain. If you, however, direct a shopper to pick a fight by making

Table 10-1 Employee Response To Being Shopped

Response	Number	Percent
Should CCF use professional shoppers?		
Yes	53	84.1
No	4	6.3
Not sure	6	9.5
	63	99.9
Would a professional shopper improve other services at CCF?		
Yes	56	91.8
No	0	0
Not sure	5	8.2
	61	100.0
No response	(2)	
How do you feel knowing that patients you interact with in the future might be professional shoppers?		
It's fine	19	35.8
Won't change anything/already doing a good job	16	30.2
Will keep us on our toes	14	26.4
Will give us feedback	2	3.8
I'm uncomfortable knowing shoppers will be coming through	2	3.8
	53	100.0
No response	(10)	

Source: Reprinted from "Improving Patient Services through a Professional Shopper Program" by W.R. Gombeski Jr., C.E. Stone, and F.J. Weaver in *Journal of Health Care Marketing*, Vol. 6, No. 3, pp. 64–68, with permission of American Marketing Association, © September 1986.

unreasonable or inappropriate demands, you may get a clue about an employee's skill in complaint handling, but the detrimental effect on employee trust and morale will be widespread.

It is important to publicize the positive findings of the evaluation. Doing so helps dispel the fears that the real motive for observational research is to catch someone doing something wrong. A professional shopper program can become an "after-the-fact-caught-in-the-act" program. The shopper cannot award recognition to those who are deserving of it during the actual survey because it is important to maintain anonymity during the course of the research. If, however, the shopper was shown special consideration by an employee(s) that is worthy of attention, it can later be written up in the newsletter.

All observations should be detailed in the shopper's report. Recommendations for improvement should be shared individually with the management of the departments involved.

The professional shopper concept can be applied in many different ways. Cleveland Clinic also called appointment secretaries of medical departments to identify the number of rings before the telephone was answered and to assess the helpfulness and courtesy extended to the caller. This application is particularly useful if you develop standard telephone protocols and wish to assess periodically conformity to the prescribed rules. A professional shopper program can identify needs for further training in various departments and when procedures or policies can be amended to produce greater efficiency or satisfaction. It is also a useful method to determine the effectiveness of changes that have been made.

A VISIT BY MRS. TIMM

Although observational research is not widely or regularly practiced by many hospitals, a popular film has encouraged many hospitals to engage in a variation of the professional shopper theme. "A Gift from Mrs. Timm," a film that was produced several years ago by Dartnell Corporation in Chicago, features an elderly woman who wanders through the hospital in search of the president's office. Unbeknownst to those with whom she interacts, she is carrying a shopping bag filled with cash. Although her deceased husband instructed her to make a contribution to the hospital in his will, her efforts to do so are thwarted by rude and inconsiderate behavior exhibited by an emergency room nurse, a billing clerk, and a radiologist. She leaves the hospital without accomplishing her mission. The story line of this film has become the inspiration for similar mystery guest programs in hospitals.

In one hospital, a volunteer was recruited to wander through the hospital as a test to see how many employees would take the initiative to offer her assistance. For 2½ hours, she wandered around looking bewildered. Only one employee asked if she could be of assistance. In another hospital, Mrs. T, who was dressed in unfashionable clothes and carried a large shopping bag, put a patient gown over her clothes and sat in a high-volume patient area for 15 minutes. During that time, she was amused to discover that, although many employees gave her strange looks (and one passing employee even exclaimed, "What a get-up!"), no one stopped to ask her what she was doing. Few of the "Mrs. Ts" that wander through the hospitals report that employees are rude, yet these experiments point out how few employees actually take the initiative to assist patients.

The University of Nebraska Center in Omaha, Nebraska, developed a "Mrs. Timm Mystery Guest" program. The purpose of the program is two-fold. First, the audits conducted by the mystery guest help the hospital identify strengths and weaknesses in service delivery in the various departments visited. Second, this program is used to recognize employees who provide exceptional service.

At the University of Nebraska Medical Center, friends and family of employees, local amateur actors, and volunteers have been recruited to appear as mystery guests. The guests are briefed on the purpose of the program and the role they are to assume. The visitors then complete an evaluation form detailing their impressions of the hospital's services. This form, which also identifies the University Hospital & Clinic's Standards of Hospitality and Caring, is shown in Exhibit 10-1.

Exhibit 10-1 Mystery Visitor Evaluation

Evaluation of Visit

Date: ——————————— "Mystery Visitor" ———————————

University Hospital & Clinic
Standards of Hospitality and Caring

Philosophy of Caring

We believe in the dignity and worth of all individuals, including those who serve as well as those who are served, and strive to achieve excellence in care through the principles of courtesy, respect, and concern. We are proud of our institution, our professions, and our service to others.

Area Visited:

1. What was the approximate time of your visit?
2. Was the area busy at the time of your visit?
3. How long did you have to wait before someone offered assistance?
4. How many people did you approach for help?
5. Were you able to identify people by UNHC name badges or some other form of ID?
6. Were the individuals you approached:

   - Professionals (i.e., nurses, doctors, etc.)
   - Clerical (i.e., receptionists, secretaries, etc.)
   - Service (i.e., maintenance, food service, etc.)?

7. Were you treated with courtesy and respect?
8. Did anyone interrupt their work or go out of their way to help you?
9. If directions were given, were they clear and understandable?
10. Rank the areas you visited on a scale of 1-3 with 1 being given to the area where you felt someone best demonstrated the Philosophy of Caring.

In your opinion, who is the one individual you encountered during your visit who best demonstrated the Philosophy of Caring to you?

Are there any comments you would like to make regarding your experience with this project?

Source: Courtesy of University of Nebraska Medical Center, Omaha, Nebraska.

A mystery guest or professional shopper program can serve to remind employees of the need to be proactive and responsive. Additionally, it is an excellent way to evaluate service delivery and to identify areas of improvement.

ENVIRONMENTAL SURVEYS

The environment of a hospital plays a significant role in how customers regard their total experience. A useful tool for assessing the hospital's physical structure and ambience is the Environmental Survey, which uses the ''shopper'' technique. You can recruit your employees to participate in this enlightening observational research survey, which is found in Appendix 10-A.

The decor and cleanliness of the environment create impressions, sometimes conscious and otherwise subconscious, that influence the overall impression of the hospital and its commitment to quality. Just as a messy bathroom, dirty tray tables, and worn seat cushions can leave a passenger with questions as to the integrity of the airplane's engine maintenance, so similar inattentiveness can cast doubt on the perceived quality of the care that is being delivered in the hospital.

Because you enter the hospital on a routine basis, you may not notice things that are apparent to a first-time visitor. Your familiarity with the surroundings and layout of the hospital obscures your ability to experience your environment in the same manner that patients and other guests do. The Environmental Survey in Appendix 10-A is designed to help you take an objective look at the hospital's physical plant, although you still will not be able to view your surroundings entirely as do those who enter for the first time.

The end result of the survey is to identify ways in which the environment can be enhanced. You may not have the financial resources to make major changes in the design and decor of the hospital. There is value in conducting the survey, nonetheless, because it may open your eyes to things you do have the power to change.

Conducting the Survey

You can assign members of your committee to complete the survey, or you may want to designate an incoming group of new employees to conduct it. New employees will be more objective, and the survey activity can help sensitize them to what patients and other visitors experience. On the other hand, members of the committee may have a better perspective because they are sensitized to guest relations and the purpose of the survey.

You might also consider having people from outside the hospital conduct the survey. Spouses of board members; contributors; local managers from hotels, restaurants, grocery stores; and other service businesses are excellent candidates. Stringfellow Memorial Hospital in Anniston, Alabama, invited an environmental design specialist to participate in the survey. By maintaining a special sensitivity to design codes and suggesting specific changes that may have otherwise been unnoticed the specialist brought valuable insight to the hospital.

Each participant should be given a packet of survey forms to use as he or she analyzes specific areas of the hospital. You may want to modify the questions or add new ones to fit your needs.

The survey sections address these areas:

- hospital exterior
- lobby
- admitting areas
- hallways and stairwells
- elevators
- patient rooms and bathrooms
- reception areas
- surgical waiting room
- physicians' lounge
- departments and offices
- gift shop
- snack bar/vending area
- other areas
- cafeteria

The committee should first identify the specific parking lots, walkways, hallways, stairwells, elevators, patient rooms, patient floor lounges, departments and offices, and special service areas, such as the outpatient surgery facility, birthing center, breast clinic etc., to be surveyed by the participants. These areas must be noted on the appropriate form.

The participants should be advised to read through the entire survey packet before they conduct the audit so that they are familiar with the scope of the survey and aware of the dimensions that will be used in the evaluation.

The participants are asked to record the time they begin the survey. The time may be important, for instance, when bathrooms are consistently rated as dirty during certain periods of the day. This knowledge may indicate that regular scheduled cleanings are not sufficient to meet the demand.

Some areas can be surveyed by several people. With others, you may want to limit access.

Each participant should be encouraged to conduct the survey alone because the presence of others can inhibit one's ability to be objective. If a number of people will be conducting the survey independently, they can be directed along a course that you design by numbering the sheets to indicate the progression they should follow.

Once the participants have completed the survey, the forms should be returned to the person who has been designated to tally the results and make an aggregate list of *Useful Comments* and *Suggestions*. The data should be distributed to and reviewed by the committee, and a report of recommendations specifying what the committee recommends to change (along with proposed costs) should be directed to the administrative staff.

NOTES

1. David Elsner, "She's a Guest It Doesn't Pay to Displease," *Chicago Tribune,* 1 April 1986.

2. William Gombeski, Cheryl Stone and Frank Weaver, "Improving Patient Services Through a Professional Shopper Program," *Journal of Healthcare Marketing* (September 1986): 64–68.

Appendix 10-A

Environmental Survey Instructions

The attached environmental survey gives you an opportunity to take a sharp look at many aspects of the hospital's physical environment.

Please read through all of the questions before beginning, and keep the sheets in the numbered order in which they have been given to you. You will be following the route prescribed by this order. The relative ease or difficulty you experience traveling to and from the various areas will indicate if the signage is adequate and whether, in some instances, employees take the initiative to assist you in finding your way. Don't be afraid to look lost (or to ask for directions) if you become confused.

Feel free to make notations of things that are significant to you—even if there is not a corresponding question on the checklist. If you overhear a compliment or complaint or inappropriate discussion on the elevator or in another public place, be aware of how those observations affect your overall impressions. You will be asked at the end of each section to share your suggestions on ways in which to improve or enhance the area.

You will be asked to respond to questions by circling either yes or no and in some instances to circle N/A if the question is not appropriate or applicable. Please return the completed environmental survey to:

_____

_____

Take your time and THANK YOU for your participation!

Hospital Exterior   Time: _____

To complete a survey of the grounds and exterior facilities, you should approach the hospital in your car on the way to work and park in the visitor's parking lot. If you are unable to do so, you may simulate your approach by using your feet!

What do you see as you approach the hospital?

Is the hospital's sign clearly visible?	YES	NO	N/A
Do the lights on or around the hospital sign work?	YES	NO	N/A
Is the flag in front of the hospital in good condition?	YES	NO	N/A
Are the signs directing you to the visitor parking lot visible and clear?	YES	NO	N/A
Are the signs directing guests to the emergency entrance clear?	YES	NO	N/A
Are the signs directing guests to the outpatient clinic entrance clear?	YES	NO	N/A
Is it easy to find a parking place?	YES	NO	N/A
Are the sidewalks clear of snow, ice, fallen leaves, mowed grass, etc?	YES	NO	N/A
Are the grounds and lawns well maintained?	YES	NO	N/A
Are the signs directing you to the main entrance clear?	YES	NO	N/A
Is the entrance covered or sheltered from exposure to inclement weather?	YES	NO	N/A
Are the main doors to the hospital easy to open?	YES	NO	N/A

SUGGESTIONS OR COMMENTS:

Lobby   Time: _____

When you enter the lobby, is it easy to identify the information desk?	YES	NO	N/A
Do the volunteers/personnel extend a greeting?	YES	NO	N/A
Do the volunteers/personnel acknowledge your presence in a timely manner?	YES	NO	N/A
Take a seat in one of the lobby chairs. Is it comfortable?	YES	NO	N/A
Is the upholstery clean?	YES	NO	N/A
Are the plants attractive?	YES	NO	N/A
Is the lighting adequate for reading or filling out forms?	YES	NO	N/A
Is the carpet clean?	YES	NO	N/A
Is the floor clean?	YES	NO	N/A
Are the walls clean and attractive?	YES	NO	N/A
Are the pictures on the wall straight?	YES	NO	N/A

Does the area smell fresh?	YES NO N/A
Is the area well ventilated?	YES NO N/A
Are ashtrays available?	YES NO N/A
If smoking is not permitted, are there signs to this effect?	YES NO N/A
Is the noise level in the lobby acceptable?	YES NO N/A
Is there adequate seating available?	YES NO N/A
Are magazines available?	YES NO N/A
Are magazines current?	YES NO N/A
Are the magazines in neat order?	YES NO N/A
Are pay telephones accessible?	YES NO N/A
Are phone directories available at the phones?	YES NO N/A
Are the phone areas neat?	YES NO N/A
Is the phone receiver clean?	YES NO N/A
Are the public restrooms easy to locate?	YES NO N/A
Is the restroom clean?	YES NO N/A
Is there an adequate supply of soap?	YES NO N/A
Is there an adequate supply of hand towels?	YES NO N/A
Is there an adequate supply of toilet tissue?	YES NO N/A
Is there graffiti on the back of the stall door?	YES NO N/A
Is the restroom well ventilated?	YES NO N/A

USEFUL COMMENTS OVERHEARD WHILE
CONDUCTING THE SURVEY IN THIS AREA:

SUGGESTIONS FOR IMPROVEMENT:

Admitting Area   Time: _____

Go back to the main lobby from wherever you are. . . . Now that you are back
in the lobby, locate the admitting department.

Was it easy to find?   YES NO N/A

Approach the admitting area. Sit down and observe the environment, the guests
who enter, and their interactions with staff.

Is the chair in which you are sitting comfortable?	YES	NO	N/A
Is the upholstery clean?	YES	NO	N/A
Is the carpet clean?	YES	NO	N/A
Is the floor clean?	YES	NO	N/A
Are the pictures on the wall straight?	YES	NO	N/A
Does the area smell fresh?	YES	NO	N/A
Is the area well ventilated?	YES	NO	N/A
Are the plants attractive?	YES	NO	N/A
Do guests appear to know what to do when they arrive?	YES	NO	N/A
Are they greeted in a timely manner?	YES	NO	N/A
Can you overhear what is being said in the other booths or areas near you?	YES	NO	N/A
Is the overall noise level acceptable?	YES	NO	N/A

USEFUL COMMENTS OVERHEARD WHILE
CONDUCTING THE SURVEY IN THIS AREA:

SUGGESTIONS FOR IMPROVEMENT:

Hallways and Stairwells   Time: _____

Specific hallways, stairs, and elevators have been selected for your travel
during this survey segment.

Direct yourself to the following hallway: _____

Are the signs easy to read and understand?	YES	NO	N/A
Are safety mirrors installed at hall intersections?	YES	NO	N/A
If you hear a page, is the volume appropriate?	YES	NO	N/A
Are there stray wheelchairs, supply carts, or trash in the hallway?	YES	NO	N/A

Locate the following stair entrance: _____

Walk up/down to: _____

Is the stairwell clean?	YES NO N/A
Is the stairwell well lit?	YES NO N/A
Exit the stairwell. Is the door easy to open?	YES NO N/A

USEFUL COMMENTS OVERHEARD WHILE
CONDUCTING THE SURVEY IN THIS AREA:

SUGGESTIONS FOR IMPROVEMENT:

Elevators   Time: _____

Locate the following elevator(s): _____

Is there a floor directory or hospital legend near the elevator?	YES NO N/A
Push the button and get on board. Are the elevators clean?	YES NO N/A
Are the elevator light boards in working condition?	YES NO N/A
Get off at any floor. As you exit the elevator, can you identify which floor you are on?	YES NO N/A
Is there unsightly graffiti in the elevator car?	YES NO N/A
Is the elevator permit visible?	YES NO N/A
Is there a no smoking sign?	YES NO N/A

USEFUL COMMENTS OVERHEARD WHILE
CONDUCTING THE SURVEY IN THIS AREA:

SUGGESTIONS FOR IMPROVEMENT:

Patient Rooms and Bathrooms   Time: _____

Locate a patient room on the following unit: _____ Do not enter an occupied room.

Is the patient room pleasant?	YES	NO	N/A
Is the patient room clean?	YES	NO	N/A
Does the patient room have a guest chair?	YES	NO	N/A
Sit in the chair. Is it comfortable?	YES	NO	N/A
Is the temperature of the room comfortable?	YES	NO	N/A
Are the decorations in the patient room—pictures and wall coverings—attractive?	YES	NO	N/A
Look out the window. Is the window clean?	YES	NO	N/A
Is the view pleasant?	YES	NO	N/A
Are the blinds or drapes in good working order?	YES	NO	N/A
Enter a patient bathroom. Is it clean?	YES	NO	N/A
Are the towels adequate?	YES	NO	N/A
Is the texture of the bath towel comfortable?	YES	NO	N/A
Leave the patient room and approach the nursing station. As you approach, does someone on the unit extend a greeting to you?	YES	NO	N/A
Is the nursing unit neat and orderly?	YES	NO	N/A

USEFUL COMMENTS OVERHEARD WHILE
CONDUCTING THE SURVEY IN THIS AREA:

SUGGESTIONS FOR IMPROVEMENT:

Patient Floor Reception Areas   Time: _____

Go to the reception area or lounge on: _____

Have a seat. Is the chair comfortable?	YES	NO	N/A
Is the upholstery clean?	YES	NO	N/A
Is the upholstery in good condition?	YES	NO	N/A
Are the plants attractive?	YES	NO	N/A
Is the carpet clean?	YES	NO	N/A
Is the floor clean?	YES	NO	N/A

Is the area well ventilated?	YES	NO	N/A
Are ashtrays available and easily accessible for smokers?	YES	NO	N/A
If smoking is prohibited, is there a visible sign to that effect?	YES	NO	N/A
Is the noise level acceptable?	YES	NO	N/A
Are magazines available?	YES	NO	N/A
Are the magazines current?	YES	NO	N/A
Are magazines arranged neatly?	YES	NO	N/A
Is the lighting adequate for reading or writing?	YES	NO	N/A
Is the television reception clear?	YES	NO	N/A

USEFUL COMMENTS OVERHEARD WHILE
CONDUCTING THE SURVEY IN THIS AREA:

SUGGESTIONS FOR IMPROVEMENT:

Physicians' Areas   Time: _____

The physicians' lounge is located: _____

Is the physicians' lounge clean?	YES	NO	N/A
Is the physicians' lounge neat?	YES	NO	N/A
Take a seat in a chair or on a couch. Is the seating comfortable?	YES	NO	N/A
Are the plants attractive?	YES	NO	N/A
Is the lighting adequate for reading or writing?	YES	NO	N/A
Is the carpet clean?	YES	NO	N/A
Is the floor clean?	YES	NO	N/A
Are the pictures on the wall straight?	YES	NO	N/A
Are the blinds or drapes in good condition?	YES	NO	N/A
Is the window clean?	YES	NO	N/A
Does the area smell fresh?	YES	NO	N/A

Is the area well ventilated?   YES NO N/A

Are ashtrays available for smokers?   YES NO N/A

USEFUL COMMENTS OVERHEARD WHILE
CONDUCTING THE SURVEY IN THIS AREA:

SUGGESTIONS FOR IMPROVEMENT:

Departments and Offices   Time: _____

Go to the following department: _____

Is the office orderly?   YES NO N/A

Is the wall space cluttered?   YES NO N/A

Are trash cans visible?   YES NO N/A

Are personal objects and belongings in view?   YES NO N/A

Are food and drinks in view?   YES NO N/A

Are ashtrays in view?   YES NO N/A

USEFUL COMMENTS OVERHEARD WHILE
CONDUCTING THE SURVEY IN THIS AREA:

SUGGESTIONS FOR IMPROVEMENT:

Gift Shop   Time: _____

Go to the main lobby. Find your way to the gift shop.

Is the gift shop easy to find?   YES NO N/A

Did a gift shop volunteer extend a greeting to you when
you entered?   YES NO N/A
Are the display cabinets and shelves well dusted?   YES NO N/A
Is the overall appearance of the gift shop neat and
clean?   YES NO N/A

USEFUL COMMENTS OVERHEARD WHILE
CONDUCTING THE SURVEY IN THIS AREA:

SUGGESTIONS FOR IMPROVEMENT:

Snack Bar/Vending Area   Time: _____

Go back to the main lobby. Find your way to the snack bar or vending area:

Is the snack bar easy to locate?   YES NO N/A
Is the snack bar clean?   YES NO N/A
Are the table tops and counters clean?   YES NO N/A
Are napkins and utensils available?   YES NO N/A
Are there 24-hour vending machines in the vending
area?   YES NO N/A
Are there trash receptacles in the vending area?   YES NO N/A

USEFUL COMMENTS OVERHEARD WHILE
CONDUCTING THE SURVEY IN THIS AREA:

SUGGESTIONS FOR IMPROVEMENT:

Other Areas   Time: _____

This section of the survey asks you to visit the hospital library, the loading
dock area, and a meeting room or classroom. Put on your walking shoes.

The hospital library is located: _____

Are the chairs in the library comfortable?	YES NO N/A
Is the lighting adequate?	YES NO N/A
Is the library neat in appearance?	YES NO N/A
Are the periodicals stocked on shelves in order?	YES NO N/A

The loading dock is located: _____

Is the loading dock swept and free of debris?	YES NO N/A
Is there a sign for those delivering materials directing them to the purchasing office?	YES NO N/A

A classroom/meeting room is located: _____

Is the meeting room neat?	YES NO N/A
Are the blackboards clean?	YES NO N/A
Are the chairs and tables in order?	YES NO N/A
Is the lighting adequate for reading or writing?	YES NO N/A
Is the room well ventilated?	YES NO N/A

USEFUL COMMENTS OVERHEARD WHILE
CONDUCTING THE SURVEY IN THESE AREAS:

SUGGESTIONS FOR IMPROVEMENT:

Surgical Waiting Room   Time: _____

Go to the surgical waiting room located on: _____

Is the room clean?	YES NO N/A
Is seating adequate?	YES NO N/A
Is seating comfortable?	YES NO N/A
Is the lighting adequate for reading or writing?	YES NO N/A
Are telephones easy to find?	YES NO N/A
Is there an adequate supply of reading materials?	YES NO N/A

Are magazines arranged neatly?	YES NO N/A
Is the television reception clear?	YES NO N/A
Is the television low so as not to disturb uninterested guests?	YES NO N/A
Are physicians able to confer with family members in private?	YES NO N/A

USEFUL COMMENTS OVERHEARD WHILE
CONDUCTING THE SURVEY IN THIS AREA:

SUGGESTIONS FOR IMPROVEMENT:

Cafeteria   Time: _____

Is the cafeteria pleasant?	YES NO N/A
Is seating adequate?	YES NO N/A
Is there a sufficient supply of silverware and napkins?	YES NO N/A
As you proceed through the line, do servers smile and make eye contact?	YES NO N/A
Are smoking and nonsmoking areas well marked?	YES NO N/A
Does the cashier make eye contact with you?	YES NO N/A

USEFUL COMMENTS OVERHEARD WHILE
CONDUCTING THE SURVEY IN THIS AREA:

SUGGESTIONS FOR IMPROVEMENT:

Source: K.E. Peterson & Associates, Chicago, Illinois.

Chapter 11

Complaint Management: Silence Is Never Golden

Although the goal of guest relations is to decrease the unsatisfactory experiences that create complaints, the goal of your customer satisfaction feedback system should be to *increase* the number of reported complaints. Complaints present valuable opportunities to create customer satisfaction and loyalty *if* they are resolved appropriately.

A nationwide Louis Harris poll showed that 25 percent of a 1,500-person sample had tried at some time to make a complaint about some aspect of hospital care, and of these, 59 percent were dissatisfied with the hospital's response.[1] Patient satisfaction cannot be achieved unless you have an effective system for soliciting, responding, resolving, tracking, and preventing complaints.

Every manager is responsible for the service entity's performance in meeting and exceeding customer expectations. For that reason, every manager is accountable for patient satisfaction and complaint resolution as well. However, although the decentralization of accountability is necessary to ensure consistent levels of satisfaction with the services delivered, it is still wise to establish a centralized complaint management function. If you do not have a centralized complaint management system, either in your patient representative department or in the administrative office, it is essential to identify someone to assume responsibility for complaint handling. This does not strip the individual department manager of his or her responsibility for service delivery and customer satisfaction. It does provide the capability, however, of preventing complaints and increasing future satisfaction and quality service delivery.

SOLICITING COMPLAINTS

Silence is never golden to a customer-responsive service business. The absence of complaints rarely means an absence of dissatisfaction. Every business must work especially hard to get customers to complain, because most people do not believe that businesses care about solving problems when they arise. According to a study by the Technical Assistance Research Programs, the reasons most often cited for failure to complain include:[2]

- not worth the time or effort (55.6 percent)
- not knowing where to go; what to do (13.5 percent)
- not believing that anyone cares, so why bother? (21.1 percent)

Although hospitals have their shares of dissatisfied guests, few complain. In addition to the reasons identified above, patients often feel intimidated and vulnerable. So exaggerated are their perceptions of the potential misuse of power, in the face of their loss of control, that some patients fear retaliation from the staff if they complain.

You have a responsibility to inform patients how to complain. Complaining is a patient's right, and it makes good sense from both a patient satisfaction and a risk management standpoint. The American Bar Association's Report of the Commission on Medical Professional Liability reports that, regardless of the severity of the claim or complaint, the frustrated patient is much more likely to resort to litigation than one whose rights, or even whims, have been patiently regarded.[3]

To reduce the frustration that patients experience, you must let them know how to complain and then respond by taking their complaints seriously. A complaint is an expression of dissatisfaction when an expectation is not met. Although it may be trivial to the employee, it is a very real problem to the guest and should be taken seriously.

For every complaint received, at least 6 serious complaints and up to 50 less serious complaints go unreported. The first step in complaint management is to remove the perceived or real barriers that discourage the expression of complaints.

The biggest barrier is the patient's ignorance. If patients do not believe anyone cares, let them know you do! If they believe it is not worth the time or effort to complain, make it worth their effort. If they do not know how or where to complain, inform them! Let patients know that their satisfaction is important to you. Inform them that you want to hear from them when they are not satisfied.

Campaigns

One method of soliciting complaints is to initiate a campaign that lets people know you are interested in learning if problems occur during their visit. Obviously, you cannot parade around with a button on your lapel that says "Please complain." A much better strategy is to communicate the message subtly.

Announce your desire and commitment to create guest satisfaction. Then, parenthetically, inform the patients that if they are not satisfied, you want to know. Suppose, for example, that your patient satisfaction surveys indicate a relatively high level of overall satisfaction (more than 90 percent) with hospital services. One possible approach for developing a solicitation campaign is to advertise your near-perfect results. For instance, if your surveys indicate that 94 percent of your patients are satisfied, adopt the slogan: "94 percent, but we're not satisfied." Similar to the successful Avis Car Rental campaign of many years ago, this approach declares, "We try harder."

If your employees wear buttons that say "94%," it is likely that patients and visitors will be curious as to what the number means. How should employees explain it? Consider the impact of the following message:

> Our surveys indicate that 94 percent of our patients are satisfied. Although that's pretty good, we're not satisfied. We are striving for 100 percent. You can help us achieve that if you will remember to let us know if you are not satisfied with any aspect of our service or performance while you are here. Please call our patient hotline at extension 1094.

The "94%" theme and the pledge to deliver superior service can be printed on tent cards that are left in patients' rooms to instruct them on how to report problems or to request information or special services.

As many hospitals have learned, it is best to educate your employees about the campaign so that they know exactly how to explain the program and give an appropriate response when questions about it are asked.

Hot Lines

Most guests will express their complaints in one of two ways:

1. verbally: in person or over the telephone
2. written: on the patient questionnaire or in a letter

In most cases when patients complain verbally, you have an opportunity to prevent long-lasting dissatisfaction because you can take decisive action within a relatively short period of time to solve the problem. Written complaints are much more difficult to resolve because you have lost both physical proximity to the patient and the ability to react within a time frame that is conducive to an optimal outcome.

If you want to decrease the numbers of complaints expressed in writing, you must open wide the channels for verbal communication. You must also inform patients of ways to get in touch with someone who can assist them.

Special telephone extensions known as "hot lines," "warm lines," or "care lines" are becoming quite common. Typically, they are direct lines to the patient representative's office or to the administrative offices. If you have such a line, make certain that a *human being* answers that line 24 hours a day. If you are really serious about complaints, you cannot use a recording. Remember that a timely response is a key factor in building satisfaction. If necessary, you can train the evening or night shift nursing supervisor or switchboard operator to receive the telephone calls and to initiate immediate "holdover" steps until the patient representative or member from administration resumes investigation and resolution activities.

Develop a form to help you document calls made to your hot line. A sample form used by Two Rivers Community Hospital, in Two Rivers, Wisconsin, is shown in Exhibit 11-1.

Guaranteed Service Programs

A guaranteed services program ensures customer satisfaction by offering money back to patients if they or their physicians are not satisfied with any aspect of the service. There are two important exclusions to this promise, however. The

Exhibit 11-1 Calls for Patient Care Representative

tr
Two Rivers
Community Hospital

Call Received by _____ Date _____ Time _____

Caller's Name _____ Caller's Phone or Room # _____

Nature of Problem _____

Check appropriate box:

Urgent _____ Non-Urgent _____   Call back within _____ hours

Caller sounded:

Angry_____   Anxious_____   Confused_____   Pleasant_____   Calm_____

Call referred to:	Extension	Home Phone	Time Referred
Marion Nilles _____	181 or 444	794-1808	_____
Jack Gospodarek _____	187	793-4815	_____
W. L. Sperry _____	140	793-2027	_____
Lorraine Sperry _____	141	793-2027	_____

Please refer call immediately if caller states it is urgent of if caller sounds angry or anxious.

Comments: _____

Source: Courtesy of Two Rivers Community Hospital, Two Rivers, Wisconsin.

hospital does not guarantee the outcome of the medical treatment, nor does it include services delivered by physicians in the guarantee.

There are several benefits to a money-back guaranteed services program. Because it is a program that needs promotion, it can be a method of encouraging patients to express complaints and dissatisfactions. The potential reduction in the number of liability claims or suits that is the result of bringing concerns to the attention of staff before they have the chance to escalate into more serious problems is an important benefit. If publicized correctly, the program can demonstrate to employees that the hospital has confidence in their performance. Employees, themselves, may feel more inspired to work to achieve satisfaction because there are tangible, monetary rewards for doing so. In many programs, budgeted money that is not refunded to dissatisfied patients is shared with employees. A guaranteed service program is particularly useful in helping the hospital identify problem situations when they occur, rather than after the fact.

In most programs, patients are told that, if they are unhappy with a hospital service, they should notify the appropriate hospital representative within 24 hours. Physicians also are instructed to report a problem on behalf of their patients. The problem is then investigated, and an attempt is made to correct the problem. If the patient or physician is still not satisfied, the cost of the service is deducted from the patient's bill.

You cannot institute a guaranteed service program without establishing clear procedures and defining guidelines. The guidelines established by Canonsburg General Hospital and West Allegheny Hospital, both affiliates of Canonsburg Hospital System, in Pennsylvania, are shown in Exhibit 11-2. Because of its potential fiscal impact, it is essential that the hospital think through the program carefully and evaluate every implication with the help of the chief financial officer before putting it into operation.

When instituting a guaranteed service program, typically a sum of money is set aside and designated for refunds to dissatisfied patients. Most hospitals are quite proud of the fact that, by the end of the year, the initial contribution is primarily intact, with only a fraction of the total sum used to reimburse dissatisfied patients. However, it is important not to delude yourself into thinking that the absence of claims for refunds necessarily signals satisfaction. Many patients who may be dissatisfied will not complain, regardless of what incentives are offered. They may not think that it is worth the time or effort, or they may be fearful that complaints will provoke unfavorable consequences. Interestingly, many hospitals that have guaranteed service programs have found that few of the patients who register complaints actually want any money back. Those who do call the telephone hot line are often motivated to do so because they want someone to listen to their complaint.

At Glendale Adventist Medical Center, a 604-bed hospital in Glendale, California, a $25,000 kitty was set up from which refunds were to be paid to any patient

Exhibit 11-2 Patient "Guarantee Services" Program

Services Covered	Refund Amount
Environmental Services (inpatient only). Dissatisfaction with cleanliness of room that is remedied to patient's satisfaction.	Up to 50% of room charge.
General Hospital Services (inpatient only). Discharge delay due to hospital control.	Up to 50% of the charge of the room and board for the time of delay.
Medical Records Services (inpatient and outpatient). Delay in sending copies of medical records to private physicians, insurance carriers, and attorneys.	Up to $4, plus 50 cents per page for photocopying.
Nutritional Services (inpatient only). Dissatisfaction with meals that is not remedied to patient's satisfaction.	Up to 50% of the meal charge.
Plant Operations and Maintenance Services (inpatient). Dissatisfaction with room temperature and/or hospital controlled maintenance items not remedied to patient's satisfaction.	Up to 50% of the room charge.
Waiting Times (inpatient).	
Admissions—30 mins. from registration to patient room.	$10.
Nursing—1 minute to answer call.	$10.
Intensive Care Unit—immediate response.	$10.
X-ray—10 minutes.	Up to the hospital charge for test.
Laboratory—10 minutes.	" "
Physical Therapy—10 minutes.	" "
Waiting Times (outpatient).	
Medical Imaging, Laboratory, EKG, Stress Lab, Physical Therapy—all 10 minutes.	Up to the hospital charge for test.
Registration—10 minutes.	$10.
Security Services (inpatient and outpatient). Covers only those items given to hospital personnel.	Reimbursement (deduction) based upon appraisal.

Source: Reprinted from *Hospital Guest Relations Report,* Vol. 1, No. 2, p. 3, with permission of St. Anthony Hospital Publications, © February 1986.

with a "justifiable complaint" about service or treatment. In one year, 539 inquiries were processed, and a total of $2,806 was refunded. Some complaints did not require a refund. In one instance, a woman who came to Glendale Adventist Medical Center under a $900 alternative birth center package designed to cover all costs of a normal birth received a bill for $1,200. Through the justifiable complaint program, she received a credit on excess charges. In another incident, an elderly patient was transferred to a new room, and in the process his bathrobe was lost. A nursing unit coordinator went shopping on her lunch hour and bought the patient a new robe, the cost of which was reimbursed by the program.[4]

Other examples of reimbursed occurrences in other hospitals include:

- Laboratory tests are lost and a patient's surgery is delayed. The hospital refunds money for the additional 2 days of room charges.
- A patient has to wait too long for an x-ray or a laboratory test. A portion of the cost of the procedure is deducted.
- A patient receives cold food on his tray, and the hospital is not able to rectify the problem quickly enough to satisfy him. The cost of the meal is subtracted from the bill.

An essential element of your internal promotion strategy for a guaranteed services program is education of your employees. Written information should not be the primary method of communicating to your employees. Conduct sessions to explain the program mechanics, as well as to communicate its benefits. A guaranteed services program constitutes a vote of confidence in employees' abilities to deliver service and should be explained that way.

Most hospitals have an informal guaranteed services program. Few hospitals would argue that costs incurred through no fault of the patient, such as additional time hospitalized because of lost tests, should be assumed by the patient. Yet, a formal program provides the hospital with an opportunity to go public with its commitment to satisfy customers. And it can be used advantageously, as Columbus Hospital in Chicago found with its advertising campaign promoting its guaranteed services program. An advertisement is shown in Exhibit 11-3.

Publicity and advertising may alert the general public, but it is important to inform patients of its existence through internal promotion. Buttons, tent cards, and brochures can be used for that purpose.

RESPONDING TO COMPLAINTS

The channels that you establish internally for complaint resolution will vary, depending upon the size of your hospital and the degree to which you have already centralized the complaint management function or plan to do so in the future.

The preliminary investigation of the complaint sets the response system into action. Once the complaint and all issues pertaining to the complaint have been defined, an appropriate response must be formulated. Everything should be done to decrease response delay, both in terms of the number and duration of delays.

Exhibit 11-3 Service Promotion

ONLY A HOSPITAL WITH A STAFF LIKE OURS CAN MAKE A GUARANTEE LIKE OURS.

IF YOUR FOOD'S COLD CALL US ON IT.

IF YOUR ROOM'S TOO WARM CALL US ON IT.

IF SOMEONE WAS RUDE CALL US ON IT.

IF WE MADE YOU WAIT CALL US ON IT.

You're going to like the way we care for you at Columbus. But if any Hospital service doesn't quite meet your expectations or those of your physician, either of you can pick up the phone and call our special hot-line number. We'll get to work on it right away. Whether it's a cold dinner, a fuzzy TV picture, a long wait for x-rays, or whatever —we'll solve the problem and try to make up for your inconvenience with some extra-special treatment. And if you're still not satisfied, you won't be charged for that service.

It takes an exceptional staff to make an offer like that. A staff like ours. We're so confident we'll treat you right, we guarantee our performance to you and your physician. And just to keep us on our toes, we wear buttons to remind ourselves—and you—of this unique guarantee.

We're proud of the high level of satisfaction we offer you at Columbus Hospital. But we're even prouder of the fact that should we ever slip, you can call us on it. And that's a guarantee.

2520 North Lakeview Avenue, Chicago, IL 60614 312/883-6666

Columbus Hospital CO

IT TAKES A STAFF LIKE OURS TO MAKE A GUARANTEE LIKE OURS.

Source: Courtesy of Columbus Hospital, Chicago, Illinois.

Roles of the Patient Representative

The patient representative is the most likely candidate to manage the patient satisfaction feedback system and to be responsible for the complaint and risk management processes. Most patient representatives routinely make rounds and meet with new patients to provide orientation to the hospital's services. The patient representative can communicate the hospital's commitment to quality service and can respond to any needs the patient may have. He or she can instruct the patient on how to communicate problems or needs. Having a staff member personally deliver this important message will increase patients' use of formal channels to communicate dissatisfactions.

As defined by the National Society of Patient Representatives, the patient representative's primary assignment is to serve as the liaison between patients and the organization as a whole. Patient representatives provide a specific channel through which patients can seek solutions to problems, concerns, and unmet needs.[5]

Some hospital administrators do not believe that one person or persons should be specifically designated to work in the patient's behalf because all employees should be expected to do so. Philosophically, this attitude is admirable. In reality, it may be detrimental to the overall attainment of patient, physician, and employee satisfaction. Although not every hospital should have a patient representative program, it is important to understand the following ways in which patient representatives can support and assist the hospital's guest relations program and how they can solicit complaints.[6]

The patient representative can function to:

- Investigate and direct inquiries and complaints to appropriate hospital staff members and act as an intermediary to hospital administration in behalf of patients and their family members.
- Assist in referring patients to appropriate services and resources and respond when other alternatives are not available.
- Assist in providing the mechanism for investigating patient care complaints that may involve the hospital or medical staff.
- Evaluate the level of patient satisfaction with the hospital experience.
- Collect data, channel information about patient care problems, and make recommendations for changes in hospital procedures and policies that create dissatisfaction or inefficient or ineffective service delivery.
- Encourage understanding and adherence by both staff and patients to the hospital's philosophy on patients' rights and responsibilities.
- Participate in the assessment of responses to incidents that, if not properly responded to, could provoke serious controversy or legal problems.
- Interpret hospital policy and procedures to the patient and family.

The scope of the patient representative's role therefore extends beyond handling crises.

Many patient representatives distribute business cards to patients so that they understand whom to call if they encounter a problem or need information or services. Tent cards holding the patient representative's business card can be placed in patient rooms, reminding patients to contact the patient representative should the need arise.

Employee's Roles

Because every employee assumes a role in creating guest satisfaction, every employee assumes a role in complaint handling. How a situation is handled initially has a great deal to do with the eventual outcome. Often, a problem will fester, anger will intensify and the situation will escalate, becoming more volatile and difficult to resolve because it has not been dealt with effectively. Therefore, employees need to be informed adequately and trained thoroughly in procedures for complaint handling and resolution. They should be provided with instructions that will enable them to identify when a complaint should be referred to someone else, either because it exceeds the scope of what they or their department can affect or because the potential for legal litigation against the hospital or physician may exist. They should also be trained how to resolve complaints.

Responses to Verbal Complaints

A complaint handling system should include an appropriate means of follow-up. Here is where lessons can be learned from other businesses that have designed very sophisticated response systems. The response system provides a way to confirm that a response to the complaint was offered and that the patient (or other guest) was satisfied with the outcome. It also identifies if further follow-up is necessary. The follow-up system demonstrates the organization's good will, as much as it is a means of ensuring that a positive outcome is perceived by the guest. For example, when a guest calls the front desk about a problem, many hotels instruct front desk clerks to initiate a return telephone call to the guest within 20 minutes. This follow-up call is made to ensure that the person or department to whom the problem was referred contacted the guest or otherwise explained what would be done about the problem.

Hospitals can implement similar response systems, although the follow-up response time may be at a longer interval, depending on the situation. What happens when a patient is dissatisfied with the cleanliness of the room and voices complaints directly to a nurse? How can you ensure that this problem will be reported to the proper authority? On a busy day, a nurse may very well feel that the room is clean enough and that the patient is being unreasonable. His or her motivation to respond may not be strong. To ensure the appropriate response, you must train employees on proper procedures, develop a hospital-wide system of accountability, and provide incentives. For this specific example, that complaint procedure would set into motion the following actions:

- The nurse completes a complaint card, noting the date, time, patient name, room number, description of the complaint, and his or her name and extension number. The nurse telephones the housekeeping supervisor and alerts him or her of the patient's dissatisfaction, noting the time of the telephone call on the card.

- The housekeeping supervisor is expected (as communicated by policy) to visit the patient within 1 hour. If unable to visit the patient within that time frame, he or she is expected to estimate when the visit will be made and to communicate that expectation to the nurse. The nurse will note that information on the card.

- The nurse tells the patient that he or she has contacted the housekeeping supervisor, who will follow up the complaint.

- Following the visit, the housekeeping supervisor notifies the nurse, retrieves the card, writes down the response to the patient noting the time and date, and signs the card.

- The housekeeping supervisor deposits the card in a collection box. At the end of the day (or the beginning of the next day), these cards are retrieved by the patient representative, administrator, or other person assigned the responsibility to visit the patient within a period of 24 hours to confirm that appropriate follow-up occurred.

In this example, the nurse and the housekeeping supervisor become a team, and together they work to resolve the patient's complaint. Yet, to make such a system work, you have to provide an incentive. The nurse may feel too busy to report the problem to the supervisor or department head. What motivation does the nurse have to follow through, other than the intrinsic satisfaction of knowing that he or she responded appropriately? The supervisor may want to mask chronic performance problems and therefore may not report the complaint. What incentives will encourage reporting the complaint and following through to meet the guest's expectation?

Consider this incentive to encourage teamwork to resolve patients' complaints. At a monthly department head meeting, hold a raffle of completed complaint cards. Award the winning team $100 or two movie tickets and dinner for two at a local restaurant for each team member. You can also give lapel pins and publish photos of winners in your newsletter. Rewards can be large or small, monetary or fun. The basic objective is to draw attention to the importance of working together to create satisfaction.

Responses to Written Complaints

If a patient cites a complaint on a guest questionnaire or in a letter, you have an opportunity to demonstrate that you take the complaint seriously and that you will do something about it. If guests identify themselves by name on the questionnaire, call them to gather more information and to ensure follow-up. If you respond in this manner, your contact will probably exceed their expectations. Many people who complain on questionnaires find that it is a therapeutic opportunity to "write their mad out." They probably do not expect to hear from you unless you have a specific question on the survey asking if the guest would like someone to contact him or her regarding any aspect of the care. Then you have set an expectation to which you should immediately respond.

When a guest writes a letter, your response is especially important. A person who takes the time to sit down and write you a letter is expressing something important to him or her. You are wise to respond, both when the guest has been complimentary and when he or she has expressed a problem.

Most consumer affairs departments have standard response letters stored in their word processing software. When a guest complains (or, for that matter, when he or she compliments), a staff member can easily pull out the standard letter that would be an appropriate response. The letter can be personalized with name and address, as well as salutation. The software can be coded to insert the guest's name within the body of the letter. Or, standard paragraphs can be used in the beginning and at the end of the letter. The staff member may wish to type in a paragraph or two in the body of the letter relating specifically to the problem or need identified. If you have the capability to do so, develop your internal word processing capabilities so you can respond in a personalized manner to every letter you receive or, at the very least, to every complaint.

Do not let the mail do for you what you could better do over the telephone or in person. It is much better to call someone if the complaint is obviously serious and appears to be valid. You may telephone only to say, "I received your letter, Mr. Jacobson. I understand something happened that upset you, and I just wanted you to know that I am looking into it right away. Would you be able to answer a few questions so I can gain further insight into the problem?" You do not necessarily need to apologize initially. Your apology may come later, if appropriate.

The initial telephone call or letter should come from the person to whom the letter was addressed. If the size of your hospital and the volume of your complaints are too large to allow the president to return every telephone call personally, this responsibility can be delegated to another member of the executive staff or to the appropriate department manager. In this response, immediate reference is made to the president. For example: "Mr. Smith, the president of our hospital, was very upset to learn of the problem that you experienced concerning the _____.
Mr. Smith asked me to follow up right away, as I am the administrator (manager)

over that department.'' If you plan to investigate the complaint further, inform the guest what can be expected from you and when you will be back in touch with him or her.

In any case of potential liability, be very careful what you say. Although the tone of your voice should be understanding and contrite, you do not need to say, ''I am sorry.'' You may be implying that you were at fault or negligent. Under more benign circumstances, however, there is nothing wrong with apologizing. ''Mr. Jacobson, I was very sorry to learn you had a problem . . .'' or ''Mr. Jacobson, I understand that you are upset about this situation and I regret very much that it occurred. We have met with those involved and are proceeding with disciplinary action. Is there anything I can do in the meantime to restore your faith in General Hospital?''

A patient who expresses a problem or complaint in a letter will be very aware how long it takes you to get back in touch with him or her. Remember, response time is critically important in rebuilding the relationship.

TRACKING COMPLAINTS

The management of information is a critical component of an effective complaint management system. Record keeping is important because you cannot refine your delivery systems or address performance problems if you are unaware of what is at the root of repetitive complaints.

If you manage the information manually, you can develop forms and procedures that will enable you to use and interpret the data more effectively. It is important to complete the information carefully and regularly according to a well-designed logging system. Neither a manual nor a computer system will work if you do not keep accurate records.

Sinai Hospital in Detroit, Michigan, has produced several forms to make its record keeping easier and the information more useful in terms of complaint prevention and problem solving. The Patient Problem Report shown in Exhibit 11-4 is completed any time a patient concern or complaint is brought to the attention of the guest relations representative.[7] The Monthly Activity Report shown in Exhibit 11-5 shows the sources and modes of inquiries made during the month and the total number of problems occurring in each of the departmental areas. The Annual Summary shown in Exhibit 11-6 shows the numbers of complaints received each month by category and has a column for the total for the year.

Whether you use a paper-based or computerized system, you should log and classify complaints. Complaints should be classified according to a number of categories, which may correspond to those used in your quality assurance and risk management programs. Computerized logs and complaint classification systems

Exhibit 11-4 Patient Problem Report

Patient Problem Report

Date _____

Patient's name _____

Patient's record number _____Room no. _____ Phone no. _____

Patient's home address and home phone number _____

(Address) _____

(City, state, zip code) _____

(Phone)

Describe patient's problem or concern. Be specific. Note when, how, from whom you learned of the problem.

_____

_____

_____

_____

List other persons, services, or departments involved. _____

_____

_____

Describe action taken to solve problem. _____

_____

_____

_____

Source: Reprinted with permission, from *Patient Representation in Contemporary Health Care,* copyright 1985 by the American Hospital Association.

---

have gained popularity recently due to the low cost of high-capacity microcomputers and the availability of appropriate software. A computerized system provides you with the ability to manipulate the data which enables a more accurate analysis of trends and more rapid problem solving.

You may also have access to the hospital's computer information system. Ask a management information specialist to design or modify the mainframe computer's data base to meet your needs. If that is not possible, you can use a personal computer and data base software system. You do not have to be a computer whiz to be able to maintain an automated complaint management system, although if you are not computer literate, you will probably need some assistance in creating the data base. Computers have become a part-time avocation of many people, and you may not have to look far to find someone in your hospital who can assist you in designing the system.

Exhibit 11-5 Patient Representative—Monthly Activity Report

Monthly Activity Report

Month of _____ , 19____

Inquiry Data

Source of inquiry. Record total number of inquiries received from each group listed.

Patient _____
Employee _____
Family or friend _____
Physician _____
Other _____

Mode of inquiry. Record total number of inquiries received via each of the following.

Telephone _____
Letter _____
Interview _____
Page or beeper _____
Other _____

Patient Problem Area Data

Record the total number of patient problems occurring in each of the following areas.

	Inquiries this month		Inquiries this month
Accounts receivable	_____	Lost and damaged property	_____
Administration	_____	Nursing	_____
Admitting	_____	Occupational therapy	_____
Billing or charges	_____	Parking	_____
Business office	_____	Physical therapy	_____
Community relations	_____	Physician	_____
Coronary care unit	_____	Pulmonary laboratory	_____
Diet—food	_____	Recovery room	_____
Diet—instructions	_____	Respiratory therapy	_____
Diet—tray delivery	_____	Roommate or room problem ...	_____
Discharge	_____	Social services	_____
Electrocardiogram (EKG)	_____	Speech therapy	_____
Electroencephalogram (EEG) ..	_____	Surgery	_____
Emergency department	_____	Translation	_____
Employee attitude	_____	Transportation	_____
Engineering	_____	Ultrasound	_____
Environmental services	_____	X-ray	_____
Financial counseling	_____	Other (specify)	_____
Gastrointestinal laboratory ...	_____	_____	
Hemodialysis	_____	_____	
Intensive care unit	_____	_____	
		Total	_____

Guest Relations Rep. Signature

Source: Adapted with permission of Sinai Hospital, Detroit, Michigan.

Exhibit 11-6 Patient Representative—Annual Summary

Annual Summary of Problem Areas, 19___

Patient Complaint Received About:	Number of Complaints Received each Month												Total for Year
	Jan.	Feb.	Mar.	Apr.	May	June	July	Aug.	Sept.	Oct.	Nov.	Dec.	
Billing or charges													
Employee attitude or behavior													
Food													
Hospital rules													
Housekeeping													
Lack of communication													
Nursing care													
Physician													
Preparation for tests													
Room													
TV													
Waiting for transportation from one area of hospital to another													
Waiting in admitting or emergency departments													
Other (specify)													

_____
Guest Relations Rep. Signature

Source: Adapted with permission of Sinai Hospital, Detroit, Michigan.

Specific information relating to the floor or unit on which the patient is hospitalized; the date of the complaint; the department responsible for resolving the complaint, such as the food service department for problems relating to the food; and the specific nature of the complaint, such as incorrect food temperature, food delivered late, not what the patient ordered, can be entered with codes. Once the system is set up and then maintained with accurate and regular input of information, your data base can become a management tool to identify sources of recurring complaints.

For example, you may want to know how many patients have been dissatisfied with their roommates. The data can be sorted to provide that information. You can also go a step further. Suppose you would like to receive information on the number of roommate complaints that resulted in room changes. If the program has been appropriately designed, a search will provide that information. The data can be further sorted if you need more specific information, such as the incidence of room changes that occurred on various units over a period of 3 months. Remember that the objective should be to have a useful system; you do not need to make it too sophisticated.

Accessibility of the system and the desire to make it work by entering accurate information on a regular basis are two important components of a successful computerized program.

Remember that you are dealing with perceptions of reality. Your investigation of a complaint may result in a conclusion that another source was the real cause of the complaint or that the patient's perception of the problem was inaccurate. Although the patient's perception is what counts, you should also account for ill-conceived perceptions of a department's or individual's performance.

When you can identify recurring problems, you can begin analyzing your service delivery system. You must continually strive to develop ways to prevent problems from occurring in the future. This is what complaint management is all about.

SUMMARY

The information you gather in your complaint management system should become a part of the total information system you manage to gauge levels of patient satisfaction. Recurring problems should be analyzed and recommendations made of changes that will prevent future occurrences. Complaints impede satisfaction. The key to creating satisfaction is to identify ways to prevent complaints, as well as to resolve them quickly and effectively.

Also remember that although this chapter has focused on the patient, you may be dealing with a physician, family member, visitor, or even a telephone caller!

Regardless of why your guests complain, by responding quickly and effectively you can build satisfaction.

NOTES

1. Norma Shaw Hogan, *Humanizing Health Care* (Oradell, N.Y.: Medical Economics Company, 1980), 95.

2. Technical Assistance Research Programs (TARP), *Consumer Complaint Handling in America: Final Report* (Washington, D.C.: White House Office of Consumer Affairs), 1980.

3. American Bar Association Patients' Rights and Responsibilities, *1977 Report of the Commission on Medical Professional Liability* (Chicago: American Bar Association, 1977): 19–24.

4. Charles C. Keely, Jr., "The Gourmet Hospital," *PSA Airlines* (March 3, 1985): 62–65, 111.

5. *Patient Representation in Contemporary Health Care,* (Chicago: National Society of Patient Representatives of the American Hospital Association, 1985), 25–28.

6. Ibid., 24–26.

7. "Essentials of Patient Representative Programs in Hospitals" (Chicago: National Society of Patient Representatives of the American Hospital Association, 1985).

Chapter 12

Patient Satisfaction Surveys: Perception Is Reality

"I believe I received competent medical care."

Suppose you are a patient and you are asked that question on the hospital's patient questionnaire. How would you answer?

Most patients have little to no ability to evaluate the quality of medical care that they receive. Yet, statements similar to this one appear regularly on questionnaires, inviting the patient to agree, to disagree, or to profess total ignorance by checking the "don't know" box. Although no one can deny that quality medical care is an important dimension of patient satisfaction, the questions asked to determine whether patients perceive that they receive good care should be based on the criteria that they most frequently use to evaluate competency and quality.

If you are to receive value from your efforts to measure patient satisfaction, you must first ask the right questions—those that patients are qualified to evaluate. The dimensions you measure must be the ones that *patients* feel are the most important. Second, you must ask questions that will enable you to improve service delivery. A questionnaire is nothing more than a public relations gimmick if it does not isolate problems and prepare you to remedy sources of dissatisfaction.

If you want quality information about the quality of the patient's experience, you must *design* a feedback system to achieve results. This chapter explores several ways in which patient satisfaction feedback can be gathered.

DESIGNING A QUESTIONNAIRE

Patients generally return satisfaction questionnaires if they are exceptionally satisfied or exceptionally dissatisfied. Those whose expectations have merely been met will generally not respond unless you do some gentle prodding. You will have to work to cull responses from a broad cross-section of patients. If you do not hear from "middle of the roaders," you will not have quantifiably sound data.

For feedback to be of value, you should receive a good rate of return and it should ask the questions that will accurately evaluate if your systems and people are performing to meet customer expectations. Far too many hospitals are led to believe they are doing better than they actually are simply because the data on which they rely are invalid or inconclusive. It is highly unlikely that any hospital satisfies 97 percent of its discharged patients, yet there are several hospitals that claim that they do. It is far more accurate to presume that they satisfy 97 percent of those who returned their questionnaires, and even that may be inaccurate.

Encourage Patients To Respond

The method of distribution will affect the number of questionnaires that are returned each month. Questionnaires can be mailed out to every discharged patient or to a random sample of discharged patients. If you distribute questionnaires through the mail, you will want to make sure that you send them within a relatively short period of time following the patient's discharge. The longer the span of time, the more likely it is that the patient will either discard the questionnaire or not be able to provide an accurate assessment because time has distorted his or her perceptions. Although mailing questionnaires is a costly alternative, the response rate is typically good. A cover letter expressing the value of the feedback helps increase the number of responses.

A more common practice is to make the questionnaire available by placing it in the patient's room or to display it prominently in the admitting and/or business office. This method of distribution does not guarantee a high rate of return, simply because it is left to chance. You can increase the rate of return if someone *personally* asks the patient to complete the questionnaire. This can be done by the patient representative, the head nurse, an administrator, or the business office clerk.

The design of the questionnaire also influences the probability of response. The following questions are useful in determining whether you have designed a questionnaire that encourages response.

- *Is the questionnaire attractive?* Patients are more likely to respond to questionnaires that are typeset rather than typewritten, printed rather than photocopied. The print should be easy to read. Effective use of white space (areas in which print does not appear) will contribute to a clean appearance.
- *Is the questionnaire too long?* If it appears that it will take a long time to complete the questionnaire, patients are less encouraged to respond. The physical length of the questionnaire is not as significant as the numbers of questions asked. A questionnaire that measures 8″ by 22″ (unfolded) is not

necessarily too long if the layout is clean and the number of questions is appropriate.

- *Is the questionnaire confusing?* Confusion occurs and disincentives to respond exist if directions are unclear or if the design is cluttered or inconsistent.
- *Is the questionnaire easy to return?* A postage-paid, self-mailer is your best bet in making the return easy.

Patients should be able to recognize immediately that your questionnaire is a satisfaction survey. This can be accomplished by using a simple slogan or invitation, such as "Your Opinion Is Important to Us," "Please Share Your Comments on Our Services," or "We Want to Know How You Feel." Avoid cute slogans, such as "We'd Like to X-Ray your Opinion!" Do not challenge the patient to disagree by using such a slogan as "94% of Our Former Patients Rate Us Excellent. Do You Agree?" or "We Care."

Include a *short* message from the president, inviting the patient to complete the survey. Do not propagandize with platitudes about your desire to achieve excellence, the quality of your services, and the value of patient opinions. The following paragraph effectively and concisely communicates a message that encourages response without going overboard:

> To enable us to carry out our mission to provide quality patient care and service that will exceed our patients' expectations, we need the kind of information only you can provide. I hope you will take a moment to complete this questionnaire. We value your opinion and will use your comments in confidence to improve our services.

Use a photograph of your president on the questionnaire; patients will have stronger personal identification with the request. Then add the president's personal signature, and make his or her office the return address. This ensures patients of confidentiality and increases their confidence that their opinions will be taken seriously.

Ask Patients To Rate Your Service Performance

The patient should be given the opportunity to *rate* your service performance. You will receive more accurate feedback if you allow people to rate services on a numerical scale, rather than providing only the options of "yes," "no," or "don't know." A scale of 1 to 5 is better than 1 to 4 because the middle (3) indicates neutrality, sometimes because of the patient's lack of opinion or lack of experience. However, you may need to add a specific ''not applicable'' or ''no opinion'' to the side of many evaluative questions.

Several different rating scales can be used, but it is best not to mix their use on the questionnaire.

Quality Ratings

Quality ratings measure the perceived value of a particular service dimension or characteristic. You can rate quality in the following manner:

- ( ) poor
- ( ) fair
- ( ) average
- ( ) good
- ( ) excellent

Occurrence Ratings

Occurrence ratings measure frequency of a desired occurrence or the consistency of a desired action. You can provide a scale of three or five on occurrence ratings:

- ( ) never
- ( ) seldom
- ( ) sometimes
- ( ) almost always
- ( ) always

Or:

- ( ) infrequently
- ( ) sometimes
- ( ) always

Agreement Ratings

Agreement ratings are used to measure the respondent's concurrence with a statement. An example of an agreement rating is provided below.

- ( ) strongly disagree
- ( ) disagree

- ( ) neutral
- ( ) agree
- ( ) strongly agree

Expectation Ratings

Expectation ratings can apply to both the quality and the occurrence of certain standards. To rate against expectations, use these phrases:

- ( ) much worse than I expected
- ( ) worse than I expected
- ( ) as I expected
- ( ) better than I expected
- ( ) much better than I expected

Evaluations are always intended to measure postoccurrence perceptions of how well your services met predetermined expectations. Expectations are variable, but they are really what counts. It is for this reason that evaluating experiences against expectations is becoming a popular method.

Maintain consistency in your format. If you select quality ratings, try to structure your criteria that way. Avoid going back and forth from quality ratings to expectation ratings, for example. However, due to the nature of some of your questions, you will probably need to mix occurrence ratings (always, sometimes, never, etc.) with another rating scale.

Request Patients To Evaluate Your Service

The first step in developing the content of the survey instrument is to ask yourself the following questions: On what dimensions do patients evaluate their hospitalization experience? What factors contribute to patient satisfaction and what factors detract from it? Of what value will the information be to us in targeting areas of improvement? What do we want to know? What does the patient want to tell us?

On a general inpatient questionnaire, three basic criteria relating to departmental performance should be assessed. These criteria are generally the most significant in influencing overall satisfaction with a department's service performance;

1. Were your needs attended to promptly? (responsiveness)
2. Were the employees courteous? (courtesy)
3. Were procedures or therapies explained? (information)

Riverside Hospital in Newport News, Virginia, has developed an excellent patient satisfaction survey that specifically measures departmental performance in the areas of information, responsiveness, and courtesy. The survey is shown in Exhibit 12-1.

Another way to structure the survey is to ask a specific question and include all appropriate departments/individuals to be evaluated, as is shown in Exhibit 12-2. This approach is suitable for teaching hospitals that desire feedback on physician and student performance on specific dimensions. Please be aware, however, that many physicians are strongly opposed to this. You should also realize that many patients will have a difficult time distinguishing between attendings, residents, interns, and students. The color of lab coats worn can be used for identification.

The environment and food are two important dimensions that should also be evaluated by patients. The performance of food service and housekeeping can be evaluated by asking questions relating to the room and the meals. Meals are typically evaluated on occurrence factors (never, occasionally, frequently, always) as shown in Exhibit 12-3.

You may want to differentiate between those patients who were and those who were not on special diets, which may affect their satisfaction with the quality and taste of the food. If so, ask the question, "Were you on a special diet?"

The room can be evaluated according to several different dimensions, as is seen in Exhibit 12-4. You can also ask the patient to identify whether the person who cleaned the room was friendly or courteous. Housekeepers routinely spend the greatest amount of time with hospitalized patients, and their attitudes can make a difference.

Encourage Comments!

Provide space for the patient to write comments after each section. Do not wait until the end of the questionnaire to include a comment section. Remember that the comments can be very insightful and may identify service improvement ideas.

Gather Information About the Respondent

You should have separate questionnaires for inpatients, those who receive care from your outpatient surgery center, and those who are treated in the emergency room on an outpatient basis. The following questions target informational needs that are appropriate for inpatient questionnaires:

- *Who is the respondent?* The name of the patient is less important than the demographic profile. Statisticians frequently like to interpret responses

Exhibit 12-1 Departmental Performance Measures

If you received services from the following list of departments, please grade each of the three sections:

Department	Were your needs attended to promptly? (circle one if appropriate)					Were the personnel courteous and helpful? (circle one if appropriate)					Were procedures or therapies explained to you by the staff? (circle one if appropriate)				
Registration/Admitting Dept. (Before and during your admission)	1 (poor)	2	3	4	5 (excellent)	1 (poor)	2	3	4	5 (excellent)	1 (poor)	2	3	4	5 (excellent)
Emergency Room (If you came to us through this department)	1 (poor)	2	3	4	5 (excellent)	1 (poor)	2	3	4	5 (excellent)	1 (poor)	2	3	4	5 (excellent)
Nursing (Throughout your stay with us)	1 (poor)	2	3	4	5 (excellent)	1 (poor)	2	3	4	5 (excellent)	1 (poor)	2	3	4	5 (excellent)
Operating Room/Recovery Room OR Labor & Delivery Services	1 (poor)	2	3	4	5 (excellent)	1 (poor)	2	3	4	5 (excellent)	1 (poor)	2	3	4	5 (excellent)
Laboratory (Specimens, blood tests, labwork)	1 (poor)	2	3	4	5 (excellent)	1 (poor)	2	3	4	5 (excellent)	1 (poor)	2	3	4	5 (excellent)
Radiology (X-rays, ultrasound, scans, nuclear medicine, radiation therapy)	1 (poor)	2	3	4	5 (excellent)	1 (poor)	2	3	4	5 (excellent)	1 (poor)	2	3	4	5 (excellent)
Transportation (Staff that assisted you to your therapies or surgery)	1 (poor)	2	3	4	5 (excellent)	1 (poor)	2	3	4	5 (excellent)	1 (poor)	2	3	4	5 (excellent)
Business Office (Cashiers, billing clerks)	1 (poor)	2	3	4	5 (excellent)	1 (poor)	2	3	4	5 (excellent)	1 (poor)	2	3	4	5 (excellent)

Source: Courtesy of Riverside Hospital, Newport News, Virginia.

Exhibit 12-2 Evaluation of a Specific Dimension

Please tell us how well each of the following staff explained your illness, diagnosis, and/or treatment.

	Excellent	Good	Satisfactory	Fair	Poor
Personal physician	( )	( )	( )	( )	( )
Nurse	( )	( )	( )	( )	( )
Intern/resident	( )	( )	( )	( )	( )
Medical student	( )	( )	( )	( )	( )
Other _____	( )	( )	( )	( )	( )

Exhibit 12-3 Evaluation of Food

	Always	Sometimes	Never
Did you receive the food you selected on your menu?	( )	( )	( )
Was the food served in an appetizing and attractive manner?	( )	( )	( )
Was the taste and quality of the food good?	( )	( )	( )
Were the meal temperatures satisfactory?	( )	( )	( )

Exhibit 12-4 Evaluation of Room Environment

	Poor	Fair	Satisfactory	Good	Excellent
Comfortable	( )	( )	( )	( )	( )
Attractive	( )	( )	( )	( )	( )
Clean	( )	( )	( )	( )	( )
Quiet	( )	( )	( )	( )	( )
Temperature	( )	( )	( )	( )	( )

Comments:

according to the respondent's age and gender, as noticeable differences in responses frequently occur between men and women and among patients of varying age groups. You will probably find, for example, that women are more critical than men and older patients are more satisfied than younger patients.

- *How was the patient admitted?* Was the patient a scheduled admission through the admitting office, did he or she unexpectedly arrive through the emergency room, or was she a maternity admission?
- *When was the patient admitted?* By asking the patient to identify the day of the week and approximate time of admission, you can better interpret the data you receive. For example, patients who are admitted on Sunday afternoons will probably wait longer periods of time than those admitted on Friday mornings. If patients report dissatisfaction with the admitting process, it is advantageous to be able to determine relative levels of satisfaction by days of the week or by shift. Doing so will enable you to pinpoint staffing level needs.

You may wish to ask patients to provide the dates on which they were admitted or discharged. This question is sometimes included as a means of identifying trends on a month-to-month basis. It may also help you identify reasons for reports of dissatisfaction. If, for example, construction was underway in obstetrics during the period of time mentioned, you may assume that dissatisfaction with noise or ambience issues was a temporary aberration prompted by explainable circumstances. Including a code on all questionnaires that signals the week they were mailed will give you similar information.

You can also ask the patient to identify the duration of the hospitalization to ascertain whether patients who are hospitalized longer are generally less satisfied than those who are hospitalized less than 5 days.

- *Where was the patient located?* You can ask the patient to identify the room number or floor on which he or she stayed. Another method is to ask the patient to identify the type of care received, such as medical, surgical, orthopedic, pediatric, or psychiatric.

The questionnaire can be designed to gather other useful information about hospital selection. Examples of such questions include:

Did your doctor give you the choice of more than one hospital?   ( ) yes   ( ) no

Did you ask your doctor to admit you to this hospital?   ( ) yes   ( ) no

You may want to ask a question to determine whether patient satisfaction is perceived to be better than at a previous time. Although many variables can shape a patient's overall experience, you may be able to spot a trend over time that tells you that you are gaining ground in your guest relations efforts. For example, include this question:

If you were hospitalized at General Hospital previously, would you say that your present experience was:
( ) More favorable
( ) About the same
( ) Less favorable

You may want to learn the extent to which satisfaction or dissatisfaction will influence future market action. For example, ask this question:

If you needed to be hospitalized again, would you request
General Hospital?   ( ) yes   ( ) no

You do not have to make any apologies for this question. Do not begin with a qualifier, such as, "While we hope you will not have to be hospitalized again, if you. . . ." You do not hope that the patient will be rehospitalized. However, you do hope that, if hospitalization does recur, the patient will select your organization. This information can be learned by phrasing the question another way, as seen below:

Would you recommend General Hospital to your relatives or
friends?   ( ) yes   ( ) no

If the patient is willing to recommend the hospital to family and friends, he or she is probably willing to return as well. The significance of this question is that it makes a statement regarding the actions you hope will result from the patient's satisfaction.

Your questionnaire should always invite the patient to discuss further any aspect of the care. In doing so, you may uncover a problem that the patient is unwilling, for whatever reasons, to record on the questionnaire. For example, ask:

Would you like someone from administration to call you to
discuss your care further?   ( ) yes   ( ) no

If yes, please provide your telephone number. _____

Once that box has been checked, the patient will expect a telephone call so it is important to ask for the telephone number following the question.

You may provide space on the questionnaire for the patient to fill in his or her name and address, but the patient may either forget or decline to do so. He or she may not realize that by failing to provide you this information, any follow-up is impossible.

You can also provide a space where respondents can identify an employee(s) whom they would like to acknowledge for special recognition. Always share these kudos with employees.

COMMON DESIGN FLAWS

Asking the right questions in the right way to gain the information you are looking for requires some work. Because people are relying on written instructions without the benefit of verbal clarification, much room is left for interpretation. The more ambiguous the question, the greater the chance of collecting misleading data. Even if the question is not ambiguous, you have no way of knowing if the respondent is basing his or her answers on the same criteria you used to formulate the question.

Beware of the following design flaws:

- *Evaluation of insignificant factors:* Always ask yourself whether you are isolating significant factors that influence overall satisfaction. A second, but equally important, question is to ask yourself whether you will be willing to remedy the source of dissatisfaction isolated by the question. For example:

	Strongly Disagree			Strongly Agree	
The bed was comfortable.	1	2	3	4	5

What, in fact, will the hospital do if the majority of patients say the beds are uncomfortable? In addition, to what degree does bed comfort influence overall satisfaction? Probably not much.

- *Improper use of rating scales:* This is a minor infraction, but it is interesting to note the number of times that errors, such as the following, appear in questionnaires.

	Strongly Disagree			Strongly Agree	
There were no disturbing noises.	1	2	3	4	5
There were no unpleasant odors.	1	2	3	4	5

Asking for a degree of agreement in these questions is unimportant. Either there were disturbing noises and/or unpleasant odors, or there were not. It is more important to ask what kind of noises and odors were present and where did they occur.

- *Improper grouping of multiple service dimensions:* Be careful to isolate different performance factors.

	Strongly Disagree			Strongly Agree
The admissions people were prompt and courteous.	1	2	3	4	5

By wording a question in this way, this hospital has grouped together two very important factors—promptness and courtesy. The employees may have been courteous, but may not have been prompt. Or, they may have been prompt, but not courteous. Ask two questions to isolate satisfaction ratings in two different dimensions.

However, it is possible to group similar characteristics together. For example: "The admitting staff was friendly and courteous."

- *Lack of specificity:* If a question is too general, you may not be able to interpret the response accurately and isolate problems that need to be addressed.

- *Inclusion of inappropriate questions:* Some questions are simply not appropriate or useful on a questionnaire. For example:

	Strongly Disagree			Strongly Agree
The prices at General Hospital are reasonable.	1	2	3	4	5

You may have the most reasonable hospital prices in town, but patients rarely consider hospital charges to be reasonable. Even if the patients consistently rate the hospital charges as too high, will you lower your charges? In essence, this question relates to perceived value. The question should really be worded, "Were the charges you paid reasonable for the quality of care you received?" Nonetheless, it is not appropriate to ask this on a questionnaire.

DETAILED SERVICE SURVEYS

A basic patient satisfaction survey is intended to provide you with feedback on general dimensions that contribute to patient satisfaction. However, you can design surveys that are much more specific and diagnostic.

If you have ever been a passenger on an airline while it is conducting market research, you may have had the experience of completing one questionnaire while on the way to your destination and another, different questionnaire on your return flight. Airlines seek very specific information from passengers and will frequently administer several different detailed surveys simultaneously so as not to burden passengers with lengthy, time-consuming survey responses.

If you are really serious about patient satisfaction measurement, you may want to develop several different questionnaires to enable you to obtain more detailed and specific information. For example, you can ask patients to respond to very specific questions relating to expectations of performance on a departmental basis. Review the sample questions included in Appendix 12-A.

It is best to request that patients complete detailed questionnaires while they are hospitalized, but you will have to ensure anonymity of the patients if you expect them to be truthful. If you mail detailed questionnaires, they must be sent immediately after the patient's discharge. The longer you wait, the more difficult it is to obtain feedback on specific criteria.

A detailed departmental services survey can also be initiated by the department manager, either on the telephone or in person. For example, the radiology administrator, on a monthly basis, can be expected to survey ten patients. The purpose of the survey is to solicit feedback from the patient about his or her satisfaction with the services provided by the radiology department. The radiology administrator should check with the nurses' station before visiting the patient to ascertain which patients who may have received services from the department earlier that day are feeling well enough to participate.

If the radiology administrator's department provides services on both an inpatient and an outpatient basis, telephone calls can be initiated to a specified number of patients who received the services on an outpatient basis. The outline of questions shown in Exhibit 12-5 can be used.

RESPONSE TO FEEDBACK

Your response system should be structured to respond and remedy recurring sources of dissatisfaction that are identified when monitoring satisfaction levels on the service dimensions you have defined. You should also be prepared to respond to those patients who identify problems or express dissatisfaction on their questionnaires.

Marriott Corporation's Office of Consumer Affairs receives over 15,000 guest questionnaires a week. Data are entered and the satisfaction levels for each of the hotel sites are monitored. When the satisfaction levels deviate from the norm, regional operations officers and hotel general managers are notified. They are held accountable to remedy the situation.

Exhibit 12-5 Telephone Interview Script

Script	Response
Hello, <u>patient's name</u>. My name is Henry Wodsworth and I am the administrator of the radiology department at General Hospital.	SMILE!
If it is convenient for you, and you feel well enough, I was wondering if you would be willing to spend 5 or so minutes with me on the telephone so that I might be able to learn of your impressions and opinion of the services we delivered to you on an outpatient basis on _day_?	Pause for response If not convenient, ask if you can call back. If not interested, thank the caller.
Thank you very much. Do I understand correctly: Dr. _____ is the physician who ordered your scan?	_____ Yes _____ No
M_____, did you personally make the appointment, or did Dr. _____'s receptionist make it for you?	_____ Patient _____ Doctor _____ Don't remember
Did the receptionist who scheduled the procedure explain where our department was located in the hospital? (and offer to give you directions to the hospital)?	_____ Yes _____ No _____ Don't remember
Did she verify our billing policy over the phone and request that you bring all of your insurance information?	_____ Yes _____ No _____ Don't remember
Did you encounter any problems finding our department once you were in the hospital?	_____ Yes _____ No
When you arrived, did our receptionist greet you in a warm and friendly manner?	_____ Yes _____ No _____ Don't remember
Did our receptionist introduce herself to you? Do you remember her name?	_____ Yes _____ No _____ Don't remember _____ Receptionist's name
Do you remember whether she called *you* by name?	_____ Yes _____ No _____ Don't remember
Did the receptionist explain that the radiologist would send a separate bill to you?	_____ Yes _____ No _____ Don't remember
Can you estimate how long you had to wait between the time you registered and the time one of our technicians came out and escorted you back into the dressing room where you changed your clothes?	_____ Less than 5 minutes _____ 5–10 minutes _____ 11–20 minutes _____ 21–30 minutes _____ Over 30 minutes _____ Don't remember

Exhibit 12-5 continued

Script	Response
Did you feel that amount of time was excessive?	_____ Yes _____ No _____ No opinion
I do know that on _____, about the time you were scheduled, we had several other unexpected procedures come up, which created delays. Did the receptionist alert you to the delay and estimate how long the wait might be?	_____ Yes _____ No _____ Don't remember
Did the technician introduce herself to you?	_____ Yes _____ No _____ Don't remember
Did she call you by name?	_____ Yes _____ No _____ Don't remember
Did she explain, to your satisfaction, the procedure before she began?	_____ Yes _____ No _____ Don't remember
Do you remember whether she asked you if you had any questions?	_____ Yes _____ No _____ Don't remember
If you had any questions, did you feel the technician did a good job of answering those questions?	_____ Yes _____ No _____ No opinion
Did you feel the technician was gentle in handling you during the procedure?	_____ Yes _____ No _____ No opinion
Once you were done, did the technician tell you what to anticipate as far as expelling the barium we injected?	_____ Yes _____ No _____ Don't remember
I have just two more questions, M_____. Overall, did you feel that the staff was responsive to your needs?	_____ Yes _____ No _____ No opinion
Is there anything we could have done to make the procedure easier for you?	
Thank you for your time, M_____. Do you have any other questions I can answer?	

Whenever a guest cites a problem on a questionnaire, a letter from Bill Marriott is sent to the guest if the guest's name and address is on the form. The problem is also sent to the attention of the general manager for follow-up. Follow-up letters are not sent to every guest who completes a positive evaluation, but many of the questionnaires are answered if the guest has cited an extremely positive experience or if an employee(s) has gone out of his or her way to assist the guest in unusual circumstances.

Such a response system is not inexpensive, but it is a measure of good will that Marriott officials believe pays excellent dividends.

Be certain that, if you receive complaints, you follow them up. Recognize also that when a guest reports a very positive experience that you have a potential supporter. You may want to keep a data base with the names and addresses of those who have completed positive evaluations for future fund-raising mailings.

SUMMARY

If used and managed appropriately, the feedback provided on a guest question-naire can be very helpful in identifying and recognizing excellent performance by a department, isolating service delivery and performance problems, and developing special services and service improvements. However, a questionnaire that merely serves as a ''public relations piece'' is a costly piece of paper for two reasons. It wastes printing and postage, and it also costs you valuable information that could help you in your service management efforts.

Appendix 12-A

Detailed Departmental Service Survey

	Strongly Disagree				Strongly Agree	

Laboratory

The laboratory personnel exhibited a caring attitude.	1	2	3	4	5	n/a
Their instructions and/or explanations were clear.	1	2	3	4	5	n/a
The lab technician warned me when a procedure would cause pain or discomfort.	1	2	3	4	5	n/a
The lab technician used terms that I understood.	1	2	3	4	5	n/a
The lab technician appeared to be proficient in drawing blood.	1	2	3	4	5	n/a
The procedures performed by the lab technician could have been less painful.	1	2	3	4	5	n/a
The lab technician(s) introduced himself/herself by name.	1	2	3	4	5	n/a
The lab technician(s) called me by name.	1	2	3	4	5	n/a

Comments:

Nursing

When I arrived in my room, a nurse oriented me to my room and procedures.	1	2	3	4	5	n/a
Shift changes were explained to me.	1	2	3	4	5	n/a
The nursing staff's explanations, instructions, and answers to my questions were helpful.	1	2	3	4	5	n/a
The nursing staff seemed to be genuinely interested in helping me.	1	2	3	4	5	n/a
The nursing staff treated my family and visitors courteously.	1	2	3	4	5	n/a
The nursing staff clearly explained to me what I should do after leaving the hospital to continue my recovery.	1	2	3	4	5	n/a
The nursing staff attempted to make me feel at ease before my surgery.	1	2	3	4	5	n/a
The nursing staff was prompt in responding to my calls.	1	2	3	4	5	n/a
There were an adequate number of nurses available to respond to my needs.	1	2	3	4	5	n/a

The nursing staff introduced
themselves by name.   1   2   3   4   5   n/a

Comments:

Patient Relations

When the patient representative visited
me, I clearly understood how he/she
could help me.   1   2   3   4   5   n/a

I called on the patient representative
for assistance with a problem.   1   2   3   4   5   n/a

The patient representative was prompt
in following up my problem.   1   2   3   4   5   n/a

The patient representative explained
what he/she would do to resolve my
problem.   1   2   3   4   5   n/a

The patient representative solved my
problem or adequately referred it to
someone who could.   1   2   3   4   5   n/a

I was satisfied with the manner in
which my problem was solved.   1   2   3   4   5   n/a

The patient representative was helpful. 1   2   3   4   5   n/a

The patient representative was
courteous.   1   2   3   4   5   n/a

Comments:

Chapter 13

Assessment: Six Basic Steps

In the early 1980s—during the period of guest relations' formative development—decisions about how to develop and implement a guest relations program were easily made. There were few options from which to choose because few approaches had been developed and even fewer had been attempted. Consultants did not know much, but they knew a bit more than their uninformed clients. Laying their expertise at the client's doorstep, consultants would lead hospitals into experimental plunges into the unpredictable and unknown and would emerge relatively unscathed. The end result had little to do with inspired ideas or brilliant methods. Implementing guest relations programs in the early years was made easy by the fact that the hospital's culture absorbed new ideas easily. Relationships were unstrained, organizations were unstructured, and hospital life was uncomplicated.

Today, there is more at stake, which deters risk taking. There are also more layers of authority that slow, if not stall, decision making. A greater timidity about making and implementing decisions exists. Few hospitals feel that they can make mistakes that will jeopardize their credibility, marketability, and viability.

So if you are contemplating a guest relations program you will want to leap out of the starting gate with the confidence that the course you have charted is one that will direct you to your desired outcomes. Analyzing different guest relations programs and evaluating them according to criteria that are important to your hospital will increase your chances for success. The plunge will be more predictable and the returns will be higher.

If you have never implemented a guest relations program, there are six basic first steps:

1. Gain knowledge, through research, of the various approaches that have been developed for guest relations and service management.

2. Evaluate available programs and methodologies against specific criteria, and identify possible approaches for in-house development.
3. Evaluate your hospital's internal state of readiness, and identify the potential sources of discontent within the organization that may undermine your program's effectiveness.
4. Collect and review feedback that will enable you early on to focus your attentions on specific needs and deficiencies.
5. Educate administration and board members about the levels of support and resources needed to implement an effective program, and solicit their involvement in drafting the foundational strategies.
6. Recommend for approval an approach that will most suitably meet your specific needs.

FORMING THE TASK FORCE

A task force can assist you in implementing these steps. The task force should be composed of at least 6 members and no more than 15 from the following departments: administration, nursing, human resources, marketing or public relations, patient relations, and training/education. In addition, four to nine managers, supervisors or employees from other front-line departments should serve on the task force. If you are an academic medical center and plan to include the university and research-affiliated personnel in your effort, it is important to have representatives from these divisions as well.

Although the number of task force participants will be influenced by the size and scope of your institution, the decision-making process invariably becomes more difficult with larger groups. If your task force is carefully selected to be truly representative of the various entities that comprise your institution, a small task force should suffice. Depending on the intensity of the search and the scope of its responsibilities, this task force will need to meet at regular intervals for 1–3 months.

CONDUCTING PRELIMINARY RESEARCH

The task force should initiate a focused investigation into the area of guest relations and service management. This research will yield a broader understanding of the subject and a greater awareness of what special needs should be considered when choosing a guest relations methodology and approach. Research resources include:

- *Articles:* A selective bibliography is included in the back of this book. There are several excellent guest relations newsletters, which are filled with good ideas. For an exploratory journey into the broader domain of service management, read several of the suggested articles and books on the subject. (See Appendix B.)

- *Professional societies and industry associations:* Sessions on guest relations and related topics are offered at the annual conventions of national and regional industry associations, such as the American Hospital Association, the Healthcare Forum (formerly the Association of Western Hospitals), the New England Healthcare Assembly, the American College of Healthcare Executives, and many others.

  If you are seeking an in-depth workshop, a local program may deliver what you need. Ask your department managers to be on the look out for sessions that may be sponsored by their professional societies. Although groups of human resource managers, patient representatives, or marketers may be the most obvious sponsors of these programs, do not be surprised if you find one offered by the local chapter of admitting or radiology administrators. Encourage task force members and management staff to attend these sessions when they participate in conventions and meetings.

  Many regional and state hospital associations sponsor expanded workshops that are conducted by consultants in the field. Check with the office of your state organization to see if such programs are offered.

- *Audiotapes:* An alternative to attending a conference or meeting is to contact the sponsoring organization to find out if, and when, audiocassette tapes of the sessions will be available for sale. Listening to these tapes, of course, eliminates the opportunity to ask questions and confer with speakers and fellow attendees, but it is more cost effective than attending.

- *Vendor-sponsored conferences and seminars:* Several worthwhile conferences and seminars are sponsored by independent consultants and companies. The length and format of most seminars allow sufficient time to explore various topics, to ask specific questions, and to receive advice. In addition, you have the opportunity to interact with other conference participants.

  When deciding whether to attend such a conference, try to determine in advance, from the brochure or a subsequent telephone call, if the conference will give you substantive information on a broad range of issues or if it is merely being conducted to showcase the consultant's programs and services.

- *Networking with colleagues:* Although some of your counterparts in competing hospitals may not want to disclose the approaches they used, many colleagues in other institutions will probably be happy to talk with you about what they learned during their experience of implementing a program. This is a very effective means of investigation and is generally more insightful than relying solely on the references that may be provided to you by vendors.

- *Brochures:* Simply reading brochures and other related materials provided by vendors can be very enlightening. Talk with these vendors as if you know nothing about the subject. Let them educate you about their suggested approach, and question them on why they feel their approach is better.

DEVELOPING CRITERIA

When developing the criteria by which you will evaluate the approach most suitable for you, it is important to consider the particular characteristics of your internal culture.

Such institutions as rehabilitation centers, psychiatric and chemical dependency clinics, and extended care facilities, for example, have specialized missions and unique concerns. Large, urban hospitals have different characteristics from small, rural ones; academic medical centers vary significantly from community hospitals. These differences, along with their social and political implications, should be evaluated in terms of the content and approach of proposed guest relations programs. Potential obstacles to success should be candidly addressed.

From your investigations, you should be able to identify a list of criteria that can be used to qualify and disqualify potential vendors. If you are planning to design the program in-house, the research will help you develop its objectives, content, and approach.

Do not make the criteria too specific. If you are going to rely on the expertise of outside consultants who have had extensive experience implementing guest relations programs, you should remain open to their suggested approaches. You should expect to receive explanations of why consultants recommend certain approaches. The logic revealed in their explanations, combined with your knowledge acquired from researching the subject, will often steer your program on a path different from the one initially expected.

At the outset of its investigation, Harper-Grace Hospitals in Detroit developed the instrument, shown in Exhibit 13-1, to help them evaluate guest relations programs according to the criteria it established. This type of an evaluation tool can be very helpful in making objective decisions when a variety of approaches are put forth for consideration.

USING OUTSIDE CONSULTANTS

With your investigation underway, you will need to discuss whether in-house personnel will develop and conduct the entire program or whether you will retain a

Exhibit 13-1 Evaluation Sheet

Harper Hospital "Guest" Relations Program

Name of Program: _____

Date Reviewed: _____

Reviewer: _____

Harper Hospital Guest Relations Program Selection Criteria	Score	Comments/Notes (number @ to selection criteria)
1. Strong focus on developing good teamwork and management skills. (*Goal:* Supervisors at all levels will have needed skills for modeling, coaching, and disciplining with dignity.)		
2. All aspects of program reflect respect for and value of employees. (*Goal:* Employees will be listened to and their concerns will be responded to and acted on when possible.)		
3. All employee groups are included, with program components addressing differing needs. Administration and department heads will be the first group approached. (*Goal:* Modeling and commitment).		
4. Includes workable strategy for good interdepartmental cooperation and communications.		
5. Introduced as a strategy to move the whole organization from good to excellent and to give employees a way to "make a difference" to the overall well-being of the hospital.		
6. Includes economic education for all employees. (*Goal:* "Guest" relations understood as a necessary economic/job security/competitive strategy.)		
7. Includes mechanism for long-term plan development and communication. (*Goal:* Individuals at all levels see program as a real change, backed by sincere administrative commitment).		

Exhibit 13-1 continued

Harper Hospital Guest Relations Program Selection Criteria	Score	Comments/Notes (number @ to selection criteria)
8. Standards for behavior clearly set and communicated, with consistent consequences and reward throughout organization.		
9. Positive feedback emphasized over negative.		
10. Approach combines "straight-talk" with humor.		
11. Immediate and visible actions are taken to solve real problems that become evident. (*Goal*: Communicating commitment and importance of first-line employees.)		
12. Includes physician group in some way.		
13. Programs reflects an urban hospital reality in setting, participants, and examples.		
14.		
15.		

SCORING: (Assign points for each criterion item)
10 points   Program definitely meets criterion.
 6 points   With minor adjustments, program will meet criterion.
 3 points   Consideration of the criterion given, but approach probably won't meet Harper Hospital's needs. Significant modifications needed.
 0 points   Does not meet criterion, not amendable. Completely unacceptable.

Source: Courtesy of Harper-Grace Hospitals, Detroit, Michigan.

consultant. Consultants are not absolutely essential, but the right consultant can bring you valuable experience and insights. Developing a program can be a time-consuming project. Even if you develop the program internally, you may want to retain an outside consultant to provide guidance and to deliver presentations to the administrative and management staff. It is difficult to be a prophet in your own land. The messages delivered by an external consultant are received with more credibility. Hiring Karl Albrecht or Tom Peters may be a little beyond your budget, but you should be able to find an effective, lower-priced consultant with knowledge of the subject.

Perhaps the one great danger of hiring even the finest consultant is the tendency of internal staff to think of themselves as adjuncts to the consultant. In reality, the reverse should occur. A qualified consultant can bring you valued insights and expertise, but only you can ensure the success of your hospital's program.

It is wise to investigate the use of consultants as part of your preliminary inquiry, even if, in the final analysis, you decide not to retain one. The following suggestions are offered to help you gather and evaluate program approaches offered by vendors and consultants.

Requesting Information from Vendors

Once you have a general idea of what type of guest relations program you are looking for, you can contact vendors and consultants. Unless you are required to call for competitive bids, a formal Request for Proposal (RFP) is not necessary. Frequently, RFP guidelines that prescribe the approach are so rigid that they leave little room for the consultants to make and justify alternative approaches that could be valuable.

If you are in the initial stages of investigation or if you intend to request a specific proposal once your preliminary screening is completed, a letter similar to the one shown in Exhibit 13-2 can be sent to vendors. Always request that a consultant telephone you with any questions. He or she should have questions. In addition, you will discover who takes the initiative to develop a relationship with you.

A sample letter shown in Exhibit 13-3 requests more specific information and is appropriate if you feel you have out-of-the ordinary needs. This letter will enable you to judge how well each vendor responds to your specific needs. If you do not receive a telephone call or if the response is "boilerplate" and does not address the requested concerns, you might question whether the consultant would be genuinely responsive to your special needs.

Questions To Ask Potential Vendors

As your inquiry into the different approaches proceeds, you will want to ask questions in a telephone interview or a sales presentation. The following questions should be considered.

What do you consider to be the most important factors or characteristics that contribute to a service program's success?

A consultant should be able to identify factors, such as the scope of program components (a shallow, unidimensional program versus a systems-oriented program that will support and sustain change), the strength of commitment from those at the top and those who serve as program leaders, the depth of an

Exhibit 13-2 Request for Information—Sample Letter

February 20, 1987

Dear Consultant:

St. Francis Hospital is a 236-bed acute care hospital owned by the Sisters of Providence of St. Mary. We are located in Anytown, Indiana approximately 35 miles from Indianapolis. As reinforcement of the mission and the philosophy of our hospital, we are interested in implementing a guest relations program.

St. Francis Hospital is soliciting proposals from a select group of consultants to develop/ provide guest relations programs. We would be interested in learning about your program and approach. Any information you can provide, such as sales literature, sample materials, and/or videotapes, would aid us in our selection.

If you have any questions, please contact me at (217) 378-4221 between 8:30 a.m. and 4:30 p.m.

Thank you for your prompt attention.

Sincerely,

Sister Mary Louis Loveland

infrastructure on which the program will be built, positioning, tone, timing, and the organization's climate/culture.

Tell us about one of your most successful clients. Why was this client successful?
Listen carefully to what the consultants say are the criteria for success. They should talk not only in terms of the instructional design or methodology, but should also be able to identify specifically what the hospital did to make the program succeed.

Have you ever introduced a program that failed? Why did it fail?
Beware of any consultant who does not admit to having introduced a program that was marginally successful or that failed. Listen to see if that consultant understands and can relate the reasons for failure.

Exhibit 13-3 Request for Proposal—Sample Letter

December 1, 1986

Dear Consultant:

General Hospital is a full-service, acute-care hospital with over 2,000 employees. We serve a multi-cultural, multi-racial, and multi-lingual clientele and our employees also reflect this diversity. General Hospital is interested in implementing a guest relations program to create skills and reinforce awareness that will enable our staff to be more responsive to the needs and expectations of our patients, physicians, visitors, and each other.

As chairman of a 12-member task force that has been selected to research and identify the approach that General Hospital will utilize, I would like to ask you to supply information about your firm and the services you provide.

We would like to request a proposal that will provide us with general information on your program(s) and approaches. In addition, we ask that your proposal specifically address the need for information on the following topics:

- What is your approach to implementing a guest relations program?
- What preliminary steps do you recommend that the hospital take prior to starting the program?
- What role do you play in this phase?
- What follow-up activities do you recommend and what is your role in assisting our hospital in implementing these?
- What kinds of audio-visual aids and materials do you utilize in the training phase?
- What specific programs do you offer for members from administration and management to support their skills in reinforcing guest relations?
- What specific programs do you offer for physicians? Their office staffs?
- If your program does not address multi-cultural differences, can special adaptations be made? Have you worked with other hospitals with similar diversity?
- What specific time-line(s) do you suggest for implementations?

Please provide several references of programs you have completed. We would also like to receive a general idea of costs and how you structure your fees.

We would like to receive replies no later than January 15, 1988. Selection of final candidates will take place in February.

If you have any questions, please call me at (412) 555-6708.

Sincerely,

Joanne Suderland
Director of Human Resources

We are also looking at _____ and _____ programs. How would you charac-terize the similarities and differences between your program and theirs?

You cannot expect the consultant to know specifics about every competitor, so the consultant's ability to address the similarities and differences will depend on what programs you are considering. However, if the other programs are well known, you should expect that the consultant will be aware of them. Most reputable consultants will not feel a need to denigrate the other programs. Ask the consultant whether he or she feels you are comparing "apples to apples" or whether you are comparing "apples to oranges" and to explain why.

What is the structure of the program? What systems will be offered that will enable us to coordinate program phases and ensure ongoing accountability for long-term results? What are the time lines? How much time will be involved on our part?

Can the consultant identify structures for ongoing implementation? Is he or she planning to provide the materials and deliver a few presentations, but leave it to you to figure out how to develop and implement ongoing strategies? Can the consultant outline a realistic plan of follow-up?

How soon can we begin the training program after we decide?

By the time you make your final decision, you will probably be eager to begin. Depending on the degree of planning that you undertake, the timespan may be as short as 4 weeks or as long as 12 weeks. Different consultants recommend different levels of planning. If you have not done any planning on your own, do not expect to be given a go-ahead to begin training your employees immediately. Planning is critical. A consultant who is eager to meet your time frame without pausing to identify some of the consequences of starting too soon is probably more interested in short-term rather than long-term satisfaction.

How large is your firm? How many consultants provide the services? Will we be working with one individual or with several? Who supports the consultants when they are out of town?

Do not be concerned if the consultant does not have a large firm or even if that consultant is a sole proprietor without other employees. As long as you can be certain that the consultant will be able to respond to your questions and needs and is good at scheduling his or her time to be responsive to you, you can expect to receive good service. If the consulting firm has other support staff, ask if other internal people will coordinate with you and respond to needs when the primary consultant is out of town.

It is important to have continuity. Some firms have different consultants deliver various segments of the program. Other firms have one consultant who will deliver all presentations and services to you. Which structure is provided?

If there will be several consultants, how do they coordinate their efforts so that there is continuity and you do not have to re-educate each consultant?

Do you work exclusively in health care or do you provide services to other industries as well?
A firm does not have to be exclusively involved in health care to be good; however, firm principals must have health care experience if they are to be valuable to you.

What are your future goals and objectives? Are you investing in the development of new products and services?
With the recent popularity and demand for guest relations programs, there are several vendors/consultants who are thinking only about the short term. They are not returning any of their profits to the development of new programs and services for the future. Will you be able to benefit from future innovations and a long-term relationship with this consultant, or are you about to tap a dry hole?

If you feel that the consultant has answered your questions appropriately and that there is a potential "fit," then check others' opinions about this consultant.

Checking References

The vendor should be able to supply you with the names of two or three clients to call as references. It is best to ask for clients who are similar in size or scope to you. When asking for referrals, think of special characteristics of your organization— something, for instance, that you foresee as a potential stumbling block. Ask to speak to another hospital served by that consultant that had to overcome a similar barrier.

Consultants, of course, will refer to you their "best" clients; indeed, some even provide incentives to client hospitals to act as references. Although they do this to compensate the client for the time spent in supporting their sales effort, the client may not provide an entirely objective reference. However, the solution is not to call others randomly. By doing so, you may unknowingly speak with someone who may harbor resentment for not being selected to participate on the guest relations committee or who otherwise does not have the knowledge to offer an objective assessment. The best approach is to contact the references offered by the consultant, but to ask probing questions that are designed to elicit the information you need.

To identify the strengths of program approaches and the qualifications of specific vendors, ask the references such questions as the following:

- Did the consultant take time to understand your specific needs?
- Did the consultant discuss the pros and cons of alternative approaches and demonstrate flexibility in handling specialized needs?
- Is the consultant a role model? Are the consultant's own employees courteous? Do they return calls promptly and send materials when requested?
- Did the reference hospital encounter any unanticipated problems that the consultant could not handle?
- How many different programs did the reference hospital consider, and why did they choose the one they did?
- How was the program initially received? How is it working today?
- If the hospital could change anything about its program, what would it be?
- Generally, how satisfied was the reference hospital with the overall performance? Was it outstanding? What was less than satisfactory?
- How has the hospital measured the program's success? Can it be quantified?

Evaluating Costs

Cost will naturally be an important factor. It is important to be aware fully of the total expenses associated with the program. What is the cost of all proposed materials and services? What will be the ongoing costs associated with the maintenance of this guest relations program?

Programs currently in the marketplace range in cost from $600 for the do-it-yourself manual to $100,000 for the most elaborate consulting services.

The consultant may offer you a price range, rather than a fixed price. If maintenance costs are not included in the proposal, ask the consultant to identify what specific services, in addition to those provided in the proposal, are frequently requested by other clients. Doing so will help you identify whether or not the package is comprehensive enough. If the consultant suggests that he or she is not frequently called back, you can infer one of three things: either the consultant provides an adequate level of instruction and support; few of the client hospitals extend a long-term commitment to the process; or the consultant's performance is so poor that hospitals do not want to see him or her again.

Be alert to hidden costs. Although the majority of programs offered today have a fixed price for consulting that includes all telephone assistance and on-site participation, be sure to identify any and all additional costs. Is this a closed-end or open-ended agreement? To what degree will the consultant use a low price to obtain the contract and then dangle the next piece of the program in front of you for an additional cost?

When you ask the consultant to identify standard charges for additional days of consulting or for additional services requested while the consultant is on-site, as with all costs, the fees quoted should always be confirmed in writing.

If the proposed agreement states that you will be responsible for expenses, do not be afraid to ask that these be clearly defined. Some people could live for a month on what some consultants submit as a week's expenses. Clarify the expense policy in advance so that you will not encounter any surprises. Typically, a consultant should charge for round-trip coach plane fare or actual plane fare, whichever is less, lodging, and meals. Ask for a per diem or a "not to exceed" amount for meals and incidental costs. And if the consultant grabs for the dinner check in a gesture of graciousness, do not be afraid to ask if it will be charged back on the expense report.

It is natural for consultants to hope that you will be so pleased with their performance that you will invite them to make additional proposals in the future. That is to your benefit because a consultant hoping for a long-term relationship is more interested in performing to meet your full expectations. At the same time, you should be cautious of consultants who will try to create dependence so that they can build in an unjustifiable number of future visits.

DETERMINING HOW TO PROCEED

Once you have investigated the various approaches, you should determine whether you will rely on outside help or develop your program internally.

Developing your own program will save on initial costs, even though your staff will invest a significant amount of time in its planning, development, and execution. Try to estimate the amount of time that you and others will spend on program development. Place calls to other hospitals that have developed their own programs, and try to get an estimate of how long it took them. Communicate this estimate to the administration of your hospital. They should be fully aware of what costs are involved.

If you are going to recommend purchasing a program, evaluate the options before you. A standard proposal evaluation form, such as the one developed by Harper-Grace Hospitals (see Exhibit 13-4,) can be readily devised and is a good tool to help you make a comparison of the consultants' program components, features of their services, and fees.

Remember that a good program should include a well-developed training program and the tools and methodologies for implementing the systems needed to support the service philosophy long after the training has been implemented.

ASSESSING THE READINESS OF THE ORGANIZATION

While your task force members are gathering and evaluating information, they should also make a preliminary assessment of the readiness of the hospital to carry

Exhibit 13-4 Guest Relations Program

Harper-Grace Hospitals' Guest Relations Program
Consultant Group/Program Comparison Chart
(September 1986)

This chart provides a summary of two (2) Guest Relations Consultant Groups/Programs that HGH are considering.

Its purpose is to help the Harper Division Guest Relations Steering Committee and the Grace Division Guest Relations Task Force decide which consultant to use as a primary guest relations consultant and what type of guest relations program they prefer.

Comparison Factors	Comments Per Consultant Group	
	Consultant Group A	Consultant Group B
I. *Program Elements* Type Summary	Basically, a pre-packaged video program; instructs and informs. Does include six phases which gives it a system approach	Slide program with employee involvement (input). Broad awareness
Materials	Standard workbook—easy to use. Program Facilitator's Guide and Meeting Leader Guide	Not much; maybe few handouts; highly determined by organization. Facilitator's Guide
Type and length of initial all-employee meetings	Mixed employee group—four hours; video lecture and participation exercises	Three hours/overview/rationale Outlines required behaviors
Introduction management component	Four hours—same as employee sessions with some content regarding management employee role	Usually one-hour overview
Follow-up components	Has several packaged. Followup (TOPS). Brings ideas from other organizations	An a la carte assortment
Initial publicity component	Suggestions/ideas provided–organization decides specifics	Same as consultant group A
On-going communication vehicle	Provides ideas and samples	Same as consultant group A
On-going problem solving system	Provides ideas—no perfect systems	Same as consultant group A

Exhibit 13-4 continued

Comparison Factors	Comments Per Consultant Group	
	Consultant Group A	Consultant Group B
Emphasis	Philosophy of good communications and services with some examples and practice	Series of system components combine to improve the environment
***		
II. *Consultant Characteristics:* Knowledge and credibility	Very—this is their only business. Extensive experience	Yes—added plus of being Hospital; negative = own workload / 75 past clients Small to large clients
General responsiveness (HGH experience)	Excellent!!! At least weekly	Very questionable; much better since site visit
Reference check (comments)	Very well; liked but not a panacea	Excellent—poor experience
Consultant office staff support	Excellent (competent and friendly) "A model"	Questionable; seems disorganized and untrained "learning how to transfer"
Image	Very good	Okay
Working consultants	Total of 3	Total of 3–4 with overall project manager
***		
III. *Costs* Initial materials	$25,000 (Harper and Grace)	$30,000
Initial segments	$5,000	Development costs?
Initial consultant fees	$10,000	$10,000 Planning, focus group and management presentation
Follow-up segments	Packaged segments are individually priced	$20,000
Total 12 month estimate	$40,000	$50,000–$60,000
***		
IV. *HGH Objectives* Approach—straight talk with humor	Some humor in videotape scripting	Slide pictures provide some humor
Includes economic education segment	Not really	Yes definitely

Exhibit 13–4 continued

Comparison Factors	Comments Per Consultant Group	
	Consultant Group A	Consultant Group B
Standards of behavior clearly set and publicized	Advocates statements and presentation by CEO	Required behaviors outlined
All employees included with program components addressing different needs	May be components achieved through participant exercises	Only through follow-up components
Program reflects respect for and value of employees	Professional employees may be insulted by instructions regarding topics such as Maslow's Hierarchy	Believe yes due to initial rationale provided
Focus on developing teamwork	Through video instruction segments and participant exercises	One of required behaviors and through overall program effect and some of the follow-up segments
Focus on management skills	Through follow-up program	Same as consultant group A
Reflects urban hospital reality	?? Probably not	Very much
Includes visible actions taken on problems	Provides suggestions	Provides suggestions
Includes physicians	One of their packaged follow-up programs and provides other suggestions	Same as consultant group A

Source: Courtesy of Harper-Grace Hospitals, Detroit, Michigan.

out the future program. They will probably already have a "seat of the pants" feeling about this readiness, but it is important to solicit comments in a formalized manner and to group together the ideas expressed.

Four factors will help you foresee how various groups within the hospital might react to a guest relations program and to what degree this might affect the timing of the program. These four factors are described below:

1. *Administration:* Is there turbulence in the administrative ranks? Is the administration characterized by turnover or polarized support? A change in leadership invariably alters the delicate balance of the internal culture. A

new administrator needs time to become established. A new administrator may be fully committed to guest relations, but if the program is used as an early pronouncement of new values, it can backfire. The troops generally distrust the intentions of new generals who sound bugles. Actions speak louder than words. It might be better to postpone the launching of the program until after the new administrator has settled in.

2. *Reductions in hours, wages or benefits:* Layoffs, forced reduction in hours, and reduced wages or benefits are always unsettling events. A grieving period invariably follows. It is best to wait until sufficient time has passed before you announce an ambitious program to improve service. Be sensitive to the predictable low ebb of morale at the time. Waiting for a period of time may be the best strategy. Do not wait too long, however. Employees have been known to grieve far longer than is healthy or necessary.

3. *Union organizing or union negotiations*: If you are aware of any serious attempts at union organization, you should be careful about proceeding with guest relations training. If union negotiations are in an active phase, planning can proceed but you should postpone formalized training until issues are resolved or at least, the activity settles down. Attempts by employees to organize typically signal discord within the ranks. Employees involved in active organizing have lost at least some degree of faith in the management practices of the organization. It is better to restore their faith by facilitating formal and informal discussions between management and employees. Otherwise, training sessions may become the forum for the expression of volatile and emotional issues.

4. *Lukewarm Support:* The paradox here may be that the administration is responsible for your task force's existence, but it may not be prepared to adequately support the effort. You can attempt to educate administrators about what the program will involve and what it will take to do it right. Be prepared, however, to change your approach. Do not launch a full-scale effort if you do not have high-level support. An aborted attempt, or one that is being undercut, does no good. If the top administration cannot be convinced of the value of the comprehensive program, some facets of the program can be implemented independently.

You cannot expect all conditions to be favorable. It is sometimes best to forge ahead if you are confident that the commitment to the program is sincere and long lasting.

TARGETING INITIAL NEEDS

Concurrent with your activities to ascertain the organization's readiness should be a parallel thrust of determining where to focus your initial attentions. Research, especially consumer preference research, can help you identify positive and negative perceptions about your hospital and its service mentality. You can more adequately direct your efforts to overcome deficiencies when you know what they are.

The general attitude and morale of the organization may provide compelling reasons to alter your strategy of implementation as well. You can survey employees' perceptions and opinions with the questionnaire that is included in the following chapter. Focus groups can be conducted to determine the employees' mindset and to identify potential sources of resistance. Members of the task force can also mingle informally with employees to gather information about their receptivity and attitudes.

Of course, these methods are highly subjective and may not provide conclusive information about when and how to proceed. If however, morale seems to be overwhelmingly negative, it is best to identify what issues are festering within the organization and what can be done to resolve them.

Another approach to gathering information is to assemble groups of managers and ask them open-ended questions that will encourage discussion about service management. The feedback can direct you in designing a program or strategy. Questions that can be asked of department managers are listed in Exhibit 13-5.

Exhibit 13-5 Sample Open-Ended Questionnaire

---

1. In your opinion is there a need to improve patient satisfaction in your department?
2. Is there a need to improve *staff* satisfaction?
3. Compared to other needs that you can identify, is the need to improve patient satisfaction more or less important?
4. Where would a patient relations program realistically fit into your list of departmental needs priorities?
5. What about a staff satisfaction program?
6. What types of activities would you recommend be included in a patient relations program?
7. What resources would you need to implement these recommendations in your department?
8. What impediments might make it difficult to implement these recommendations?
9. What incentives would make your staff more interested in implementing and continuing a program of patient relations?
10. In your opinion, what activities or actions by other departments could significantly affect your department's ability to satisfy its patients?
11. How could the administration help ensure the success of a patient relations program?
12. What could the administration be doing to improve *staff* satisfaction?

Source: Reprinted with permission of Irwin Press, Ph.D., Press, Ganey Associates, Notre Dame, Indiana.

RECOMMENDING THE PROGRAM TO ADMINISTRATION

Once you have completed your assessment of programs and of your organizational readiness, you should plan to make a presentation to your administrative staff. This presentation should be for the purpose of recommending the service program that, in the opinion of the task force, will meet the hospital's needs. Any pertinent articles written about the subject should be shared. General comments, solicited through the assessment research, can also be presented at this time.

At this meeting, alert administration not only to the benefits of instituting a service program but also to the potential problems that may occur. This meeting is also a time to educate the administration about the level of support that should be extended to make the program successful. The following process can be used in preparing the presentation:

- *Research:* Identify your process of researching the topic of guest relations and service management—what resources were used and what methods were employed. If you conducted consumer preference research or other methods of market research, share those findings.
- *Evaluation:* Identify the basis by which you evaluated available programs and what you learned in the process of conferring with consultants, checking references, and talking with staff of hospitals that had implemented service programs. Share the criteria used to evaluate the programs, and identify clearly the approach that you feel is best suited to your needs.
- *Assessment:* Identify what you learned from your organizational assessment. What conditions are favorable and what obstacles might you confront? Educate administrative staff members about the critical factors that will contribute to the success of your program. Identify what remedies the task force suggests to address each potential problem.
- *Recommendation:* Share with the administrative staff your recommendations. Identify the program that the task force recommends for implementation. Describe its approach and project costs. Separate the costs associated with the amount of time that employees will spend in the planning of the program and those for the actual execution of the plan. Many institutions neglect to compute the actual costs of a program, which far exceed the amount of money spent purchasing a program.

Persuade administration members that they must play visible and active roles in implementation of the service program. They should be clear about their roles and understand that their support is critical.

One way to generate this commitment is to involve executives and key board members in a service strategy planning retreat. The focus of the retreat should be to identify strengths, weaknesses, opportunities, and threats (SWOT) as they relate to service. From that, a service mission, service strategies, and action steps can be derived. Values can also be reviewed and measured against market research that may show that the hospital is perceived to operate by different values than what they (executives) perceive.

The strength of the organization's culture is determined by the extent to which organizational values are perceived to be well-defined and effectively communicated to the employees. When the culture is strong, employees view the organization as having a clear set of norms, values, and sense of direction. When the culture is weak, employees do not believe that the hospital has very well-defined sets of norms, values, or sense of direction. When a hospital image is not well-defined, there tends to be substantial variation in the way employees behave. It is for this reason that you will never be able to lead your employees and the organization itself to be more service-driven if strategic service planning is not done at the outset.

SUMMARY

Conducting an evaluation of the approaches, methodologies, and the readiness of the internal culture to assimilate a service or guest relations program is a valuable initial effort that will reap future benefits and prevent failure. Likewise, educating your administration and gaining strong support are necessary initial efforts to ensure the success of your program. Once you have followed these steps, you are ready to turn responsibility for the program over to a steering committee.

Chapter 14

Planning: Drafting a Blueprint

Careful planning is necessary if you are to implement a successful service program. By clearly defining your goals and objectives at the outset, you will be able to chart a course of action that will enable you to achieve them. These objectives need to be translated into specific strategies and tactics. It is during this planning phase that you can also begin gathering baseline data that will enable you to measure the success of your efforts.

GETTING STARTED

A steering committee should be formed to assume responsibility for planning the program. The composition of this steering committee should be similar to that of the task force (as described in Chapter 13), although you may want to enlarge the committee to include more employees from the rank and file. The results of the task force's investigation should be clearly understood by all members of the steering committee. Identify to the members the criteria that were used to select the service approach. If you selected an outside consultant, review the proposal and the firm's qualifications when you first meet. If you purchased a prepackaged program, review the various components. If you are planning to develop your program in-house, review its basic objectives. Regardless of which option you selected, you will need to develop strategies and programs further.

GATHERING INSIGHT AND IDEAS

If your efforts are to be directed at improving customer/guest satisfaction, you should be able to identify the primary expectations of your customers and their perceptions of how well you are doing in meeting them. Research should be undertaken to uncover areas in which you could do better. The task force that was initially formed may have initiated such research. If it did not and you have no outside sources of valid information, it is wise to initiate this research during the planning phase.

As has been identified in preceding chapters, the value of research cannot be overstated. You may decide to conduct patient, physician, and/or employee focus groups to gain insight into their perceptions of service. Interviews or surveys can also be employed to gather information on what strengths and weaknesses exist and where you should focus your attentions. The feedback you solicit can help you define the primary objectives of your program.

For example, one group from which you can gain significant insight and direction is physicians and their office staffs. By asking questions that will enable you to focus more adequately on their needs, expectations, and perceptions, you will demonstrate a sincere interest and commitment to creating satisfaction.

Begin by making an appointment to meet with a physician at his or her office. When you meet, briefly describe the general goals and objectives of your program. Allow time for the physician to ask questions, and then ask the following four questions:

1. What do your patients tell you they like about their hospital experience and the ways in which they are treated at General Hospital?
2. What do your patients tell you they do not like about their hospital experience and the ways in which they are treated?
3. As a physician, you are one of our customers (guests). What do you like about the ways in which we provide services and support to you in your practice of medicine?
4. What could we do to improve service and support to you?

This interview should be kept short, but if you have a willing and interested participant, you can use the time to obtain reactions and support for proposed ideas. Other questions include:

- If we were to develop a special program, similar to the program we are sponsoring at the hospital, would you be interested in sending your employees?
- Our committee is evaluating several nationally recognized practice management consultants because of the interest that has been expressed by physicians in a variety of different topics. Some of the topics that have been suggested to use include _____. What is your level of interest in each of these topics?
- We are thinking about subscribing to this practice management newsletter on behalf of the physicians on our staff. (Share a sample copy with the physi-

cian.) This would be delivered directly to your office. Does it look like something you would be interested in?

- Would you mind if I spent a few minutes with your office manager (or receptionist)? I am interested in asking her a few questions about how she feels General Hospital can support your practice and the patients.

Physicians' employees are excellent sources of information! If the physician approves, spend some time with key employees. Questions that can be asked of the person who works most closely with the patients to schedule surgeries and admissions are presented in Chapter 17.

Physicians are not the only group from which to solicit information and ideas. Patients, volunteers, and employees can be requested to provide feedback as well. Some of the specific methods for collecting this feedback were discussed in Chapter 9.

DRAFTING AN ACTION PLAN

The basic objectives and outcomes of your program implementation should be defined early on. From those objectives, specific programs, activities, and initiatives can be produced to make up an action plan. This action plan will identify what needs to be done and by whom. It will influence, to some degree, what subcommittees and task forces are formed, what responsibilities are assigned to various individuals, and when those are to be completed. The action plan will become the blueprint for implementing your program.

The following objectives are offered as examples that may be used in drafting the initial strategy and action plan:

- To adopt service as a strategy for achieving the hospital's goals and to integrate guest/provider satisfaction into its mission and values.
- To create awareness of, and commitment to, guest/provider satisfaction from every "audience," including administration, management, employees, trustees, physicians, and volunteers.
- To enhance the effectiveness by which the hospital communicates its mission and values to patients, employees, physicians, and the community it serves.
- To ensure that internal and external communications reflect the values and service orientation of the hospital.
- To improve the flow and clarity of communications among administration and managers and employees.
- To provide measures by which the administration can evaluate service delivery and performance improvements by departments.

- To analyze the systems for delivering service within the hospital and to modify those systems that are inefficient or ineffective in meeting guests' or employees' needs.
- To encourage the communication of problems and complaints experienced by guests to individuals who can assist them and to overcome the root causes of recurring complaints.
- To emphasize the need for a service orientation and interpersonal skills during the screening and hiring process of new employees.
- To emphasize service and organizational values during the initial orientation of new employees.
- To develop the awareness and skills that will enable employees to meet the needs and exceed the expectations of guests.
- To provide ongoing training that emphasizes contact skills and enhances the personal and professional development of managers and employees.
- To expand employees' knowledge of the functions of other departments within the hospital in an effort to facilitate better internal service delivery.
- To communicate pride through the appearance of the facility, the appearance of employees, and their professional conduct.
- To provide incentives/rewards for service performance to both managers and employees.
- To develop special guest services that will distinguish the hospital from competing hospitals.

These aforementioned objectives, and others of your own design, are used to develop the action plan. To translate objectives into actions, review each objective against the following checklist:

- Identify what, if anything, is being done presently.
- Generate ideas for improving present practices or services.
- If the need is not presently addressed, identify general guidelines for what can be done.
- Assign the responsibility for implementing a change or idea to a task force, subcommittee, or individual.
- Identify when, if appropriate, the assignment should be completed.
- If there is a need to investigate further, identify a date by which person(s) should respond with review and recommendations.

From every objective identified, an action should result. Consider the following examples.

To expand all employees' knowledge of the functions of other departments in the organization.

What is being done now? What could be done to improve employees' awareness of the functions of other departments? The committee members may suggest periodic open houses in each department, feature articles in the in-house newsletter or magazine, displays in the lobby, an exercise during the training program that encourages employees to identify which department(s) they internally serve and how, and so on.

To ensure that internal and external communications reflect the values and service orientation of the hospital.

When was the last time that patient brochures, newsletters, questionnaires, employee handbooks, signage, and other communication formats were reviewed with a critical eye for the service message? Do these internal and external communications reflect the values of the organization? Are the messages warm and inviting, or cold and uncaring? Who should review these? How should proposed changes be reviewed and implemented?

By analyzing each objective, specific action(s) will result. An idea brought forth by the committee may inspire another objective. Although there is a limit to brainstorming, the strength of your program will be built on creativity and innovation. Promote creative thinking to its fullest.

Some of the objectives are easy to address, whereas others will take a significant amount of investigation, planning, and time in execution. For example, *To analyze the systems for delivering service within the hospital and to modify those systems that are inefficient or ineffective in meeting guests' or employees' needs* is not a simple process. You must first develop a reliable method for isolating the structures or systems that are deficient or inefficient. You must then establish what can be realistically done to overcome them. The proposed solutions must be analyzed for their feasibility, consequences, and benefits. Then, their implementation must be approved if they require an expenditure of time or money.

It is important to analyze every objective before assigning the dates for project completion. So many ideas will be generated that it will be easier to prioritize those once all have been reviewed. A schedule, detailing what planning activities need to be initiated, by whom, and by what date they need to be completed, should be drafted. This schedule will probably be revised several times during the planning process. To avoid delays that will hold up other activities, be realistic. You may want to get the program started right away, but careful planning is essential.

For several years, the steering committee at Jewish Hospital in Louisville, Kentucky, has developed annual plans that have guided its guest relations program direction. Committee members develop an action plan and meet regularly to review the progress that has been made in implementing the plan. Goals are defined, and specific actions to accomplish the goals are delegated to appropriate persons on the committee. Jewish Hospital's 1988 plan is shown in Exhibit 14-1.

DEVELOPING A POLICY STATEMENT

A written policy or statement of purpose that clarifies the structure, scope, and standards of your service or guest relations program is important in enabling employees to understand its purpose and to be committed to the program. The policy statement should describe:

- the purpose of the program
- the structure of committees
- the identities of steering committee members
- the identity of the coordinator
- the general responsibilities of the coordinator
- the program components/requirements
- the standards of expectation
- the outcomes expected

Mesquite Community Hospital in Mesquite, Texas, drafted a two-page administrative policy statement (shown in Exhibit 14-2) for its guest relations program. This policy is included in departmental policy manuals.

GATHERING BASELINE DATA

Obviously, if the goals of your program are to improve service delivery and satisfy the expectations of the guests, you must develop ways to measure if you have been successful. The first step is to identify baseline information that will enable you to monitor the improvements.

Measuring patient satisfaction will give you feedback as to whether the program has resulted in greater patient satisfaction. Because physician satisfaction and employee satisfaction can also be affected by a service program, their feedback should be solicited as well. Departmental satisfaction with those services delivered by other departments should also be assessed.

For the purpose of measuring the success of a service program, quantitative measures are sufficient. Levels of satisfaction and dissatisfaction on several dimensions can be monitored on a regular basis. It is relatively easy to solicit and receive this feedback from your patients on a monthly basis through the distribu-

Exhibit 14-1 Statement of Intent

Jewish Hospital
Statement of Intent
1988

DEPARTMENT Guest Relations Committee

Key Result Areas	Objectives	Activity	Measurable Results	Responsibility	Completion Dates	
					Planned	Actual
Organizational Effectiveness	1. Continue to increase management accountabilities for guest relations	1. Continue the use of focus groups by product line	1. Focus groups held four times per year	Patient Relations	Ongoing	
		2. Develop a Close to the Customer program involving the management staff	2. Close to the Customer program implemented	Education/ Employee Committee	Second Quarter	
		3. Implement Mystery Guest program	3. Mystery Guest program implemented twice per year	R.I. Shircliff/ D.K. Molnar	Second Quarter	
		4. Develop Guest Relations Departmental Audit Program	4. Department audit program developed and implemented	Facilities Committee/Service Committee	First Quarter	
		5. Continue to monitor Patient Survey Data	5. Corrective action on file for depts. as required by standards.	Service Committee/Guest Relations Committee	Ongoing	

Exhibit 14-1 continued

DEPARTMENT Guest Relations Committee

Key Result Areas	Objectives	Activity	Measurable Results	Responsibility	Completion Dates Planned	Completion Dates Actual
Market Share	2. Position JH Systems as being leaders in guest relations	1. Submit for publication two articles that publicize key efforts	1. Articles submitted for publication	R.L. Shircliff/ D.K. Molnar	Third Quarter	
		2. Conduct a regional guest relations conference as a joint venture with a guest relations consulting firm	2. Seminar held	R.L. Shircliff/ D.K. Molnar	Fourth Quarter	
		3. Develop and market consulting capabilities	3. Selling guest relation consulting services	R.L. Shircliff/ D.K. Molnar	Fourth Quarter	
		4. Continue to maintain relationship with K.E. Peterson and Associates	4. Consulting contract reviewed	R.L. Shircliff/ D.K. Molnar	Ongoing	
		5. Develop guest relations/community relations tour program	5. Tour program activated	Cindy Stewart/ Alice Bridges	Ongoing	

	6. Implement Phase III of Image Consultant program	6. Departments involved in Phase III Image Consultant develop and implement appearance standards	R.L. Shircliff/ D.K. Molnar	Ongoing
	7. Develop a guest relations program for physicians offices	7. Program offered twice per year	Carol Reis/Patient Relations	Second Quarter
Market Share	1. Conduct a guest relations facility audit to serve as a basis for 1989 improvements	1. Facility audit completed	Facilities Committee	Second Quarter
3. Continue to implement facilities modifications that enhance our capability to serve patients and guests	2. Plan and implement key projects for 1988	2. The following projects are implemented A. Renovation of radiology holding/registration areas B. Full revision of major signage (interior/exterior) C. Provide one telephone per bed D. Refurbish ER waiting area	Facilities Committee	

Exhibit 14-1 continued

DEPARTMENT Guest Relations Committee

Key Result Areas	Objectives	Activity	Measurable Results	Responsibility	Completion Dates Planned	Actual
			E. Install electronic directory			
			F. Continue annual patient room upkeep program			
			G. Continue to implement master plan for replacement of patient furniture			
Market Share	4. Continue to develop improved and unique services for patients and guests	1. Improve the security of patient valuables	1. Decrease in loss of patient valuables	Services Committee	First Quarter	
		2. Provide access to audio/video equipment	2. Equipment available upon patient request	Services Committee	Second Quarter	
		3. Implement postdischarge telephone calls to all inpatients and outpatients	3. Postdischarge telephone calls made to all patients	Community Relations	Third Quarter	

Goal	Objective		Measure	Responsible	Timeline
		4. Improve visibility and use of valet parking	4. Valet parking utilization increased	William Reichart	First Quarter
Organizational Effectiveness	5. Continue to develop and implement communication strategies to emphasize guest relations	1. Develop a monthly guest relations theme communicated through impressions, bulletin boards, etc.	1. Monthly theme developed and implemented	Education/Employee Committee	First Quarter
		2. Develop an incentive-based employee suggestion system	2. System implemented		Third Quarter
		3. Develop an action plan from the results of the 1987 Employee Attitude Survey to reduce/eliminate barriers to positive guest relations	3. Action plan developed and implemented		First Quarter
		4. Implement the Departmental Recognition Program	4. Evaluation of effectiveness of Departmental Recognition Program		Second Quarter
		5. Pilot and evaluate the use of quality circles in four departments	5. Evaluation on quality circles completed		Fourth Quarter

Exhibit 14-1 continued

DEPARTMENT Guest Relations Committee

Key Result Areas	Objectives	Activity	Measurable Results	Responsibility	Completion Dates	
					Planned	Actual
		6. Develop patient printed materials that are user-friendly and max-imize effectiveness	6. Evaluation annually of all patient printed materials (as updates are sched-uled)		Ongoing	

Source: Courtesy of Jewish Hospital Systems, Inc., Louisville, Kentucky.

Exhibit 14-2 Administrative Policy

Policy Number:
Policy Date:
Review/Revised:

Subject: Guest Relations, ''My Caring Hospital''
Department: Marketing/Community Relations
Purpose: To set standards for the operation of Mesquite Community Hospital's Guest
              Relations Program, ''My Caring Hospital.''

Mesquite Community Hospital is a community of individuals where relationships between a
variety of people within individual departments play an important part in the successful delivery
of healthcare services to our patients and other customers. This hospital is committed to
providing an environment where each employee shall display a caring attitude, and demonstrate
responsiveness to meet the needs and exceed the expectations of our customers. Guests or
customers include, but are not limited to, patients, visitors, physicians, fellow employees, and
volunteers. Therefore, Mesquite Community Hospital has established ''My Caring Hospital,''
a formalized guest relations program to ensure all employees are introduced to and recognized
for the value of their personal interaction skills.

1. The responsibility for overseeing the guest relations program rests with the Guest
   Relations Steering Committee. This committee consists of 12 members who serve a
   minimum of 1 year. Permanent members of the committee include: The Director of
   Marketing/Community Relations, The Assistant Director of Marketing/Community
   Relations, the Assistant Administrator of Patient Care, and the Assistant Administrator
   for Financial Services or the Associate Administrator. Other members of the committee
   shall be determined with a goal of including representatives from a variety of different
   departments within the hospital.
2. The Guest Relations Steering Committee will meet monthly, with provisions for special
   meetings more frequently on an as-needed basis.
3. The chairperson of the Guest Relations Steering Committee will be the Director of
   Marketing/Community Relations. This person is responsible for scheduling meetings
   and guest relations training sessions and providing overall direction to the committee.
4. The Guest Relations Steering Committee will have four standing subcommittees to
   include: Promotion, Recognition, Accountability, and Audit. These subcommittees will
   meet on an as-needed basis.
5. All employees will be briefed in new employee orientation on the hospital's commitment
   to guest relations and required to attend a formal 4-hour guest relations orientation
   program. New employees will be scheduled for the guest relations orientation program
   after they complete their initial 90-day employment period. All employees should attend
   the guest relations orientation program within 6 months of their employment date. Each
   class session will be conducted by two facilitators selected on a voluntary basis from
   employees on staff at the hospital.
6. Individual employees who demonstrate their positive commitment to customer/guest
   relations shall be recognized for their contribution.
7. All employees will be evaluated on their guest relations skills in conjunction with their
   annual performance ratings. Expected customer/guest relations performance standards
   will be included in the employee handbook and on all job descriptions by June 1, 1987.

Exhibit 14-2 continued

> Employees who fail to meet the established customer/guest relations standards will be counseled by their supervisor with an emphasis on identifying the unacceptable behavior and setting agreed upon methods of improvement. Employees who fail to improve in previously identified deficiencies shall be subject to the progressive disciplinary process as outlined in the employee handbook.
>
> Date: _____   Reviewed/Revised: _____
> Approved by: Administration   Date: _____
>
> _____
>
> Raymond P. DeBlasi,
> Administrator
>
> _____
>
> Katie Pirtle, Director
> Marketing/Community Relations
>
> *Source:* Courtesy of Mesquite Community Hospital, Mesquite, Texas.

tion and collection of patient questionnaires. Departmental satisfaction with internal service delivery is also easy to collect. Employee satisfaction is not as easy to track because opinion surveys are not routinely administered. However, employee satisfaction can be monitored on an ongoing basis through simplified survey techniques, as discussed later in this chapter. Physician satisfaction is the most difficult to monitor quantitatively.

Review or design carefully your measurement instrument(s) from the outset. If you alter the measurement instrument in several months, keep in mind that doing so will skew the data. To monitor improvement, you should be consistent throughout the monitoring period. However, do not let this requirement of consistency keep you from improving your instruments or methodologies later on if such a change will significantly improve the quality of your feedback.

Patient Satisfaction Feedback

If you feel that your present questionnaire sufficiently reflects dimensions of service delivery, you can use the data that have been collected over the past 3-6 months as a benchmark. Keep in mind that there are three primary measures that are easy for patients to evaluate, which correlate directly to their perceptions of service delivery. These identify whether employees of various departments (1) responded to the patients' needs promptly, (2) exhibited courtesy and respect, and (3) offered explanations and information.

Physician Satisfaction Feedback

Physicians have a variety of needs and expectations to which you can and should respond. When you provide quality care and good service to patients and when employees exhibit cooperation, respect, and courtesy to them, two of their primary expectations are satisfied. How will you know if you are successful in meeting those expectations? An example of a survey instrument that monitors physician satisfaction with hospital services can be found in Chapter 9.

Departmental Satisfaction Feedback

Survey instruments that provide a benchmark on the effectiveness of internal service delivery can be developed and administered. See Chapter 9 for more details.

Employee Satisfaction Feedback

Measuring employee satisfaction can be done in a number of ways. For the purpose of establishing a baseline from which to monitor employees' perceptions, attitudes, and satisfaction, a survey as is shown in Exhibit 14-3 can be used.

This survey is not a substitute for the major employee opinion survey that you may conduct periodically. Rather, it is designed to measure employee satisfaction in those areas that will frequently influence the employee's attitude about working for the hospital. From these findings, you can infer the degree to which the hospital is responsive to the needs and expectations of employees.

The survey can be administered every 6 months. By distributing the survey to a random sample of employees before the service program is implemented, you can later see if the changes that are taking place as a result of the program are positively influencing the attitudes and perceptions of your employees.

CREATING AN IDENTITY FOR THE PROGRAM

To identify the service program in the minds of its various audiences, you should create an identity for the program. It can be a logo, a slogan, or a special name. Acronyms are frequently used. You may have a slogan that was used in an advertising campaign that you would like to adopt for your program identity. Be creative. "We care" may be a sincere pronouncement, but try to develop an identity that is more special. Do not be gimmicky.

Exhibit 14-3 Employee Survey

1. People in this community have a good image of our hospital.	Strongly Disagree 1	Disagree 2	Neutral 3	Agree 4	Strongly Agree 5
2. I would choose to be hospitalized in this hospital.	Strongly Disagree 1	Disagree 2	Neutral 3	Agree 4	Strongly Agree 5
3. Most patients are satisfied with the treatment they receive here.	Strongly Disagree 1	Disagree 2	Neutral 3	Agree 4	Strongly Agree 5
4. I enjoy working at this hospital.	Strongly Disagree 1	Disagree 2	Neutral 3	Agree 4	Strongly Agree 5
5. I am challenged by my work.	Strongly Disagree 1	Disagree 2	Neutral 3	Agree 4	Strongly Agree 5
6. I feel I am an important person to this hospital.	Strongly Disagree 1	Disagree 2	Neutral 3	Agree 4	Strongly Agree 5
7. Most employees show a caring attitude.	Strongly Disagree 1	Disagree 2	Neutral 3	Agree 4	Strongly Agree 5
8. Employees in other departments are cooperative with our department.	Strongly Disagree 1	Disagree 2	Neutral 3	Agree 4	Strongly Agree 5
9. Employees in my department are cooperative with each other.	Strongly Disagree 1	Disagree 2	Neutral 3	Agree 4	Strongly Agree 5
10. I understand how other departments operate.	Strongly Disagree 1	Disagree 2	Neutral 3	Agree 4	Strongly Agree 5
11. Other departments understand how our department operates.	Strongly Disagree 1	Disagree 2	Neutral 3	Agree 4	Strongly Agree 5
12. My supervisor treats me fairly.	Strongly Disagree 1	Disagree 2	Neutral 3	Agree 4	Strongly Agree 5
13. My supervisor expresses appreciation for my contributions.	Strongly Disagree 1	Disagree 2	Neutral 3	Agree 4	Strongly Agree 5
14. I get the information I need to do my job well.	Strongly Disagree 1	Disagree 2	Neutral 3	Agree 4	Strongly Agree 5

Exhibit 14-3 continued

		Strongly Disagree 1	Disagree 2	Neutral 3	Agree 4	Strongly Agree 5
15.	I am informed of changes that will affect me or my job.					
16.	I understand my job and what I am expected to do.					
17.	My job is important in helping people who are sick.					
18.	In my department, there are not enough employees to do the work well.					
19.	Courteous behavior is expected of employees here.					
20.	This hospital treats physicians as valued customers.					
21.	In my department, our suggestions are welcomed.					
22.	I am encouraged to think of ways to improve the quality of our service.					
23.	This hospital values the employees.					
24.	I get enough training on how to deal with patients.					
25.	I have enough freedom in my job to make decisions on my own.					
26.	Overall, morale is high among employees.					
27.	Most employees are proud of where they work.					
28.	Employees show good telephone manners.					
29.	I think volunteers serve an important role in this hospital.					

Exhibit 14-3 continued

30. Employees in my department look professional.	Strongly Disagree 1	Disagree 2	Neutral 3	Agree 4	Strongly Agree 5
31. I am worried about my job security.	Strongly Disagree 1	Disagree 2	Neutral 3	Agree 4	Strongly Agree 5
32. This hospital will be strong in the future.	Strongly Disagree 1	Disagree 2	Neutral 3	Agree 4	Strongly Agree 5

33. One idea for making the hospital experience nicer for patients is:

34. One idea for making the hospital experience nicer for visitors is:

35. One idea for making this hospital a nicer place for physicians to work is:

36. One idea for making this hospital a nicer place for employees to work is:

37. One idea for making this hospital a nicer place for me to work is:

38. I have worked at this hospital for _____ years.
39. I am a _____ full-time _____ part-time employee.
40. I work the _____ day _____ afternoon _____ night _____ rotate shifts.
41. I work in _____ nursing department _____ nonnursing department.

Guest relations program identities that have served the following hospitals well in the past are:

- University of Alabama Hospitals, Birmingham, Alabama: "I Make the Difference"
- Shands Hospital, Gainesville, Florida: "Make the Critical Difference"
- Anderson Memorial Hospital, Anderson, South Carolina: "110%"
- Memorial Medical Center, Long Beach, California: "That Extra Measure of Care"
- Albany Medical Center, Albany, New York: "P.R.I.D.E." (People Responding with Initiative, Dedication, and Enthusiasm)
- Nebraska Methodist Hospital, Omaha, Nebraska: "Y.E.S." (Your Enthusiasm Shows)
- Mercy Hospital, Iowa City, Iowa: "E.S.P." (Extra Special People)
- Elkhart General Hospital, Elkhart, Indiana: "H.O.S.T." (Hospitality Our Special Touch)

Many hospitals have sponsored contests to choose a name for their program. These hospitals have provided attractive incentives to inspire employee creativity—from $100 savings bonds to weekend "getaways" at nearby resort hotels.

Interesting outcomes arise from these slogans. Riverside Methodist Hospital in Columbus, Ohio, developed the identity, "All You'd Expect and More," for their guest relations program. Following their participation in the training program, employees were given a small enameled pin featuring the slogan to wear on their name badges. Patients would often see the pins and inquire as to what the slogan meant. Many employees would simply reply, "Oh, it's this program we went to." Realizing that they were losing an important opportunity to promote the philosophy of the guest relations program, a short "prescription for guest relations" was developed and published in the in-house newsletter. This was a simple statement that defined what "All You'd Expect and More" meant. Employees were encouraged to memorize this prescription. To motivate them to do so, the hospital sponsored a button-spotter campaign. Spotters would approach employees and ask, "Can you recite the prescription for guest relations?" If the employee was successful in doing so, the spotter would award a prize to that employee. Chances were that if the employees could recite the prescription for guest relations, they would be better equipped to communicate more appropriately the meaning of this slogan the next time they were asked by a guest.

Many hospitals promote the program identity in their internal and external promotional efforts and advertising campaigns. The program identity can be printed on buttons, car bumper stickers, and T-shirts. Several hospitals have renamed their employee newsletters with their program identity. They have also produced employee appreciation awards with the logo/identity.

DEVELOPING A PUBLICITY STRATEGY

For many years, the introduction of the guest relations program was viewed as a spectacular media event. Everything was kept under wraps until the "big day" when the banners would go up; the newsletter, featuring a front-page story and bold headline, would be released; and the paycheck envelope would be delivered, fattened by the two-page memo written by the chief executive officer announcing the program. Short of dropping leaflets from an airplane circling the hospital's campus, every promotional gimmick was used to tout the program as a significant event in the life of the hospital. This publicity blitz would often receive a mixed response from employees.

It is best to begin apprising employees of your plans early in the planning stages. Let them know what you are attempting to do and why. Do what you can to encourage employees to contribute to the development of the program. It is essential that you position the service program initially, so that the rumor mill does not take over and distort the purpose and motivations behind the program.

Your efforts may be met with resistance. Some employees will feel insulted by a guest relations program. Others will prefer to watch from the sidelines to see if this is yet another "here today-gone tomorrow" program that lacks substance and staying power.

You need to anticipate resistance and take steps to prevent it. Of course, one of the best ways to overcome resistance is to make certain that the program does have substance and that it will be supported by those at the top. Early proclamations about the greatness of the program may be viewed as propaganda by the cynics and skeptics. Do not let this reaction discourage you from publicizing the program, however. Position the program positively and let employees know that you are building on strengths. Publish statistics and comments that will reveal patient satisfaction with the services you provide. Educate employees as to the reasons why patient, physician, and employee satisfaction is so important in today's competitive marketplace.

The newsletter editor at Albany Medical Center in Albany, New York, thoughtfully developed a list of questions that were used to interview the program coordinators and consultants, and from this interview a story was developed for the internal newsletter. The questions, relating to their P.R.I.D.E. guest relations program, are shown in Exhibit 14-4. Do not forget to include in your article comments from your chief executive officer and other top management staff.

Plan several articles for inclusion in your newsletters. Advise employees of the many facets of the program. In addition, plan events that will involve administrators and/or managers in communicating the hospital's and department's commitment to guest/customer satisfaction.

There are many other ways that the goals and objectives of your program can be shared with employees. To communicate the goals and standards of Jewish Hospital's service commitment (Louisville, Kentucky), ad slicks were distributed internally to employees. The message, "No single goal is as important to our future as guest relations," was delivered by Henry Wagner, president of the hospital's parent company, JH Systems (Exhibit 14-5). This promotional piece emphasized the fact that it takes the personal commitment of everyone in the organization to achieve this corporate goal. The text of the promotional piece also reiterated the seven standards of excellence that had been defined as cornerstone expectations of the guest relations program.

It is essential that all employees understand your goal, the organization's values, and what they can do to embody the values and make the goal a reality. In addition to the published messages, an excellent strategy is to schedule short presentations during the introduction phase of the program to communicate the goals and objectives of your program and to solicit employee input.

Exhibit 14-4 Interviewing Questions—Albany Medical Center (AMC)

QUESTIONS ADDRESSED TO INTERNAL PROGRAM COORDINATORS

1. What is the PRIDE Program?
2. What is its purpose?
3. What is the significance of the name "PRIDE"?
4. Who on the hospital staff will be involved?
5. What will be expected of them?
6. How long will this program last?
7. What results are you trying to achieve?
8. Who has worked on this program or had significant input?
9. What would happen if Albany Medical Center does not begin this program?
10. Is this a way of trying to make employees feel good about the place by glossing over some of the areas of concern?
11. I understand there are built-in incentives to get employee input on how to break down institutional barriers that might prevent them from doing the best they possibly can. What do you mean by institutional barriers, and how does this part of the program work?
12. What would make you say this program was a success? What are the criteria for judging success of a guest relations program?
13. What effect will it have on how we treat our patients?
14. What effect will it have on how we treat our physicians?
15. Will physicians be involved?
16. Many employees in the college and many in the hospital do not deal directly with patients. Why do they need to be involved with a guest relations program?

QUESTIONS ADDRESSED TO EXTERNAL CONSULTANT

17. Is this a charm school course to teach people to smile more?
18. What is your role in this program?
19. How did you get involved in guest relations?
20. Why are guest relations programs needed in hospitals?
21. Are most major academic health science centers such as AMC also instituting guest relations programs?
22. What were the results of the most successful program you've been involved with and how does that program differ from here? How was the situation at that institution similar to AMC?
23. What difficulties, if any, do you see in accomplishing the goals of the program?

Source: Courtesy of Albany Medical Center, Albany, New York.

Exhibit 14-5 JH Systems Standards of Excellence

JH SYSTEMS STANDARDS OF EXCELLENCE

"No single goal is as important to our future as guest relations."

Henry C. Wagner, President, JH Systems, Inc.

These words from Mr. Wagner underscore the importance that we place in achieving excellence in guest relations.

The goal of our guest relations program is to deliver high-quality health care services in a professional, compassionate, and courteous manner while respecting the dignity and individuality of each person who comes in contact with our organization.

To turn this goal into a reality, there are seven standards of excellence:

1. Presentation of professional image– We at JH Systems feel it is important for employees to present a professional image, in dress and actions to both our guests and co-workers.

*2. Communicate effectively–*We expect everyone at JH Systems to convey a clear, friendly message whether in person, or on the telephone.

3. Privacy and confidentiality maintained– Everyone is expected to respect the privacy and confidentiality of our guests.

*4. Go out of your way– help another person–*We at JH Systems feel that our guests are important and should be treated as such. Please take the extra step to provide assistance to a guest or co-worker.

*5. Take pride in your job responsibilities–*We at JH Systems believe that every job is important to the success of the organization. Be proud of your contribution.

*6. Be a team player–*We at JH Systems feel that working cooperatively with co-workers is important in moving our organization forward.

*7. Explain procedures–*Share your knowledge and explain procedures and activities to our guests.

Source: Courtesy of Jewish Hospital Systems, Inc., Louisville, Kentucky.

INTRODUCING THE PROGRAM

The best way to implement a service program is to foster enthusiastic support and participation from all individuals throughout the organization. This support evolves over time. Introductory sessions can be scheduled to provide a forum for communicating the goals of the program. These sessions can be used to:

- Communicate the service goals
- Articulate organizational values
- Define broad objectives of the upcoming service program
- Educate employees to changes in the industry that have fueled competition
- Identify the importance of *every* employee's role
- Solicit employee questions and suggestions

These sessions can be offered to employees, managers, volunteers, and even physicians.

Depending on what you want to cover, the introductory sessions can be between 45–90 minutes in length. Typically, it is best to schedule a meeting blitz, with sessions conducted around the clock within several days (or weeks, if your institution is especially large). The sessions should be conducted by members of your administrative team. It is a test of endurance, but many chief executive officers have themselves conducted these sessions on all three shifts. The very fact that the administrator will turn out at 2:00 A.M. to conduct a session implies a strong commitment from the top.

Slides that visually support the messages to be delivered will guide the presentations and ensure consistency in the messages delivered from one session to the next. The following is a suggested outline from which you can develop a slide presentation:

I. Competition in Today's Marketplace
    A. Hospitals are competing for:
        1. Patients
        2. Physicians
        3. Payers/contracts
    B. What has caused this competition?
        1. Business—benefit-cost management
        2. Government—prospective payment
        3. Alternative delivery centers
        4. Greater demand for customer-oriented *service*
    C. How has this affected our hospital?
        1. Inpatient utilization statistics

        a. 5 years ago
        b. 3 years ago
        c. last year
    2. Average length of stay
        a. 5 years ago
        b. last year
    3. Outpatient procedures
        a. 3 years ago
        b. last year
    4. Staffing levels
        a. 5 years ago
        b. 3 years ago
        c. today

II. What Are We Doing to Position Ourselves?
  A. Expansion and diversification of services
  B. Contract negotiations
  C. Facility improvements
  D. Managing change through values
    1. Our mission
    2. Our values
  E. Service, service, service
  F. Greater attention to customer needs/expectations
    1. What do patients expect?
    2. Word-of-mouth advertising
    3. Negative impact of dissatisfaction
  G. Systems analysis and design

III. *You* Are Important to Our Future Success
  A. Every employee makes the difference
  B. Every department delivers an essential service
  C. We thank you for the good job you are doing
    1. Patient satisfaction statistics
    2. Selected comments from patient questionnaires

IV. Our Commitment to Service
  A. Anticipated benefits
  B. Components of the comprehensive program
  C. When training program sessions will be scheduled
  D. Building on strengths

V. It Starts at the Top—We Are Committed!
  A. Open up channels of communication

   B. Develop a strategy for service
      1. Built on values
      2. Keyed to guest benefits
   C. Everyone participates and is accountable

At the end of the slide presentation, invite employees to ask questions. Some employees may pose challenging questions. Be ready to respond with honest, forthright answers. Let them know that their concerns are appreciated. Pledge your support and commitment to address these concerns. Things will not change overnight and you cannot promise that you will have a solution to every problem, but emphasize that you will pursue those that are within the realm of possibility.

Following the question-and-answer period, distribute suggestion cards and ask the employees to develop ideas on how service can be improved. A suggested format for such cards is shown in Exhibit 14-6. The employee does not have to sign his or her name on the card, but those who identify themselves and have useful suggestions can be recognized by name for their good ideas in an upcoming newsletter. If you have asked similar questions on an employee survey (Exhibit 14-3), you will not want to duplicate these questions again.

The introductory sessions, as outlined in this section, should precede training sessions by at least 4 weeks. In the intervening weeks, build greater awareness of the program by publishing articles and communicating information that will identify the program strategies more specifically and reinforce the desired organizational values.

Introductory sessions for managers should be offered before the employee sessions are held. Although you can cover much of the same material during these

Exhibit 14-6 Employee Suggestion Card

---

1. One service idea that will result in greater patient satisfaction is _____
   _____.

2. One service idea that will result in greater visitor satisfaction with our services is _____
   _____.

3. One service idea that will result in greater physician satisfaction with our services is _____
   _____.

4. One idea that will make the hospital a better place for employees to work and to provide services to our guests is _____
   _____.

Name (optional) _____Department _____

Source: K.E. Peterson & Associates, Chicago, Illinois.

---

management sessions, they will provide your first opportunity to reinforce how important each manager is to the overall success of the program. Explain that every employee will be expected to participate in training, and acknowledge that this may place an additional staffing burden on supervisors and managers. Remember that resistance will not be solely experienced within the employee ranks. Some managers will be skeptical and will view the program as an additional squeeze on their declining resources. Help your managers and supervisors understand how the service program can help them achieve their individual and departmental goals.

Once you have defined your strategies, created the infrastructure, and begun to stimulate grassroots support and involvement, you can proceed to implement your action plan.

SUMMARY

A comprehensive program will require an enormous commitment of time and resources. Do not take shortcuts during the planning phase. Mapping out your goals and strategies carefully, while simultaneously gathering feedback to refine your focus and baseline data against which to measure your effectiveness, will help ensure a more effective, successful, and lasting service effort.

Chapter 15

Training: Developing Service Competence

Certainly, the most memorable moments of truth in any consumer's experiential repertoire are those brief encounters with disrespectful, surly, rude employees. Fortunately, employees who display such contemptible behavior toward customers are definitely exceptions. Most employees understand common courtesy and live by the golden rule.

Indifference, rather than mean spiritedness, is often the most prevalent cause of performance that does not meet the expectations of service-driven employers. Those employees whose attitudes are tinged with indifference may be unaware of the impact that their attitudes and actions have on a customer's perception of service, quality and value.

Quite simply, you cannot train a person to care. For the most part, adult behavior emanates from basic values that are instilled early on by parents, teachers, clergy, and neighbors. Those employees who do not possess the inherent values that foster the expression of care, concern, and compassion toward others will not embrace those values as the result of a 4-hour training program. For this very reason, training interventions that are designed primarily to teach the "dos and don'ts" of etiquette are anathema to successful service programs. The last thing you want to do is to insult your employees by assuming that "smile" training will enable them to do a better job of serving the customers. Rather, employees need to be made aware of their roles in carrying out the service strategy and to be provided with the training that will enable them to handle customer interactions with skill and confidence. Moreover, employees must be empowered to become advocates and problem solvers and be made to feel that their positive contributions are appreciated. These are the most powerful antidotes to chronic indifference.

A wide variety of training approaches is currently being used in hospitals and other service organizations. It is difficult, if not impossible, to identify and recommend one as being the best for your hospital. The choice of the appropriate approach for your hospital will be influenced by what you want to accomplish in

227

the general training sessions and the availability of resources and support to provide targeted training in the future that will satisfy specific skill-development needs.

TRAINING OBJECTIVES

The primary objectives of training programs are to heighten employees' awareness of guests' needs and expectations and to present and develop the interpersonal skills that will enable employees to respond effectively to meet those needs. Meeting those objectives will enhance and maintain strong, supportive relationships with patients, visitors, physicians, and other employees.

Another equally important objective is to facilitate discussions among employees about how they can constructively improve interdepartmental and intradepartmental relations. Opportunities to engage in discussions with employees from other departments are limited during the normal workday. The value of mixing employees from several departments in general training sessions is shown by the comment frequently expressed by participants in guest relations training programs: "The best thing about this program was the opportunity to talk to people outside of my department."

Although a training program should have modules geared to development of specific skills, such as communication skills and complaint resolution techniques, you must work within limited time constraints. Guest relations programs on the market today vary in length from between 2 hours to 40 hours; the vast majority run between 3–4 hours. Because some employees may need specific skill building more than others, it is best to approach the general session as an awareness-building effort with a limited skill-development focus. More specific training for the needs of those within a department or particular job function can be scheduled after the general sessions. For example, a program that addresses how to handle a hostile or difficult patient will be valuable to many employees from nursing or ancillary departments who have frequent interaction with patients. Training on how to resolve billing complaints is an example of the specific training that is useful to employees in the business office.

PROGRAM FORMAT

Who Should Participate in the Program?

Quite simply, everyone should participate in the program. This means full-time and part-time employees, as well as managers, administrators, and volunteers. The importance of guest relations should make participation in the program mandatory. Physicians should be included as well; approaches for involving physicians are discussed in Chapter 16.

For optimal employee participation, do not include managers in the employees' sessions. The presence of supervisory-level personnel frequently inhibits a subordinate's willingness to contribute ideas and thoughts. Special sessions for managers should be scheduled before the general sessions for employees. If some managers are unable to attend special introductory training sessions for management, they may be individually integrated into employee sessions.

How Long Should the Sessions Last?

Keep in mind that the real costs of training are in loss of job productivity. You are paying employees while they are attending training sessions. You must make certain that every hour is invested wisely. The length of your program will depend on what you hope to accomplish and what you can afford.

The program length will also be influenced by the size of your groups. If you have 20 employees attending, the level of participation and length of time to complete discussions are greater than if you conduct the session for 8 employees. Consider this fact when scheduling night and evening shift sessions, which are generally smaller in size.

How Should You Structure the Training Sessions?

You can sponsor one program session or break the program into several sessions, covering different topics in each module. Although managers may initially feel it is too great a sacrifice to schedule an employee away for a period of several hours, most agree that a single, long session is ultimately more desirable than having to schedule the same employee for two or more shorter sessions. An important consideration that will influence how you schedule your sessions is the time it takes for a group to establish rapport. If you schedule four 1-hour sessions rather one 4-hour session, at least 10 minutes will be spent in each session "breaking the ice." Too, some employees will be unable to attend each session, which will affect the composition of your groups.

How Many Participants Should Be Scheduled for Each Session?

The number of participants in each session should be no fewer than 8 participants nor more than 30. The optimal size is 20 to 25 employees per session, although this number is too large if the primary objective of your program is to develop interaction skills. The size of available room(s) will influence the number of employees you can accommodate per session. If you are planning to use audiovisual materials, such as videotapes, your group size should be small enough to allow everyone to see the VCR monitor. The number of employees you can reasonably expect to be away from departmental responsibilities at one time will be influenced by the size of your hospital, census, and staffing levels. If you offer the sessions on all three shifts, expect your night sessions to be significantly smaller.

How Many Sessions Will Need To Be Scheduled?

The number of sessions you schedule will be influenced by the total number of employees divided by the number you anticipate per session. For example, if your hospital has 1,000 employees and you expect to be able to schedule an average of 20 employees per session, you will need to schedule 50 sessions.

Over What Period of Time Should the Sessions Be Scheduled?

You should aggressively schedule the sessions over a short, well-defined period of time. Doing so will result in a greater level of enthusiasm, awareness, and participation by all departments. Managers may prefer the sessions to be spread out over time to avoid having employees away from their departments with such frequency. If your implementation proceeds slowly, however, you run the risk of having managers become less and less supportive of employees' time away from the department. Another incentive for aggressively scheduling your sessions is to complete this phase quickly so that you can proceed to other phases of the comprehensive program.

To plan the span of time over which you will schedule the sessions, determine how many sessions you can realistically schedule each week. If you have 1,000 employees and plan to hold 50 sessions and you feel comfortable scheduling two programs a day for 5 days a week, the duration of your program implementation would be 5 weeks.

PROGRAM CONTENT

Before developing the content of the guest relations training program, you must decide precisely what you want to accomplish by it. To what degree, for example, should the training be focused on developing skills? What specific skills do you want to develop? Communication, telephone courtesy, assertiveness, or complaint and conflict resolution? How much time will you devote to creating awareness of guests' needs and expectations? The values of the organization? To what degree will you educate employees about the changes that have created a more competitive marketplace? Will you focus on building empathy? Team building? Will you offer techniques for coping with stress and relieving the "burnout syndrome?" How relevant is training to handling difficult or hostile patients?

The answers to these questions will determine how you develop the structure and content of your training program. The possibilities are many, and you must focus on the desired objectives before engaging in the involved process of designing the instruction.

If you are planning one training program for all employees, be sure that the subject matter is relevant to most personnel. It must be written and produced to be understood by employees who may not have had much prior education and training, yet it cannot be so elementary that it is boring to those who have. It is also important to remain sensitive to how you are presenting the content to employees. It cannot be presented in a condescending manner. If you plan to use cartoons and caricatures, do so carefully. Many are offensively juvenile. The same is true of audiovisual programs that present absurd and ridiculous vignettes. Although rude behavior can be amusing, the absurdity of many of the portrayals will certainly cause many viewers to become defensive. Unfortunately, many of the professionally produced films and videotapes on the market today portray guests as saints while employees exhibit exaggerated, obnoxious responses. In reality, the guests of many service establishments would benefit from a charm school course! Employees frequently deal with very difficult and demanding patients, visitors, and physicians. Remember not to exaggerate when attempting to demonstrate inappropriate employee responses.

A program designed to *involve* employees will be more constructive and meaningful. This principle suggests the use of many small and large group discussion exercises, rather than lectures. Do not tell employees how to act; let them tell you. As they do so, you can reinforce many skills and techniques. Employees will learn through self-awareness and through instruction provided to reinforce the points brought out in the discussions.

Make the program participative and *fun* and you will capture the attentions and active involvement of those who attend.

FACILITATORS

Because the effectiveness of each session depends to a great degree on the person leading it, the choice of facilitator should be carefully thought out. Facilitators may be members of the training and education department, the guest relations director, the patient representative, or department managers. In addition, consider using nonmanagement employees as facilitators. Do not exclude employees simply because they do not have previous experience in training. If you select people who have good communication skills and positive attitudes (and a certain degree of courage!) and if you spend the time necessary to train the facilitators to assume their roles, you can achieve some spectacular results. When you identify employees who presently contribute to the promotion of guest relations and you recognize them by offering them the opportunity to conduct the sessions, this assignment is viewed as a positive distinction by their peers.

Certainly, the credibility of the person(s) who conducts the training is important. A skilled instructor who is a real grouch will not be viewed favorably by the participants.

Speaking to a group of peers can be one of the most stressful activities that anyone undertakes. The fear of rejection is understandable, and those employees who are selected may experience initial stage fright. Yet, once they have led one session, most blossom in their roles.

One successful approach has been to use a team of two employees to conduct the sessions. There are several advantages to this approach. If the facilitators are inexperienced, they can rely on the support of their partners. If the team is made up of an employee from a patient care department and another from a support or ancillary department, they are together more likely to represent the interests and affiliations of the departmentally mixed groups of participants and can prevent the discussions from becoming narrow in focus.

What Criteria Should Be Used in Identifying Facilitators?

Facilitators should have these personal traits:

- demonstrate skill in interacting with others
- are role models
- exhibit positive relationships with others
- possess good communication skills
- are recognized as leaders by peers
- exhibit loyalty to the institution

The facilitators should also be:

- employees in "good standing"
- employed at least 6 months

What Method Should Be Used in Selecting the Facilitators?

The best method to select facilitators is to ask your supervisors and managers to nominate candidates from their departments. There are several reasons why this approach is desirable.

- Managers are made to feel more of a part in the planning process.
- They acknowledge and support the employee's time away from the department.
- They are more aware of employees who possess the desired qualities.

It is best to orient your managers/supervisors to the program before asking for nominations. In preparing your presentation, the following points can be made:

- Outline the program—its objectives and time frames.
- Communicate the level of support extended to the service program by the administration.
- Identify the total number of facilitators needed.
- Identify the characteristics you are seeking in a facilitator.
- Estimate the time each person will be away from the department.
- Reinforce that serving as a facilitator is an honor and distinction for the employee and for the department.
- Reinforce the need to have diverse departmental representation.
- Describe the procedure for submitting nominations.
- Describe the procedure for interviewing/selecting candidates.

Be prepared to receive a greater number of nominations than you will be able to use. The steering committee can select facilitators from those who are nominated. You may first want to interview the candidates. During the interviews, let each candidate know that it is an honor to be nominated. Explain the program and the roles that will be assumed by program facilitators, and note that there are more candidates than available positions. Ask if the person would be willing to participate on a subcommittee or in another role if he or she is not selected as a facilitator.

Develop a list of questions that will be asked of every candidate. Distribute interviewer sheets containing these questions to those who will be conducting the interviews. Suggested questions include:

- What benefits do you feel the program will bring to the hospital?
- In what ways can the hospital create a more unified team effort in guest relations?

- What qualities or characteristics do you feel General Hospital has of which we can be proud?
- What ideas do you have for improving the quality of service we deliver to patients, visitors, and physicians?
- Do you have any previous professional or nonwork experience presenting programs or speaking before groups?

Once the candidates have been interviewed, the interviewers should recommend those candidates whom they feel will be able to participate effectively in this capacity.

As an alternative to having managers nominate the facilitators, members of the steering committee may select the facilitators. This is especially convenient if your hospital is small and you have a diverse committee whose members are aware of talented candidates.

After the facilitators are identified, inform the department managers and supervisors of the choices made. Make certain that they understand and support the time commitment that each will make.

How Should Program Facilitators Be Prepared?

Facilitators will need to be given thorough instruction on how to conduct the sessions. Explain to the participants how the program should be introduced. Share group facilitation skills that will encourage discussion. These include such techniques as nodding to affirm responses, using eye contact, maintaining an open stance, and asking open-ended questions. Explain how the facilitator can get the session back on track when discussions stray from the subject. Anticipate those uncomfortable situations that may arise during the sessions. Share responses and techniques to use when a participant confronts the facilitator with verbal resistance or when a group resists voluntary discussion. Share personal anecdotes to illustrate that it is normal to experience a desire to flee from the room when uncomfortable situations occur.

Hold practice sessions during which the facilitators take turns leading group discussions. These role plays will provide opportunities for facilitators to develop their presentation skills. They will also provide you with an opportunity to coach the participants and to provide positive reinforcement.

Because facilitators will have final questions before the program begins, schedule a meeting several days before their first sessions. During this short meeting, you can review last minute details and respond to questions or concerns expressed by the facilitators.

You will need to provide a good deal of support to these facilitators. One way to involve other committee members in providing this support is to ask them to be mentors to the facilitators. It is not necessary that mentors attend all sessions, but the facilitators should always have the name of someone to call if they require assistance.

In addition, a mentor should call each facilitator after each session to talk about how the session went. This is most important during the initial stages of the program implementation. If the facilitators are inexperienced, they may need to talk about something that surfaced during the session that made them feel uncomfortable. A mentor's call will also be an appreciated gesture that acknowledges his or her support and interest.

After all of the facilitators have conducted at least one session, schedule a group meeting of all the facilitators. This will be a ''show and tell'' session in which facilitators can show that they have survived and tell others of their experiences, triumphs, challenges, and reactions. Another follow-up meeting should be scheduled at the conclusion of the general sessions. This will give you an opportunity to debrief the facilitators and to gain their insights, feedback, and suggestions. Before the final meeting, you may want to distribute a survey to enable facilitators to evaluate the program, to share what they learned during the process, and to offer any ideas or recommendations to management. A sample evaluation survey, adapted from one developed by Bethesda Hospital in Cincinnati, Ohio, is shown in Exhibit 15-1.

Do not pass up the opportunity to recognize the fine contributions of these employees who have served as facilitators. Schedule a special event, such as a luncheon or dinner, in their honor. The success of your program will depend on the many hours of time and energy they have invested. If your budget allows, give each a plaque, certificate, paperweight, pin, clock, or some such item commemorating the program. Invite members from administration and the steering committee to this recognition event, and schedule short speeches by the CEO and the program coordinator before awarding the gifts.

How Many Facilitators Should Be Used?

The number of facilitators you select will be determined by the size of your hospital and the number of sessions you can reasonably expect each facilitator to conduct per month. If your hospital is large and implementation is planned over a short period of time, you may wish to involve more facilitators. Do not, however, dilute the effort. Each facilitator gains confidence and experience each time he or she conducts a session. If the facilitator is only offered an opportunity to conduct a program every few weeks, it is difficult for that person to maintain proficiency.

Exhibit 15-1 Guest Relations Program Facilitator's Evaluation

1. The number of program sessions I conducted:
   _____ 2–3 sessions
   _____ 4–5 sessions
   _____ 6 or more sessions

2. The amount of time scheduled to conduct the program was:

   More than was needed   Just about right   Too little time

3. The meeting rooms/classrooms used for the sessions I conducted were:

   Very Adequate   Adequate   Inadequate   Very Inadequate

4. The initial session for trainers, which covered the program objectives and the trainer role was helpful to me in understanding the guest relations program.

   Strongly Agree   Agree   Undecided   Disagree   Strongly Disagree

5. The day long session for trainers provided adequate preparation for me to meet my responsibilities in implementing the guest relations program.

   Strongly Agree   Agree   Undecided   Disagree   Strongly Disagree

6. The overall response of employees who attended the sessions I conducted was positive.

   Strongly Agree   Agree   Undecided   Disagree   Strongly Disagree

7. I found the workbook which was distributed to each participant to be:

   Very Helpful   Helpful   Not Helpful

8. Helping to conduct this program has been of value to me in my job.

   Strongly Agree   Agree   Undecided   Disagree   Strongly Disagree

9. I feel a sense of pride about being employed by our hospital.

   Strongly Agree   Agree   Undecided   Disagree   Strongly Disagree

10. Helping to conduct the guest relations program has indicated to me that I have an important part in establishing a good impression of our hospital.

    Strongly Agree   Agree   Undecided   Disagree   Strongly Disagree

11. What degree of improvement in relations among departments have you noticed since the guest relations sessions were implemented?

    Great Improvement   Some Improvement   No Improvement

12. What degree of improvement in employees' approaches and responses to patients, families, and visitors have you noticed since the guest relations sessions were implemented?

    Great Improvement   Some Improvement   No Improvement

Exhibit 15-1 continued

13. Three things I liked *most* about being a facilitator: (Check only three)

_____ Meeting and working with employees I otherwise would not have known

_____ Positive responses of employees to sessions

_____ Learning about myself and how I can affect other people

_____ Confidence in speaking in front of group

_____ Challenge of presenting program in an interesting way

_____ Feeling of doing something constructive for hospital and co-workers

_____ Being chosen to participate as a trainer

_____ Attempting to improve our respect for one another

14. Three things I liked *least* about being a facilitator: (Check only three)

_____ Length of program—too long and repetitive

_____ Dealing with negative employees

_____ Time away from job

_____ Rooms and equipment poor

_____ Did not feel comfortable/qualified

_____ Explaining to others why I was a trainer

_____ Scheduling night shift after work

_____ Workbook

_____ Saturday classes

_____ Concern that follow-up will be inadequate

_____ No response

Source: Courtesy of Bethesda Hospital, Cincinnati, Ohio.

If facilitator teams are used and each team conducts 5 sessions, (assuming a total of 50 sessions are offered) ten teams (or 20 facilitators) would be required.

Alternate facilitators should also be identified. These individuals can be trained to conduct sessions if, for any reason, a regular facilitator is unable to fulfill the scheduled commitment. Expect such problems to occur. Alternates may be management/supervisory level personnel, as there is often greater scheduling flexibility at this level. You may even elect to have one to two alternates chosen from your steering committee or from the education and training department. The alternates will need to anticipate which days they are ''on call'' and should have some schedule flexibility. Because they may be asked to stand in on a moment's notice, alternates should be experienced in training or speaking before groups.

What Is the Time Commitment Demanded of Facilitators?

Each team should present between four to six sessions. If each session lasts 4 hours, this will be a time commitment of between 16 to 24 hours for each facilitator. Of course, if some teams are available and willing to conduct more than six sessions, it is fine for them to do so. In addition to the actual time spent conducting the sessions, approximately 30 minutes per session will be needed to prepare for the session and to return materials to the program coordinator. Communicate this time commitment to managers. Those who are selected as facilitators should have the full support of their supervisors and department managers.

Remember that facilitators will need training to assume their roles. The time required for training will depend on the depth of preparation you provide. In addition, the facilitators should meet periodically during the implementation period to share their experiences and observations.

SCHEDULING

In preparation for scheduling sessions, it is wise to meet with representatives from the education and training department. Review the scheduling methods they have used for training. If you do not have such a department or if established procedures for scheduling a hospital-wide training program are not in place, you may want to follow these six steps:

1. *Develop a preliminary schedule of sessions.* Use the number of day, evening, and night shift employees to calculate the approximate number of sessions to be held on each shift. Then begin scheduling sessions on appropriate days and times.

    Finding available classrooms is typically the biggest problem a coordinator confronts. If at all possible, try to reserve the same room for all of the sessions.

    You can avoid paying overtime to employees on 3-11 and 7-11 shifts by scheduling sessions during those shifts. Furthermore, employees will appreciate your efforts to accommodate their schedules. If you cannot schedule at least eight employees for night-shift sessions, consider scheduling sessions during the evening shift and request that night-shift employees come in early to attend. This is an example of when split sessions, such as two 2-hour sessions, would be appropriate to avoid having night-shift employees work 12 hours.

If some units/departments cannot afford to have an employee away for an extended time, you will need to hire relief personnel. You may find that scheduling two sessions (back to back) is efficient because the relief employee can work a full 8-hour shift and relieve each of the two employees attending a 4-hour session. You may need to add a half-hour to some sessions to provide employees with a lunch or dinner break.

2. *Communicate the preliminary schedule to the nursing department.* Because most employees to be scheduled will be from nursing, it is important to confirm with the director or head nurses that the schedule is indeed workable.

3. *Confirm a master schedule and design individual session sign-up sheets.* Develop and reproduce a form that notes the day, date, and time of each scheduled session. Assign a color to sessions scheduled on day (red), evening (black), and night (green) shifts for easy reference. Identify the number of employees you can accommodate in each session. Add at least two additional spaces. On any given day, you can expect that several employees will not be able to make the session for which they are scheduled. Divide the total number of spaces available by two, reserving one-half of the sign-up sheet for nursing and the other half for nonnursing departments.

4. *Designate a room or area for scheduling.* Post sign-up sheets on the wall and invite head nurses/nursing supervisors to schedule their employees. Once nursing supervisors have scheduled their employees, check session sign-up sheets and identify any sessions with poor attendance. If any of the sessions have fewer than four nursing employees scheduled, designate those as tentative sessions and move them to a special wall. Invite nonnursing department directors/supervisors to a session on the following day to schedule their employees.

5. *Prepare master scheduling sheets for selective distribution.* Supervisors should make notations in their own records as to when each employee was scheduled. It is not necessary to distribute the master list to all managers/supervisors.

6. *Cancel any sessions that do not achieve minimum registration.* Inform managers/supervisors of session cancellations in a memo along with other important information and changes.

It is best to ask supervisors to schedule their employees by name. If they only reserve a place in the session by writing their department name in the space(s) provided, they may not be as likely to organize the work schedules around a specific person's absence.

If you have the internal capabilities to do so, you can schedule employees by computer. Computer scheduling is advantageous for very large institutions.

Although a list can be sent to the manager identifying which sessions their employees will attend, an additional friendly invitation sent directly to the employee provides a personal touch.

PUBLICITY

A publicity strategy should be planned with the director of public relations and/or the newsletter editor. Begin sharing information about the training program with those people well in advance of the program kick-off. Encourage them to run an article about the program in your in-house newsletter at the time it is introduced. Consider introducing additional information about the guest relations/service program in a letter distributed to employees through the mail or in their paycheck envelopes.

Regardless of how you decide to publicize the program, remember always to position the program positively. The program is not being introduced to correct a problem; rather, it is a way to build on strengths.

Once managers and administrators have participated in the training program, place photographs taken during those sessions in the newsletter to let employees know that managers have been involved in the training. It is also a good idea to feature the facilitators. Have a photographer attend their special training session, and include several formal and candid shots of facilitators participating in their training.

Once the program is underway, publish comments from employees who have participated. Their first-hand impressions will validate the program more strongly than comments from program leaders. To achieve balance, you should feel free to include a less than positive comment or two.

After you have conducted a session for your medical staff, do not forget to share supportive comments from physicians. Patients' expectations are changing the way that physicians practice medicine. If appropriate, you may feature an article on that topic. If you offer a patient (guest) relations program for the staffs of physicians, include photographs of participants in those sessions.

Keep employees informed about what is planned for the future. The service program does not begin and end with training. Identify the activities and plans of the steering committee and other subcommittees.

Decide at what point, if any, you will release information about the service program to the local media. The program should be positioned positively. Its implementation is an indication that the hospital maintains a commitment to quality care. The program creates many opportunities for favorable publicity. However, be sure to let the public relations director handle the outside media coverage. The last thing you want to spot in the morning newspaper is the headline, "Well, It's About Time."

Other very visible promotions of the program are such specialty items as buttons, balloons, pins, and posters. Do not spend a great deal of money on such items, but consider their value in promoting the program. Remember: it is service, not slogans, you want to produce.

PROGRAM INTRODUCTION

The way in which the training is introduced is very important in setting the tone for the service program. Your chances for a successful program implementation will be increased if you invest time at this critical stage to make sure that everyone understands the purpose and objectives of the program.

How Should the Program Be Introduced to Employees?

If you did not schedule preliminary sessions to introduce the overall goals of your service program, you may want to begin the training sessions with an introduction by someone from administration, preferably the chief executive officer. If it is unrealistic to have the CEO personally present this introduction at every session, enlist other members of the administrative team to participate. These introductions should be ''scripted'' so that there is some consistency of message. Points that should be reinforced include:

- Acknowledge their personal participation in earlier sessions.
- Describe the hospital's commitment to the program.
- Position the programs positively.
- Note that the program's goal is to reinforce existing strengths.
- Extend appreciation on behalf of the administration for the dedicated contributions made by employees.
- Identify upcoming programs and activities that will complement the training program.

An alternative to the personal presentation by administrators is a videotaped message from the chief executive officer (CEO).

How Should the Program Be Introduced to Managers?

As previously discussed, training sessions should be scheduled for managers and supervisors before the employee sessions are held. At the managerial sessions, the CEO should introduce the program and emphasize his or her support for the programs, services, and strategies being developed for the entire service/guest relations initiative. If administrators participated in earlier introductory sessions scheduled at the outset of the program, this introduction can be brief. Employee facilitators should not conduct sessions for administrators, managers, and supervisors. If a visit by an outside consultant is not planned, the program coordinator and/or other committee members should conduct these sessions.

Although it is important that managers and supervisors participate in the same training as will be offered to their employees, you may want to add specific segments to their training that will help them more effectively execute their roles after completion of the guest relations training. If managers do not reinforce the expectations that are set forth in the training, you will receive diminished returns from training in the long run. Administrators and managers are role models. They must exhibit the skills and attitudes that are expected of employees. In addition, they provide feedback, coaching, and positive reinforcement to their employees. Specific management development training can be offered in these initial sessions or scheduled after their participation in the basic training program. Do not wait too long! If you are to validate the commitment to service and hold employees accountable, managers must be ready to provide the support.

GOAL SETTING EXERCISE

To make sure that the guest relations concepts and expectations of behavior become an integral and ongoing part of the performance of all employees, it is important to follow the training with actual goal setting. This will give employees an opportunity to translate what was covered in the training into specific goals that will improve their performance on the job. This activity is a valuable exercise in directing both the employee and his or her immediate supervisor to focus on performance improvement and recognition.

Personal and Professional Development, Inc. (Wheeling, Illinois), one of the first firms to specialize in guest relations and performance improvement programs, has developed a structured approach for posttraining goal setting. Their multiphase program—C.A.R.E.—concludes with an exercise that assists the employee and his or her immediate supervisor in setting goals.

After participating in the C.A.R.E. workshops, each employee is asked to complete a short goal setting form entitled, "You Make the Difference" (Exhibit 15-2). The form lists eight major categories of interpersonal behavior. Each employee identifies areas under each category in which he or she feels performance can be improved. From a summary of goals, the employees develop individual plans for how they will approach typical patient/guest/employee interactions that will be encountered on the job.

Exhibit 15-2 Goal-Setting Form

C.A.R.E.

You Make The Difference

Improving interpersonal skills is a never-ending process, and we can all strive to "do even better than we're doing now."

During the C.A.R.E. Workshop, you became even more aware that you are a very special person and that no matter what your job is, you are important.

Only You Can Make The Difference Between:
- A good hospital versus an *outstanding hospital!*
- A good place to work versus an *outstanding place to work!*
- Being just an employee versus being an *important member of the team!*

Please review the items listed below and the examples given for each. Ask yourself if you could apply just a little more effort and attention to any or all of the items could you "do even better than you are now." Check one of the boxes to the right of each item and briefly state your specific goal(s) or just underline one of the examples if they apply.

Remember, even a *small difference* can be of *major importance!* When you have completed this form, return it to your supervisor. He/She will arrange for a short meeting to share your ideas and to support your efforts to *make a difference!*

If I Paid A Little More Attention To:

1. Personal Appearance

For example: • Always wearing I.D. badge • Always following dress code—shined shoes, neat and clean uniforms, well groomed, moderation in jewelry and hair style.

Other goals: _____

☐ I could do even better than I'm doing now.
☐ I'm doing very well now.
☐ Doesn't apply to my job.

2. Appearance of Work Environment

For example: • Putting away supplies, folders, etc. • Hanging up uniforms • Keeping personal work area neat and clean • Not leaving coffee cups and other debris in public areas.

Other goals: _____

☐ I could do even better than I'm doing now.
☐ I'm doing very well now.
☐ Doesn't apply to my job.

3. Initial Interactions With Others (Patients, visitors, physicians, fellow employees)

For example: • Taking the first step in greeting others • Introducing oneself to patients and visitors • Calling the person by name whenever possible • Always saying please and thank you • Smiling appropriately • Having good body language and eye contact • Using appropriate phone courtesy • Looking for opportunities to pay compliments.

Other goals: _____

☐ I could do even better than I'm doing now.
☐ I'm doing very well now.
☐ Doesn't apply to my job.

4. Patient and Family Rights

For example: • Always knocking before entering a patient's room • Explaining what you are there to do • Showing a special regard for patient's modesty and need for privacy • Refraining from talking about patients in public areas. • Explaining reasons for rules and regulations • Anticipating questions and concerns.

Other goals: _____

☐ I could do even better than I'm doing now.
☐ I'm doing very well now.
☐ Doesn't apply to my job.

5. Interpersonal Interactions With Others (Patients, visitors, physicians, fellow employees)

For example: • Providing directions to others • Responding to patients'/visitors' requests for information • Showing a genuine interest in the other person • Going out of one's way to help out fellow employees especially when they are in need of help • Improving communications with other departments • Looking for opportunities to encourage and support others • Maintaining a positive attitude even though the other person is in pain or upset by something • Working well as a team member.

Other goals: _____

☐ I could do even better than I'm doing now.
☐ I'm doing very well now.
☐ Doesn't apply to my job.

Exhibit 15-2 continued

6. **Interpersonal Interactions With Others in High Stress Situations**
(Patients, visitors, physicians, fellow employees)

For example: • Avoiding responding emotionally and defensively • Listening carefully • Giving the other person our complete and undivided attention • Avoiding interrupting the other person • Letting others know that you are sensitive to their feelings • Showing a genuine interest in how they feel • Striving for mutual problem solving • Looking for win-win solutions • Reaching solutions that determine who, what and when things will be done • Follow-up.

Other goals: _____

☐ I could do even better than I'm doing now.
☐ I'm doing very well now.
☐ Doesn't apply to my job.

7. **Additional Factors Affecting The Hospital's Image and Reputation**

For example: • Avoiding complaining about hospital policies, fellow workers or supervisors • Speaking positively about the hospital and its employees to outsiders • Making suggestions for positive changes.

Other goals: _____

☐ I could do even better than I'm doing now.
☐ I'm doing very well now.
☐ Doesn't apply to my job.

8. If you would like to discuss a high-stress situation that you experience on the job, please describe it below:

_____
_____
_____
_____

Summary of Goals

Please complete this during the C.A.R.E. goal setting session between you and your supervisor.

Summary of Specific Goals: _____

_____
_____
_____
_____
_____
_____
_____
_____
_____
_____
_____
_____

Employee Name: _____ Date of Workshop: _____

Department/Work Unit: _____ Date of Goal Setting Session: _____

Supervisor's Signature _____

Source: © Copyright 1985. Personal and Professional Development, Inc. Reprinted by permission.

Employees then schedule 20- to 30-minute sessions with their supervisors to share their plans. The supervisor, in turn, offers suggestions, ideas, and reinforcement. The supervisor is expected to observe the employee's day-to-day performance on the job and is encouraged to offer positive strokes, coaching, and support. Within 4 weeks the supervisor completes the Employee Feedback Report (Exhibit 15-3) and schedules a session with the employee to review the plan and the performance improvement that has taken place. If appropriate, new goals are identified. These feedback sessions are routinely scheduled, and they become extensions of the employee performance evaluation practices.

FINISHING TOUCHES

Continuing Education Credits

You may find it worthwhile to investigate continuing education credit qualifications with the state board of nursing and other professional certification organizations. Participation in the guest relations program may qualify employees for CEU credit.

Certificates

If you distribute certificates to participants following their participation in the guest relations program, these can be designed and printed with your program identity. Certificates are meaningful awards, especially to employees who do not frequently attend workshops.

Evaluations

Evaluation forms distributed to participants at the conclusion of the program will provide you with useful feedback. In designing an evaluation, use statements to which participants can register agreement or disagreement, and provide ample space for them to write in comments.

Distribute a feedback report weekly or monthly to members of administration and the steering committee. It is especially important to note recurring themes in the employee evaluations. You may include such comments as the following:

- "I believe administration should come and work on the patient floors periodically so that they can fully understand the stress and problems that occur because of lack of staff."

Exhibit 15-3 Evaluation Form

Care.

Employee Feedback Report

Employee: _____ Department: _____

Job Title and Classification: _____ Date: _____

Directions

Indicate the level of improvement for each of the following areas in which improvement goals were established (Refer to the employee's "You Make The Difference" Form.) Use "N/O - N/A" for those items which:

1. You have not had an opportunity to observe the employee's performance.
2. Do not apply to the employee's work responsibilities.
3. Were not established as improvement objectives.

		Exceptional Improvement	Substantial Improvement	Moderate Improvement	No Improvement	N/O N/A
1.	Personal Appearance					
2.	Appearance of Work Environment					
3.	Initial Interactions With Others (Patients, visitors, physicians, fellow employees)					
4.	Patient and Family Rights					
5.	Interpersonal Interactions With Others (Patients, visitors, physicians, fellow employees)					
6.	Interpersonal Interactions With Other in High Stress Situations (Patients, visitors, physicians, fellow employees)					
7.	Additional Factors Affecting The Hospital's Image and Reputation					
8.	Overall Rating					

What specific examples or comments do you have regarding his/her efforts to "Make A Difference"?

Comments: _____

_____

_____

What additional objectives can be set for the future? _____

_____

_____

Supervisor's Signature: _____ Employee's Signature: _____

Source: © Copyright 1985. Personal and Professional Development, Inc. Reprinted by permission.

- "Until we can break down the management versus nonmanagement barriers, we will continue to have attitude problems, no matter how many guest relations programs we present."
- "The questions I want to ask are: Where are the management people? Where are the physicians? They are the ones who should hear this."

Sharing these comments with administration will make them more aware of employees' attitudes. Keep your perspective, however. Do not let the negative comments overshadow positive comments, such as these:

- "I have a friend who is a pediatrician who comes to General Hospital. He told me he has noticed a big difference since the program. I, too, have noticed an increase in friendliness."
- "It bothers me that so many people say that the hospital does not care about them as people. They fail to see so many of the good things, including this program, that General Hospital provides for us. I hope this program will continue in some way."

Evaluations can offer important insights to the facilitators. Although most of the comments will be positive and constructive, an occasional negative comment about a facilitator can pierce pride and esteem. Remind the facilitators that they will never be able to please everyone.

The ratings can also help you identify a trainer team that may not be effective. If the evaluations are low, you are well advised to consider changing the team, pairing each with a stronger partner. You should also sit in on the session to see what guidance and support you can offer to the facilitators. Finally, the evaluations will give you important information about the value that employees attach to the program.

SUMMARY

Implementing the training program requires a great deal of planning. If you develop the content of the program internally, it will require even more time and effort. Be certain to allow yourself enough time for adequate planning. Provide the facilitators with the support they will need as well. The returns on your investment of time and energy will be gratifying!

Chapter 16

Physicians: Forging New Relationships

Today's hospital administrator, faced with the intense pressures of competition and demands of service-conscious consumers, wrestles with the dichotomy of viewing physicians as customers and as hospital representatives. Clearly, physicians are the hospital's chief customers—driving business in or out of the doors. Yet, patients rarely distinguish between physicians and hospitals as different providers of service and form their perceptions of hospital quality by how employees *and* physicians perform. A patient who is visited by the physician infrequently or who receives abrupt and uncaring treatment will often transfer his or her dissatisfaction to the hospital, rather than focus it on the physician. Likewise, because patients base their perceptions of quality more on psychosocial dimensions of care than on technical expertise, the supportive and respectful relationships they witness between physicians and employees will do more to shape an image of the hospital's quality than the expert diagnosis a physician provides or the medical procedures he or she performs effectively.

These realities pose a dilemma for the hospital administrator who must decide how and to what extent physicians should be involved in the guest relations effort. If you sidestep the issue, however, expect your employees to ask, "Where are the docs?" and thereby challenge the credibility of your commitment to quality service.

Physicians will benefit from greater awareness of the expectations of patients and family members, as well as the needs and concerns of employees. The hospital should provide the information, insights and gentle prodding to see that its physicians assume their shares of responsibility. Enhanced patient care, stronger staff-physician relations, greater cooperation, complaint and risk reduction result when physicians actively participate in creating guest satisfaction.

INVOLVING PHYSICIANS

It would appear then that physician participation in a guest relations program has the potential of being a win-win situation. Yet, creating physician support of, and participation in, guest relations is not easy, because physicians are not universally convinced of the efficacy of guest relations and the pragmatic results of responding aggressively to customer needs. Although you cannot make participation mandatory, your best approach will be to provide incentives that encourage voluntary attendance and build support.

A presentation to physicians on the topic of guest relations/patient relations should be scheduled before, or soon after, the introduction of your hospital-wide program. Many successful presentations have been scheduled in conjunction with a quarterly or annual medical staff meeting and dinner. Of course, you can also deliver the presentation at a regularly scheduled medical staff meeting or, if you are an academic medical center, at grand rounds. By using the latter method, however, you are not as likely to draw many attending physicians from the community.

To gain widespread participation, first recruit the support of several members of your medical staff. Physicians will be more attentive if they see that guest relations is embraced by respected colleagues. The chief executive officer should solicit the support and endorsement of the president of the medical staff. If you have a physician member on your steering committee, he or she should be involved in helping you develop your plan of action.

Remember that physicians are, first of all, customers. The emphasis of your approach should be to tell them what the hospital guest relations program will do for them and why you are implementing it. State the reasons in terms to which the physicians can relate.

- *Service to the physician:* Physicians generally select a hospital for its service capabilities. They seek those institutions that will support them in delivering good medicine. Your program will enhance your ability to deliver service to the physicians and will thus enhance patient care and their image with patients. You have made a commitment to customer satisfaction and recognize the physician as an important customer.
- *Mutual benefits:* Through your guest relations program, you are hoping to build greater levels of patient satisfaction, reduce grounds for complaints, and therefore reduce unnecessary time spent by physicians resolving problems.
- *Risk reduction:* Satisfied patients are less likely to sue a physician and/or a hospital.
- *Business enhancement:* Satisfied patients will tell others of their satisfaction, thereby creating practice enhancement opportunities for physicians and helping hospitals maintain high occupancy rates. Discuss the impact of positive word-of-mouth advertising in shaping hospital preference and physician preference. Nearly 48 percent of the respondents to one survey said their regular physician was recommended by a family member or acquaintance.[1]

You will enlist physicians' attention and greater levels of cooperation if you build a rational case for how patient relations will benefit them in the practice of medicine. These benefits center around making more money, reducing exposure to risks, and making their jobs easier.

Promote the Program

Market the presentation to your physicians. Develop a title and short description of your planned presentation. Promote the program by distributing fliers, mailing special letters of invitation to the physicians' offices, and placing posters in the doctors' lounge or dining room.

Another way to encourage physician participation is to promote the presentation as an introduction to a patient relations program that the hospital will later sponsor for physicians' office staffs. You can suggest that, if they want to send their employees to the program, they themselves must first participate in this introductory session. That is called dangling a carrot, but it works!

Still another tack is to include guest relations in a practice enhancement seminar that you sponsor for physicians. Today, many hospitals are assisting physicians with programs about practice management and enhancement in an effort to build physician loyalty and to attract their business. Programs that focus on internal marketing—building better relationships among the physicians, patients, and staff—support practice enhancement efforts.

Develop the Content and Approach

Most physicians are very analytical and will respond better to logic, rather than emotion. Think in terms of what motivates physicians. Why would they want to invest greater effort in building patient satisfaction?

One of the best approaches is to utilize statistical data from studies that have been conducted by physicians, medical anthropologists, and behavioral scientists. Use slides to report these findings. The following research has been compiled for your benefit in developing this approach.

What Do Patients Value in Their Relationships with Physicians?

Patients overwhelmingly cite the physicians' interest in and concern about them as the most important factor in selecting and retaining a physician. This factor is important enough to cause four out of ten consumers to say that they would switch physicians if their regular physician showed less interest in them. Women are more likely than men to use poor physician behavior as a reason to change physicians.[2]

The specific reasons why people change doctors, according to a poll by Louis Harris and Associates, Inc. and Pfizer Pharmaceuticals, are varied and are listed in Table 16-1 in order of response frequency.

These reasons point up the fact that a physician's interest and concern are interpreted through various actions. What this survey did not identify, however, was how patients arrived at their conclusions. The assumption that a physician is not knowledgeable and competent is frequently the result of actions that communicate a lack of interest and concern.

In another survey that asked respondents to identify three characteristics most descriptive of what they desired in an ''ideal'' physician, qualities that supported technical competence and the proper use of tests and medications were identified much less frequently than those suggesting the psychosocial dimensions of physicians and the caregiving process. Characteristics that patients seek most often in their physicians are identified in Table 16-2.

Although these characteristics relate specifically to what patients value most in their relationships with their personal physicians, many are certainly applicable to what patients expect from primary and consulting physicians who provide care while they are hospitalized. Those characteristics that patients feel are less desirable in their physicians are shown in Table 16-3.

In and of themselves, these characteristics are meaningless unless physicians understand the underlying expectations that are most often associated with either the ideal or undesirable characteristics. Physicians may acknowledge the impor-

---

Table 16-1 Reasons Why Patients Switch Physicians

Reasons	Percentage of Adults
Didn't spend enough time with patient	51
Wasn't friendly	42
Didn't answer questions honestly and completely	40
Treatment didn't work	38
Wasn't knowledgeable and competent	37
Didn't explain problems understandably	30
Wasn't up to date with medical advances	29
Didn't treat patient with respect	27
Wasn't always available when needed	27
Fees weren't reasonable	25
Refused to accept second opinion	10

Source: Reprinted from *Practice Marketing and Management*, p.3, with permission of the Procom Unit of American Health Consultants, © May 1986.

Table 16-2 Distribution of Ideal Physician Characteristics

Characteristic	Percentage of Total Responses
Communicative	50.00
Caring	41.30
Takes time	26.09
Listens	21.74
Friendly	21.74
Thorough	17.39
Interested	15.22
Sincere	13.04
Prompt	13.04
Careful about prescriptions	6.52
Keeps cost down	6.52
Confident	6.52
Relaxed	6.52
Family-oriented	4.35
Efficient	4.35
Takes patient or problem seriously	4.35

Source: Reprinted from "The Ideal Physician: Implications for Contemporary Hospital Marketing," by A. Feler, D.S. Gochman, and G. Stukenborg in *Journal of Health Care Marketing*, Vol. 6, No. 2, p. 20, with permission of American Marketing Association, © June 1986.

---

tance of communication in building positive relationships with patients. They may be generally much less aware of what specific behaviors contribute to the perception that they communicate effectively.

Here again, a distortion in perceptions has been demonstrated through research. In one study that recorded the interactions of more than 300 patients and their physicians, it was found that, during a visit averaging about 20 minutes, little more than 1 minute was actually spent giving information. Physicians, however, estimated that they spent nearly one-quarter of the visit providing information to the patient. When asked to estimate the patients' desire for information, 65 percent of the physicians underestimated how much information the patients wanted.[3]

Regardless of the *actual* amount of time spent asking for or providing information, physicians can use several techniques to create more satisfaction through communication. Studies have demonstrated that a physician who demonstrates sensitivity to nonverbal signals has patients who are generally more satisfied than physicians who do not demonstrate this sensitivity. The effective use of nonverbal language, such as establishing good eye contact, expressing responses facially, uttering "um-hum" every few sentences, and leaning forward, can result in patients' perceptions that the physician has spent more time with them. The

Table 16-3 Distribution of Least Ideal Physician Characteristics

Characteristic	Percentage of Total Responses
Hurried	43.48
Doesn't care	26.09
Arrogant	21.74
Inattentive	19.57
Kept waiting	17.39
Doesn't explain enough	15.22
Careless with prescriptions	15.22
Ineffective treatment	13.04
Uninterested	10.87
Reluctant	8.70
Lack of knowledge	6.52
Unprofessional	6.52
Uses big medical terms	6.52
Uncertain	6.52
Unfriendly	6.52
Too concerned with money, charges too much	6.52
Inaccurate diagnosis, inappropriate tests, based on half-answers	6.52
Inefficient	4.35
No follow-up on patient	4.35

Source: Reprinted from "The Ideal Physician: Implications for Contemporary Hospital Marketing," by A. Feler, D.S. Gochman, and G. Stukenborg in *Journal of Health Care Marketing*, Vol. 6, No. 2, p. 20, with permission of American Marketing Association, © June 1986.

amount of time a physician spends with the patient is a highly desired characteristic.[4]

The importance of communication cannot be stressed enough in light of the prevailing sense of distrust that many consumers now have of the medical profession. Many patients are predisposed to sue physicians when they do not feel they have been informed or if they have felt prevented from participating in decisions. There is no question that exploitative lawyers have encouraged a more litigious society, but one cannot ignore the role that communication plays in building respect, confidence, *and* forgiveness.

One Midwestern hospital scheduled an interesting session to reinforce the message of the importance of good communication. Former patients (although not from that hospital) were invited to participate in a focus group. In the group they were asked to respond to questions about the manner in which physicians cared for them while they were hospitalized. The candid observations offered by these former patients were recorded on videotape and later viewed by physicians. The comments and observations had a greater impact than if they had been relayed to the physicians by someone else.

In your program, go easy on terminology. Most physicians have not adopted the marketing mentality and wrestle with such terms as guest, customer, and business. You do not want to alienate the physicians and cause them to ignore your message because they have a bias against marketing.

NEW APPROACHES TO PHYSICIAN TRAINING

Although the medical education of the past was not geared to help students understand and respond to the emotional, psychological, and cultural dimensions of human behavior, increasingly medical schools today are better preparing tomorrow's students to cultivate positive relationships with patients. Harvard Medical School has recently introduced an experimental curriculum designed to produce physicians who are more humane. This New Pathway program offers a required course on ethics and an alternative course of study specifically geared to helping physicians develop a more holistic approach to medicine.

At Riverside Methodist Hospitals in Columbus, Ohio, family practice residents are trained to counsel patients. They are also provided with insights that help them understand their own personalities and communication styles and how those affect patients. Riverside's Family Practice Residency Program is an indication of the hospital's emphasis on patient/guest relations. At its foundation is the belief that employees and physicians alike can play powerful roles in creating a less stressful environment that is more conducive to healing.

As a result of new approaches in training, younger physicians will be more comfortable in giving patients more information, listening to their complaints, offering them choices, and compromising with them about treatment. Some established physicians will adapt to the changes over time. Others will become increasingly frustrated and will wrestle with the disparity between how the practice of medicine used to be and what it has become.

This frustration is one of several reasons for a prevailing sense of discontentment and disenchantment within the medical profession. In one recent research study, of physicians polled, 66 percent said they would still become physicians if they had it to do over again, but only 30 percent wanted their children to be doctors and another 33 percent actually opposed their children becoming doctors. In addition to the frustration that is provoked by more demanding patients, doctors cite these sources of their discontent—the long, expensive education, the frequency of being on call, and the red tape created by government and insurance regulations.[5]

FORGING STRONGER RELATIONSHIPS

As customers of the hospital, physicians can and should expect good service that is delivered to meet their expectations. Physicians are, in reality, the hospital's chief sales force and, as such, vitally affect its survival and future success. Yet, employees often overlook the critical roles that physicians play and rarely view them as valued customers.

Just as successful manufacturers go to great lengths to identify their customers' needs and the features of their products that will satisfy those needs, so do nurses, radiology and laboratory technologists, medical records technicians, and other employees who interact regularly with physicians need to design, market, and deliver their services to meet the needs and expectations of physicians.

In Chapter 6, the service package was discussed. The primary service package contains basic services offered to satisfy customers' primary needs. The secondary service package adds value to the service package. It often contains the little extras that provide customer comfort and convenience and distinguish the hospital's services from those offered by competitors. The characteristics of the secondary service package most strongly influence the customer's decision to purchase the service, particularly when the primary service packages offered by two competitors have relatively similar characteristics. Unless the quality of care is substantially superior at one hospital, the physician will decide to admit patients to whichever hospital provides the greatest number of desired services that are part of the secondary service package. This includes those qualified and capable employees who will extend the courtesies that make the physician's job easier and more satisfying.

The directors of those departments that serve physicians as primary customers should be particularly attentive to their needs and expectations. Managers should meet with each new physician to determine his or her needs and service requirements. As discussed in Chapter 9, physicians should be asked to provide feedback to department managers in response to questions posed periodically. Written questionnaires can also be distributed.

Building better physician/employee relations is a two-way process. Although the hospital should expect all employees to treat physicians respectfully and as valued customers, physicians must reciprocate by treating employees in kind. Many nurses who have little regard for physicians often feel that physicians have little regard for their status as professionals. They feel relegated to the position of "handmaiden" and resent the expectations that they should offer their seats to physicians who enter the nurses' station or pull charts when the physicians are capable of doing so themselves. It is regrettable that these simple courtesies have developed into symbolic gestures of servitude. On the other hand, if physicians were to be more openly receptive to, and appreciative of, the observations and suggestions of nurses, these nurses might take greater initiatives to extend these courtesies. Nurses who attempt to offer meaningful and important insights into the care of a patient, but are rebuked by a gruff physician who believes they are trespassing on his or her territory, soon learn that by keeping quiet they spare themselves much frustration. Unfortunately, the quality of care suffers, and the obvious benefit resulting from collaboration is lost.

There will always be some employees and some physicians who will never find a common meeting ground. By encouraging interaction and communication on a formal and an informal basis, however, some of these barriers can be dissolved.

Physician Liaison Programs

One personalized service that strengthens the bond between hospital and physicians is provided by a physician liaison.

What are the formal and informal communications channels between the hospital and physicians? Although physicians can express and discuss concerns and issues in a variety of committee meetings and through informal discussions with administrators and board members, these sporadic encounters do not provide effective channels for collecting early information concerning issues, problems, and trends. Soliciting feedback from physicians is worthwhile because such feedback can identify issues before they become serious problems and, thus, impediments to physician satisfaction. A physician liaison who functions in the role of soliciting feedback can help build better relations with the hospital's medical staff and other community physicians.

General Responsibilities

The physician liaison has the following responsibilities:

- Identify levels of physician satisfaction and dissatisfaction with hospital services
- Provide assistance to physicians in solving hospital-related problems
- Develop physician and office staff awareness of hospital services
- Function as the primary liaison between office (physician and staff) and the hospital
- Generate commitment, through rapport building and responsiveness, for primary use of the facility by both active and nonactive admitters
- Provide assistance to the physicians and their office staffs in areas of practice management, practice enhancement (marketing), recruitment of associates, and others

- Develop and implement plans, activities, and special services for physicians and office staffs
- Offer in-service opportunities for physicians, and provide updates on hospital programs, such as cardiac rehab, radiology, ambulatory surgery, and birthing rooms, in coordination with the director of education and training

The physician liaison can also help create better relations between the physicians and the various departments. Gathering responses to the following three questions from departments that have frequent interaction with physicians can help facilitate this process:

1. What new information about your department (procedures, policies, capabilities) would you like to have communicated to physicians?
2. Have you encountered any problems or misunderstandings with new or existing physicians or their office personnel that were due to a lack of information?
3. What information should be provided (and to whom) to eliminate future problems?

It is important to select the right person for this position because it is a challenging role. The physician liaison must have the personality and maturity to develop credibility with the physicians. He or she should also have the respect of hospital peers, problem-solving skills, and patience.

Many times, a registered nurse is selected to fulfill a liaison position at the hospital. It is of benefit if that nurse has had experience working with physicians in an administrative capacity, such as on the Utilization Review Committee or has had frequent contact with physicians in a collaborative role, perhaps as a critical care nurse. However, you may not be able to afford to hire a full-time physician liaison. This role can be assumed, and often is, by a patient representative.

Team building among physicians and those employees of departments that interact most frequently with physicians is an ambitious undertaking. The physician liaison is in the position of hearing frustrations expressed by both sides and can help facilitate greater understanding and cooperation. Yet, the relationships that exist between many physicians and the employees of departments can only be repaired and strengthened by the personal initiatives of both physicians and nurses, lab and radiology technicians, and other allied health professionals.

SUMMARY

Physicians occupy unique positions within a hospital setting, serving both as customers and, in the eyes of the patients, as integral members of the hospital team. It is beneficial to physicians and hospital staff alike to involve physicians in guest relations activities and to treat them with the courtesy and responsiveness afforded all hospital customers. In doing so, the hospital has the opportunity to forge relationships of mutual respect and cooperation between physicians and employees that will enhance the hospital's image and ensure higher quality patient care.

NOTES

1. Joyce Jensen, ''Women Generally Select Their Family's Physician,'' *Modern Healthcare* (January 31, 1986): 60-61.

2. Joyce Jensen, and Ned Miklovic, ''Consumer Satisfaction with Physicians is High,'' *Modern Healthcare* (February 14, 1986): 62-63.

3. Edward Krupat, ''A Delicate Imbalance,'' *Psychology Today* (November 1986): 24.

4. Ibid., 24-26.

5. Steven Findlay, and Dan Sperling, ''Nursing Our Health Care Relationships,'' *USA Today*.

Chapter 17

Physicians' Office Staff: Practice Promotion Partners

Concurrent with your efforts to strengthen your hospital's bond with physicians should be an effort to develop a relationship with the physicians' office staffs. Those employed by physicians are valuable sources of information and ideas on how well your hospital can deliver service more effectively to meet the needs of patients. Additionally, you can be more responsive to physicians' needs and supportive of physicians' business when you take the time to develop a personal relationship with their office staff.

Patients will often select, through word-of-mouth referrals from other satisfied patients, physicians who display personal interest, sincere concern, and genuine caring. Their decision to keep seeing a certain physician is often attributed to similar characteristics, although few patients are consciously aware that these are what influence their confidence in the physician's ability. They also build relationships with the physician's office staff over time, and the strength of these relationships cannot be underestimated. A physician who understands the value of building relationships with patients and who understands how valuable the employees are to practice-building efforts is more likely to prosper amidst the competition. The courtesy and friendliness of a physician's office staff are acknowledged to be significant factors in retention of patients, as is illustrated in Exhibit 17-1. Courtesy and responsiveness are also factors that will influence the establishment of referral relationships with other physicians.

DEVELOPING THE RELATIONSHIP

The physician liaison, a patient representative, or a designated person from the guest relations steering committee should schedule short meetings with key members of each physician's office staff. It is advisable to clear these meetings first with the physician before contacting the staff person. By doing so, you let the

Exhibit 17-1 Selecting a Physician

Choosing and Retaining a Physician

It is useful to examine the factors that influence the decisions of patients to choose and then remain with their own personal family physician. A public opinion poll revealed the following responses to these questions.

"Suppose you or a member of your family became sick and didn't have a regular doctor. If you were choosing a doctor, how important would . . . be?"

Public Opinion 1982	Very Important	Fairly Important	Not Very Important	Not At All Important
The recommendation of friends and relatives	**63%**	**26%**	**5%**	**6%**
The doctor's fees compared to other doctors in your area	38%	28%	20%	12%
The doctor's qualifications and training	89%	8%	2%	1%
Advertising that tells you about the doctor	19%	17%	29%	33%
The length of time before the doctor can see you	74%	19%	4%	2%

"How important are each of the following reasons for keeping your personal physician?"

Public Opinion 1982	Very Important	Fairly Important	Not Very Important	Not At All Important
Your personal relationship with the doctor	65%	22%	9%	4%
The doctor's fees compared to other doctors in your area	35%	34%	21%	9%
The way you are treated by the doctor's staff	**75%**	**20%**	**3%**	**1%**
The length of time before the doctor can see you	66%	26%	6%	1%
The length of time you wait in the doctor's office	51%	32%	14%	3%
Your doctor's knowledge of medicine	96%	3%	0%	0%

Source: Reprinted from *Physician and Public Attitudes on Health Care Issues* by Larry Freshnock, p. 17, with permission of American Medical Association, © 1984.

physician know that you are serious about developing a stronger relationship and becoming more responsive to his or her needs.

Solicit Feedback

When meeting with this person from the office staff, briefly explain the goals and objectives of your service program. Respond to any questions that person may have. Then, ask questions to identify any unanswered concerns or issues that should be addressed by the service program. These questions might include:

- What do your patients tell you that they liked about their experience at our hospital?
- What complaints do your patients relate about their hospitalization experience?
- Do you have any impressions, given the feedback you receive from patients, that characterize their experience at our hospital compared with other hospitals in the area?
- How can we provide better service and support to you in your practice?
- We have made up a list of several specialized services that we are considering providing. Would you review these and identify those you feel would be particularly helpful to you or to your patients?
- We have also made up a list of several topics that we are considering offering as training programs for those who work in medical practices. Which of these topics would you find helpful? Can you think of any other areas in which training would be helpful?

When you finish interviewing the person, mention that you will be calling periodically to see if he or she has identified ways in which the hospital and the physician or practice staff can work together more effectively. Leave a business card and encourage the staff member to call with any questions or ideas.

Provide On-Site Tours

Employees from physicians' offices will have more of a personal identification with the hospital if you invite them to your hospital periodically. A tour of the hospital will familiarize them with its layout and will help them communicate more clearly to patients what to expect when they are hospitalized. A tour also offers you a chance to promote your latest technology or services. Do not overlook opportunities to create the impression that your hospital is uniquely qualified to respond to the needs and concerns of patients and physicians.

Open Channels of Communication

News of new developments and services should be communicated regularly. You may want to consider publishing a simple newsletter on a quarterly basis that will inform the staff of new developments of which they should be aware.

Provide Growth Opportunities

Take advantage of opportunities to sponsor worthwhile and interesting programs that will encourage the employees' personal and professional development. You can assist your physicians in building stronger relationships with patients by sponsoring a patient relations program for office staff. This program can be offered to admitting physicians on your medical staff. You may want to extend the program to those physicians who do not admit frequently to your hospital, but whose loyalty and business you would like to cultivate. A private physician's ability to provide this type of training is limited, so your efforts will be appreciated by those who recognize its value.

DESIGNING A PATIENT RELATIONS PROGRAM

Just as your hospital guest relations program's structure and content are influenced by your institution's specific needs, so will a patient relations program be developed to meet the specific needs of your physicians.

What do you hope to accomplish? Certainly, you will want to provide a program that will enhance the employees' effectiveness in dealing with patients. What specific program components will achieve that objective? Beyond that, what can you include that will enable the participant to identify more strongly with your hospital?

A checklist of questions that should be answered before developing the program might include:

- How long will the program be?
- On what days and at what times will it be offered?
- Who should be invited?
- How many can be accommodated per session?

- How many sessions will be necessary to accommodate the expected attendance?
- Who will conduct the program sessions?
- What topics will be included?
- How will we publicize the program?
- What refreshments or meals should be served?
- What follow-up will occur after the sessions?

The structure of the patient relations program will be influenced by what is a realistic length of time that employees can be away from the office practice. This factor will also influence the days and times on which you offer the program. Because many offices are closed on Wednesday or Thursday afternoons, you may find that sessions scheduled on either of those days will enable the greatest number of employees to attend.

In all probability, you will have a wide representation of medical specialties at each of the sessions. The employees of primary physicians may be very different from those who work in the offices of specialty physicians. In addition, office employees will have diverse job responsibilities. Topics that address scheduling of patients may benefit a receptionist, but be of little interest to a nurse. For that reason, the content of the program should appeal to a diverse group of participants. You may want to offer specific follow-up programs to address practice management techniques, such as collection and scheduling practices. These types of sessions are generally of specific interest to those who function as office managers within the practice.

Ask selected members from your admitting staff and other key departments that have contact with physicians and their staffs to become involved in planning the program. Because they are the ones who most frequently interact with employees of the doctors' offices, they should be available to welcome the participants to the sessions. It is also a good idea to invite the president of your hospital or another key executive to make a few introductory remarks at the sessions. This special welcome will impress those who participate.

Developing the Content

The content of the program should focus on developing the specific skills that will enable the employees to interact more effectively with patients and visitors. Initially, however, an awareness of why the program is important should be created. To what degree are the participants aware of changes that have affected the practice of medicine and the delivery of health care? Do they understand the term "marketing?" Are they aware of their roles in the "internal marketing" of the practice?

Introduction

The exercises shown in Exhibits 17-2 and 17-3 are specifically designed to introduce rudimentary marketing concepts and to present a marketing orientation to the participants. The information contained in these and all subsequent exercises is presented to reinforce the mutually beneficial goals that can be achieved when physicians and their staffs develop effective partnerships—with patients, family members of patients, referring physicians, and with the hospital.

Exhibit 17-2 Marketing Professional Services

Partners in Marketing
_____

Marketing was once a foreign term to many health care professionals. In recent years, however, dramatic changes have affected the way in which health care providers operate their businesses and think about their customers. The ways in which medical services are developed, promoted and delivered have undergone transformation. Marketing has become a respected and legitimate strategy for recruiting and retaining customers.

What is Marketing?
_____

Marketing focuses on the strategies and processes which satisfy customers' needs, desires and expectations.

Marketing is:
☐ a product strategy
☐ a pricing strategy
☐ a placement strategy
☐ a promotion strategy
☐ a positioning strategy

Marketing is not:
☐ advertising
☐ sales
☐ public relations
☐ direct mail
☐ publicity

Who are Your Customers?
_____

As a partner, you play an important role in marketing the practice and satisfying the needs and expectations of your customers. Identify your customers in the spaces provided.

_____   _____

_____   _____

_____   _____

Source: Reprinted from *Partners*, K.E. Peterson & Associates, Chicago, Illinois, © 1985.

Exhibit 17-3 Test Your Marketing Awareness

Many factors influence consumer behavior and decision making. In addition, they encourage competition and the need for marketing. How well do you understand these? Respond to the following questions by checking the appropriate box.

	True	False
1. It is predicted that there will be a surplus of 70,000 physicians by the end of the decade.	☐	☐
2. Most patients cannot evaluate the quality of medical care which they receive. Their evaluation is influenced to a greater degree by the human care which is delivered.	☐	☐
3. Today, patients are better informed and more participative in decisions that affect their health and their health care.	☐	☐
4. By the end of the decade, it is predicted that 1,000 of America's 7,000 hospitals will have to close because of lack of business.	☐	☐
5. A patient's predisposition to sue a physician or a hospital is influenced by courtesy and respect.	☐	☐
6. A satisfied patient will recommend your practice to approximately 4 to 5 other people.	☐	☐
7. A dissatisfied patient will tell approximately 9 to 10 other people about his dissatisfaction.	☐	☐
8. Marketing is just another "fad" and will fade away in a couple of months.	☐	☐
9. Physicians who are just starting out need to worry about marketing, but we have loyal and satisfied patients who will carry us through.	☐	☐
10. Marketing data suggests that it costs about five times as much to get a new customer as it does to keep an existing one.	☐	☐
11. The introduction of ambulatory/emergency care clinics was in response to consumer demand for convenience.	☐	☐
12. "Friendliness with colleagues" is the factor most frequently cited when physicians are asked why they refer patients to certain specialty physicians.	☐	☐

Source: Reprinted from *Partners*, K.E. Peterson & Associates, Chicago, Illinois, © 1985.

First Impressions

First impressions are created both visually and verbally. How does the appearance of the physician's office influence the patient's overall perception about the quality of care that is delivered? What is revealed about the values of the business? Signs about payment policies, cancellation policies, and accepted charge cards posted near the reception area leave most patients with the impression that, in that office, it is more blessed to give than to receive. The presence of 2-year-old well-worn magazines may cause the patient to question whether the physician is keeping up with medical journals and professional matters. Closed, frosted sliding glass reception windows with buzzers hardly leave the patient with the impression that he or she is welcome. Ask participants to list ways that the appearance and atmosphere of their office and exam rooms could be improved.

Personal Appearance

Just as the image of the practice is influenced by the warmth and appearance of the office, the professional image of employees is shaped by similar standards. Ask participants to identify specific characteristics that either "make" or "break" a professional image. Specific responses should be offered for the following categories: uniform, dress, hose, shoes, makeup, hair, jewelry and "other."

Telephone Courtesy

First impressions are also created over the telephone. How many times does the phone ring before it is answered? How is the phone answered? Are callers put on hold for exceptionally long periods of time? Is the image of the practice, as it is conveyed over the telephone, a positive one? It is important to discuss the importance of telephone courtesy in creating positive first and lasting impressions.

The topic of telephone courtesy may encourage discussion of how the telephone can be used to position the practice effectively. How many practices presently encourage follow-up telephone calls by the nurse the day after a patient's visit to ask if the patient is feeling better, if he or she has any questions and if the prescription was filled and to remind the patient of special instructions on taking the medication or following the treatment regimen?

This can also be a time to suggest "telephone tips" that will help staff members manage their volume of telephone calls. Do they politely discourage patients from making routine prescription refill or routine appointment requests on Monday mornings and Friday afternoons? Do they inform the patient when it is most likely that the physician will return the telephone call? How are patient telephone calls screened? The question, "What *seems* to be the problem?," may solicit the desired response, but it is often resented by patients whose symptoms are more than imaginary.

Communication Skills

Many of the telephone tips suggested above are simply communication techniques. This topic can be expanded to include other exercises that will create greater awareness of the importance of communicating effectively with patients. What specific statements, gestures, and activities leave the patient with a negative impression? How can every employee communicate more effectively? What role does listening play in effective communication? The exercise included in Exhibit 17-4 is an excellent way to reinforce the importance of listening.

Conflict Resolution

Every employee can benefit from a discussion of complaint resolution techniques. By role playing common complaint situations, you can reinforce skills that will be useful to employees in the situations they encounter in their practice.

Stress Management

Meeting the needs of others, as well as their own, can be stressful to employees. Their effectiveness is often determined by how they respond to the challenging demands of their roles.

Exhibit 17-4 Analyze Your Listening Skills

Listening requires active involvement. It is not a passive skill. Please respond to the statements below to identify the degree to which you practice effective listening skills.

	Always	Sometimes	Never
I concentrate on the message which is being delivered	☐	☐	☐
I save time by doing other things while someone is talking	☐	☐	☐
I make a special effort to stay calm when someone is irate	☐	☐	☐
I avoid distractions while another person is talking	☐	☐	☐
I maintain good eye-contact with the speaker	☐	☐	☐
I avoid making premature judgments about a speaker based on my individual prejudices	☐	☐	☐
I try to use facial expressions to confirm my interest	☐	☐	☐
I listen for the feelings the speaker is expressing	☐	☐	☐
I interrupt a speaker to get clarification of points	☐	☐	☐
I am usually thinking about what I am going to say next while someone is talking to me	☐	☐	☐
I appear rushed or impatient while someone else is speaking	☐	☐	☐
I find it difficult to concentrate because I have a lot on my mind	☐	☐	☐
I have to ask others to repeat what they said because I get distracted easily	☐	☐	☐
I get frustrated because it takes others a long time to express simple things	☐	☐	☐

Source: Reprinted from *Partners*, K.E. Peterson & Associates, Chicago, Illinois, © 1985.

Controlling distressful reactions to stressors begins with controlling perceptions. Although one cannot always control what happens, the interpretation of events and how one reacts can be consciously influenced. The exercises in Exhibits 17-5 and 17-6 will help employees identify the degree to which they are experiencing distress and unhealthy perceptions. Employees should be encouraged to offer their own methods of coping with stress, in addition to those provided.

Helpful Tips and Reminders

Your program can provide helpful tips and reminders to employees. For example, in wanting to be friendly, some employees do too much. Several years ago, an editorial appeared in the Chicago Tribune that brought into focus one senior citizen's objection to being called ''Charles'' by those he did not know. This editorial, reprinted in Exhibit 17-7, is worthy of sharing in a patient relations program.

Although employees should be encouraged to call patients by their last names unless they know the patients well, it is interesting to note that the same rule does not necessarily apply to physicians. A survey found that, although 74 percent of patients preferred to address physicians by title and last name, just 18 percent wanted physicians to call them by their last names.[1]

If time allows, you can include a section on practice promotion. This particular segment of the program is devoted to exploring ways in which the practice can be ''legitimately'' promoted. Because few physicians feel that advertising is a legitimate way to promote business, tips on other promotional approaches are useful in stimulating ideas. These include the following approaches:

Brainstorming Sessions. Operational barriers to patient satisfaction, such as policies, procedures, and inadequate services, do exist. Encourage employees to identify recurring questions and complaints, policies that the patients do not understand, and ineffective procedures and services. These can then be discussed in monthly staff meetings. Brainstorming and creative problem solving will produce positive changes. Rigid adherence to the way ''we have always done things around here'' is ineffective in creating necessary changes to meet the evolving expectations of patients.

New Patient Packets. The office computer can be used to generate a professional-looking, well-written personalized letter that is used to welcome new patients. With this letter, which is *personally* signed by the physician, a practice brochure and/or newsletter can be included.

Suggestion Boxes. How many offices encourage patients to offer their suggestions on how the practice can meet their needs and exceed their expectations? This suggestion box can also be the depository for a patient satisfaction survey.

Exhibit 17-5 Stress Test

Self-Assessment

Respond to the following statements by circling the number which indicates the level of your agreement.

		Strongly Disagree			Strongly Agree	
1.	I am very forgetful	1	2	3	4	5
2.	It seems I can never get enough sleep	1	2	3	4	5
3.	No one really understands me	1	2	3	4	5
4.	There's not much I can do about my problems	1	2	3	4	5
5.	I frequently feel irritable without a reason	1	2	3	4	5
6.	I find it difficult to make decisions	1	2	3	4	5
7.	Others are to blame for many of my problems	1	2	3	4	5
8.	I'm embarrassed by things I do and say	1	2	3	4	5
9.	I'm not happy with my job	1	2	3	4	5
10.	I'm afraid of meeting new people	1	2	3	4	5
11.	I have many acquaintances but few friends	1	2	3	4	5
12.	I often wish I were someone else	1	2	3	4	5
13.	I am afraid to try new things	1	2	3	4	5
14.	I worry about financial matters	1	2	3	4	5
15.	I am unfairly criticized	1	2	3	4	5
16.	I feel that I am a failure	1	2	3	4	5
17.	I feel inferior to other people	1	2	3	4	5
18.	I distrust people who say nice things	1	2	3	4	5
19.	When I am criticized, I feel defensive	1	2	3	4	5
20.	I don't seem to be getting anywhere	1	2	3	4	5
21.	I worry a lot	1	2	3	4	5
22.	It really makes me mad when I make a mistake	1	2	3	4	5
23.	If I had more money I would be happy	1	2	3	4	5
24.	I wish I could move somewhere and start over	1	2	3	4	5
25.	My relationship with my family is strained	1	2	3	4	5

Add up the number values. If they equal more than 78, you are probably dealing with a high level of stress. If they equal more than 100, you are not only experiencing stress, you are approaching a state known as "burnout." Burnout occurs when stressors inhibit your ability to enjoy your job, your family and friends, your life.

Some of the above statements indicate evidence of burnout. Are you forgetful? Do you have a difficult time concentrating? Sleeping? Or do you want to sleep too much? Other statements identify perceptions that can be changed.

Source: Reprinted from *Partners*, K.E. Peterson & Associates, Chicago, Illinois, © 1985.

Exhibit 17-6 Coping with Stress

Changing Perceptions

Recognize healthy perceptions and unhealthy perceptions. Work to change your attitude.

- ☐ If I make the "wrong" decision, what's the worse consequence?
- ☐ I'm not someone else, I'm me.
- ☐ Moving somewhere else and starting over would not accomplish anything.
- ☐ I may make mistakes, but then—who doesn't?
- ☐ When people say nice things they are probably sincere.
- ☐ Others are not to blame for my problems, I must take the responsibility.
- ☐ I am not helpless. I have the power to change.
- ☐ Worrying won't change the situation.

Twelve Ways To Cope with Stress

1. Change how you perceive things. A positive outlook uplifts the spirits and reinforces healthy thoughts.
2. Learn to let go. Recognize your limitations and acknowledge that there are some things that you cannot change.
3. Don't forget to laugh at yourself. Taking yourself and your life too seriously can be very stressful.
4. Listen to your inner voice and view yourself positively. Don't criticize yourself to the point of diminishing your self-esteem.
5. Introduce yourself to new places and people. New experiences and interactions increase your energy level.
6. Show others you care. Listen to them. Stress is reduced when you compare your problems with those of others.
7. Say "no" to activities that don't really interest you. When you are assertive, you are in control.
8. Exercise at least three times a week. Walk around the block. Join an aerobics class. Learn to play racquetball.
9. Eat a balanced diet to ensure that stress will not invade because your physical defenses are weakened.
10. Establish time for yourself to indulge. A long bath. A book. A craft or hobby. If you make the time, you can do it.
11. Live in the present. Don't get consumed with the dead past or the imaginary future.
12. Establish goals and work toward them. What are life-time goals? What are short-term goals?

Remember: It is difficult to meet the needs of others if you are not effective in responding to your own needs!

Source: Reprinted from *Partners*, K.E. Peterson & Associates, Chicago, Illinois, © 1985.

Exhibit 17-7 A Patient Speaks Out

On Friday morning the telephone rang.

"This is Dr. Edward's office calling to confirm that Charles has an appointment for Tuesday afternoon at 3:30."

I am no friend of this nameless receptionist or even an acquaintance of Dr. Edward, the dentist. I will go, but shouldn't someone have the courage to tell the dentists and the doctors and especially those young people who always seem to be in charge of senior citizen activities that people my age do not like to be called by their first name by people they do not know? This treatment seems demeaning and patronizing to one over 60.

Stop it! We hate it! In our day the use of first names indicated close friendship, and if and until that developed, one spoke with respect to Mr. & Mrs. Whoever. We older people wish to preserve all dignity possible, and such cheap chumminess surely destroys it.

Last winter while we were in a southwest Arizona town without a hospital, my wife had a heart attack. Two young, male paramedics in an ambulance drove her 20 miles to St. Mary's Hospital in Tucson, where she remained in the emergency room for approximately four hours while her condition was stabilized, and then she was taken to the cardiovascular intensive care unit.

"During the entire time," she told me with great appreciation afterward, "nobody called me Eva. I was always Mrs. Hampton. I was made to feel adult, competent and worthy of respect. In my fear and uncertainty and inability to function, this was a great support."

There is a young assistant in my doctor's large medical center office who takes me in routinely to have my weight and blood pressure checked before I am given a room in which to wait for the doctor. The next time she says to me, "Charles, step on the scale, please," I swear I am going to say, "Don't call me Charles!"

Source: Reprinted with permission of Charles F. Hampton.

Get-Acquainted Interviews. Growing in popularity among those physicians who are beginning new practices, the get-acquainted interviews are offered at no charge to the patient. These brief sessions enable the patient to determine whether he or she is comfortable with the physician's style and demeanor.

List Purchases. More prevalent among new practices, but certainly useful to all who are serious about recruiting new patients, is the practice of purchasing lists of new utility customers or "welcome wagon" lists that identify new families to the community. These provide names of prospects to whom introductory letters can be sent at a relatively low cost.

Thank You Notes. Whether communicated on preprinted postcards or in hand-written notes, the expression of appreciation to patients who refer new patients to the practice does not go unnoticed. Some physicians will even send bouquets of flowers to those patients who make multiple referrals to the practice. An expression of thanks should be forwarded to referring physicians on a regular basis as well.

Patient Profiles. Demographic and other characteristics, such as age, gender, zip code, average number of annual visits, referral sources, third party payers, and other information can be stored in a computer. This data can be useful to the practice that plans to develop a marketing plan.

Chart Notations. Information about patients' hobbies or special preferences can be included in the patient's record. Even those who visit their primary physician once a year or less frequently feel that the doctor/patient relationship is nonetheless special. Notations in the patient's chart about personal details will help the physician and staff remember the little things that make patients feel they are special.

Surveys. Surveys designed to provide the practice with additional information about patients' preferences and to query patients on what services would be desired can be useful. The staff can distribute these surveys in the office and personally ask patients to complete them, or they can mail surveys to a random sample of patients with a postage-paid envelope enclosed for its return. The surveys should be kept short and simple and can include such questions as the following:

- How do you usually get to the office?
- If by car, how long is the drive?
- Are our parking facilities adequate?
- Would you be willing to pay $1.00 to $2.00 for a convenient parking place?
- Are our office hours convenient?
- If we could extend our hours, what times would suit you best?
- How long have you been a patient in our practice?
- What aspect(s) of our practice do you feel we could improve?
- What do we do or what services do we provide that are particularly valued by you?

Screenings. Just as many hospitals participate in health fairs by offering initial screenings for diabetes, high blood pressure, colon-rectal cancer, and other problems, physicians and office staffs can also participate in these activities. Of course, if your hospital currently sponsors these types of screenings, it is doubtful that you will want to go out of your way to encourage physicians to do them on their own!

PROMOTING THE PROGRAM

You will need to market your office staff program both to physicians and to their employees. Because you must sell physicians on the benefits of their employees' participation, begin with communications that are directed to the physicians. Although physicians may initially express interest in this type of program, many will be cautious when it comes time to approve their employees' attendance. A letter from the hospital's chief executive officer, physician liaison, and/or medical staff president introducing the program can serve as the first announcement (Exhibit 17-8). Follow with a short presentation at a medical staff meeting. If you have the budget to do so, develop a brochure to promote the program.

Franciscan Health Care, Inc. in Milwaukee, Wisconsin, sponsored a patient relations program for more than 600 physicians' office staff members in the fall of 1986. They did an excellent job of promoting the program to area physicians. The promotional brochure is shown in Exhibit 17-9.

Exhibit 17-8 New Program Announcement

October 1, 1987

Dear Dr. Lopez:

Consumer research has shown repeatedly that the most important way to build and maintain a strong medical practice is to ensure that each and every patient who visits is left with an impression of respect and concern.

According to a published opinion poll sponsored by the American Medical Association, "the way you are treated by the doctor's staff" was cited as being a very important reason for keeping their personal physician by 75 percent of the respondents.

Your employees are important partners in building the success of your practice. General Hospital is pleased to be able to offer a unique opportunity for your office staff. We will sponsor a patient relations program workshop that will optimize your staff's personal and professional effectiveness in responding to patients' needs and expectations.

A brochure describing this program in greater detail will be arriving in a couple of days. We've scheduled the sessions at times that will be convenient for your staff to attend. They will be held at the hospital during the week of November 5th.

For more information, please do not hesitate to call Tim Carter, Director of Public Relations, at extension 497.

We hope you will support and encourage your staff's attendance.

Sincerely,

Hospital President

Exhibit 17-9 Patient Relations Program

PARTNERS: A PATIENT RELATIONS PROGRAM

One of the most effective ways to enhance your position in today's competitive health care environment is to ensure that each patient coming into contact with employees is left with a positive impression.

"Partners: A Patient Relations Program" is a four-hour seminar developed especially for physicians' office staffs. Seminar participants will learn how to become more "patient-oriented" through discussions on:

- First Impressions
- Reception
- Office Decor
- Employee Attitudes
- Employee Appearance
- Listening skills
- Verbal/Non-verbal Communication
- Telephone Courtesy
- Resolving Complaints
- Skills to Build Rapport & Respect
- Stress Management
- Personal Effectiveness

TIMES & PLACES

Participants can enroll in any one of the six half-day sessions:

- **Wed., Nov. 5, 1986**
St. Michael Hospital,
Franciscan Room
7:30 a.m.-Noon **OR** 1:00-5:30 p.m.

- **Thur., Nov. 6, 1986**
St. Joseph's Hospital, Rathskeller
7:30 a.m.-Noon **OR** 1:00-5:30 p.m.

- **Fri. Nov. 7, 1986**
Elmbrook Memorial Hospital,
Auditorium
7:30 a.m.-Noon **OR** 1:00-5:30 p.m.

Rosemary Marks

SPEAKER

Seminar speaker Rosemary Marks is a management consultant with K.E. Peterson & Associates, a nationally recognized, Chicago-based consulting firm which provides programs and services to health care institutions interested in developing and implementing patient-oriented management strategies and guest relations programs.

A graduate of Virginia Commonwealth University, Marks has a bachelor's degree in mass communications with a specialization in hospital public relations. Her past experience as a public relations practitioner includes market research, planning and implementation, as well as development and fund raising.

WHO SHOULD ATTEND

The seminar is open to office managers and staff of physicians affiliated with Elmbrook Memorial, St. Joseph's and St. Michael hospitals.

REGISTRATION & FEE

The fee is $5 per person and includes all conference materials and breakfast or lunch. To register, please complete the form printed in this brochure and mail it with a check made payable to Franciscan Health Care, Inc., to: PARTNERS, c/o Planning and Marketing, Franciscan Health Care, Inc., 3029 N. 49th St., Milwaukee, WI 53210. You will receive confirmation of your registration.

Please register by October 24. Enrollment is limited.

SPONSOR

PARTNERS is one in a series of practice enhancement programs sponsored by Franciscan Health Care, Inc.

A subsidiary of Wheaton Franciscan Services, Inc., Franciscan Health Care has four member organizations in the greater Milwaukee area: Elmbrook Memorial Hospital in Brookfield, St. Joseph's and St. Michael hospitals in Milwaukee, and Franciscan Home Health, Inc., a Milwaukee-based home health agency.

FOR FURTHER INFORMATION...

Contact the Medical Staff Coordinator at one of the Wheaton Franciscan hospitals:

- Elmbrook Memorial, 785-2031
- St. Michael, 527-5006
- St. Joseph's, 447-2197.

PARTNERS: A PATIENT RELATIONS PROGRAM

Please complete one registration form per person. If additional forms are needed, please duplicate.

Name _____ Title _____

Physician's Name _____

Physician's Hospital Affiliation(s) _____

Office/Clinic Name & Address _____

City _____ State _____ Zip _____ Phone _____

Session Preference (Check One)	Nov. 5	St. Michael	☐ 7:30-Noon	or	☐ 1:00-5:30
	Nov. 6	St. Joseph's	☐ 7:30-Noon	or	☐ 1:00-5:30
	Nov. 7	Elmbrook Memorial	☐ 7:30-Noon	or	☐ 1:00-5:30

I am unable to attend this seminar but would be interested in future practice enhancement, planning or marketing seminars. Suggested topics: _____

Please enclose with a check for $5 made payable to Franciscan Health Care, Inc. and return by October 24 to: PARTNERS, c/o Franciscan Health Care, Inc., Planning & Marketing, 3029 N. 49th St., Milwaukee, WI 53210.

Source: Courtesy of Franciscan Health Care, Inc., Milwaukee, Wisconsin.

SUMMARY

Physician office staffs are important customers of the hospital and can serve as advocates of the hospital. The hospital can strengthen relationships with this important group by building relationships with its members. By soliciting regular feedback, providing on-site tours, and offering meaningful programs and services to employees of physicians' offices, the hospital can strengthen its relationship with physicians as well.

NOTES

1. Joselyn Dunn et al., "Patients and House Officer Attitudes of Physician and Attitude," *Journal of the American Medical Association* (January 2, 1987): 65-68.

Chapter 18

Written Communications: Sending the Service Message

An organization communicates values through a variety of channels. Leaders can easily declare their values, but the veracity of their statements is certainly challenged when other statements, actions, and written communications do not support that which they profess.

The "grapevine," the ever-active, influential, and highly interpretive channel of communication present in any organization, becomes the most lively when other official channels of communication are nonexistent or vaguely defined. The grapevine will never die, but it can support rather than contradict important messages.

The most prominent evidence of whether you are clearly communicating and reinforcing your organizational values is found in your written communications. Over time, however, it is easy to become blind to how they shape and reinforce people's perceptions. A degree of objectivity can be lost when these familiar communications routinely pass before you. For example, you may quickly skim the employee newsletter and occasionally glance at the employee handbook. Although you may have been obsessed with dotting every "i" and crossing every "t" when the proposed patient handbook was presented for your first review, in all probability you have failed to scrutinize the content and style of the publication since it was printed.

Do not ignore your written publications! They are pervasive and may communicate messages that are contrary to what you would like them to be. Although you cannot control everything that is written, you can carefully review your widely distributed publications to assess the degree to which they reinforce and complement, or scramble and distort, the messages you are trying to promote.

EMPLOYEE PUBLICATIONS

Employee Newsletter

Pull the past 12 issues of your employee newsletter from the archives. Grab a cup of coffee, sit down, and spend the next several hours rereading those newsletters. To what degree do the articles that are featured in those issues support what you say you value? After completing each issue, ask yourself the question: "Given what I've read, what would I say is important to this hospital?"

The answer to that question will be determined by the content of the articles and the amount of space devoted to each story. Reading these newsletters can be rather tedious, but it is a valuable exercise. The length of the articles in column inches in the December issues of two different employee newsletters is compared in Exhibit 18-1. Both newsletters were approximately the same size and number of pages, but note their different focuses.

Whereas General Medical Center spent more space on research breakthroughs, promotions, and donations, Community Medical Center devoted more space to human interest stories, employee recognition, and guest relations awareness and skill building.

An academic medical center is likely to dedicate more coverage to research breakthroughs and physician contributions than will a nonteaching hospital. Yet, both of the publications featured in Exhibit 18-1 are from academic medical centers of similar size and scope, but their newspapers say something very different. One is clearly more "high tech"; the other is "high touch."

You might want to conduct a readership survey to see just how many of your employees find the articles in your newsletter to be interesting. Do they read the articles? What do they enjoy and benefit from the most? You may have political reasons for including many of the articles, but a newsletter that does not meet the needs of its intended readers is not of real value to your institution. Given the choice, Dan Rather might possibly want to devote more time to foreign affairs and other issues that "really matter," but news directors discovered long ago that if they were to attract the lion's share of the viewing public, they had to balance the hard news with soft features.

Included in the "soft" category of published articles are those that reinforce the importance of customer satisfaction and strengthen awareness of the organization's values. To accomplish those objectives, the following suggestions are provided:

Share Your Vision

Where is the hospital going? How will you get there? Facts and figures help tell the story. You can list comparative census statistics from year to year to remind employees that, in addition to declining resources, inpatient admissions and patient days are declining. Let them know why these changes are occurring. Educate employees about the impact of alternative delivery centers, prospective payment, and joint ventures. Few may hold MBAs, but most have some interest in the future direction of their employer.

Exhibit 18-1 Newsletter Audit

Community Medical Center

Hanson Discusses Medical Center's Goals: 15 inches
Thanks!—United Way Goal Met: 15 inches
Board of Trustees Elects Officers: 7.5 inches
Length of Stay Remains Stable: 3.5 inches
New Breakthrough in Diabetes Control by Dr. Stable: 10 inches
When Guests Complain: 4 inches
Telephone Tips: 7.5 inches
Employee of the Month: 7.5 inches
Employees Recognized by Patients: 15 inches
New Ideas for Patient Care and Comfort: 15 inches
New Faces at Medical Center: 15 inches
Auxiliary Members Organize Toys for Tots: 7.5 inches
Auxiliary Donates Transportation Van: 7.5 inches
Swenson Retires after 30 Years: 7.5 inches
Medical Center Receives Grant: 7.5 inches
Employees Caught in the Act: 5 inches
For Your Health—Stress Reducers: 10 inches
Administrative Resident Named: 5 inches
Louise Oster Turns Tragedy into Triumph: 15 inches

General Medical Center

United Way Campaign Appeal: 15 inches
In-vitro Fertilization Breakthrough by Dr. West: 30 inches
35-Year Service Award to Henry Stump: 7.5 inches
Dr. Westerland Retiring: 15 inches
Blue Cross and Medical Center Join Together: 15 inches
Hospital Bowling League Wins Second Place: 5 inches
Hospital Receives $30,000 Grant for Study: 15 inches
Gomez Named Employee of the Month: 7.5 inches
New Vice President-Finance Named: 10 inches
Service League Donates $30,000: 15 inches
Cholesterol-Conscious Recipes: 20 inches
Letters from Patients: 15 inches
New Tax Laws: 10 inches
Haskins Promoted to Vice President of Development: 8 inches

Relate and Update Guest Relations Activities

What is the status of your guest relations program? In what direction are you now moving? Be certain that you use the newsletter to communicate what is going on behind the scenes to show your ongoing commitment to the service program.

Include Awareness and Behavior Reinforcers

Every issue should contain tips and techniques that will reinforce effective contact skills and keep employees focused on their roles in creating satisfaction. You can select a multitude of topics, from teamwork to telephone tips, complaint resolution skills to stress management skills, and professional appearance to confidentiality. Keep on the lookout for new statistics and market research that will provide insights into customer expectations and market trends. One newspaper that regularly features interesting tidbits of information on patient expectations is *USA Today*.

Whenever you are reading a periodical, viewing television or a movie, or talking with a friend, a sentence, paragraph, quotation, or anecdote may strike you as being insightful, profound, absurd, or interesting. If you can translate the thought or interpret the message in the context of service, it may inspire new awareness and insight for someone whose senses have become dull. Be on the lookout for those phrases that reveal truths.

Provide Human Interest

Feature patients who are willing to have their stories told, and tell those stories in a way that will provide insights into their needs and expectations. Share their gratitude for employees' care and concern. Exalt their triumphs over disease in order to reinforce employees' sense of pride and purpose. Introduce new employees, physicians, *and* volunteers with photographs and short descriptions of their past experiences, families, hobbies, etc., if space allows.

Recognize Employees Who Contribute

Share patients' appreciation as expressed in their letters to the president and their comments on the questionnaires and over the telephone. Identify employees who are "caught in the act" of caring. Applaud employees who go the extra mile. When you feature your "Employee of the Month" and other employees who may be honored for length of service, focus on their personal values that parallel your organizational values.

Celebrate Ideas and Innovations

Continually identify what you are doing to make the hospital a better place for patients, physicians, employees, and volunteers. Recognize those employees who contribute their ideas and suggestions. Focus on how departments are excelling in service delivery, solving problems, and becoming more innovative.

Orient Employees to Other Departments

Every department is important. Provide your readers with an orientation to each department's functions and how each contributes to guest relations.

Employee Handbook

After you review the newsletters, study a copy of your employee handbook. Read it carefully. How warmly do you welcome new employees? Do you clearly communicate your expectations of appearance and actions? Do you state that service is important in your hospital? Do you otherwise state your mission and values? Be mindful of how you state the messages. If you discover a proliferation of "You should not," "You cannot," "You will not," and "Do not" phrases, is the style too dictatorial? Rephrase the sentences to retain their emphasis but to lighten the tone. Commands may work well in the military, but you are not supervising a battalion of soldiers.

PHYSICIAN PUBLICATIONS

If you publish a newsletter for physicians, do you include information about guest relations? Inform your physicians about your program and your continuing commitment to care for the patients they entrust to you.

Include information that may be of interest and value to physicians in the care and treatment of patients. You do not want to "preach" the gospel of service to your physicians through the newsletter, but there is nothing wrong with including factual and important information about communication techniques and other patient/physician or physician/employee relations topics. It is particularly effective to include outcomes of research studies that more clearly indicate patient expectations. For example, in 1986, several physicians from Harvard Medical School conducted a study on patients' expectations of physician appearance. The survey of 200 patients revealed that patients want physicians to look like physicians. Sixty-five percent of the patients said physicians should wear white coats. Fifty-three percent disapproved of physicians wearing jeans, and twenty-seven percent disliked them wearing sneakers. If you summarize and report this research in your physician newsletter, you can subtly remind them that their credibility is undermined by informal or inappropriate attire.[1]

PATIENT PUBLICATIONS

Patient Handbook

Pick up a copy of your patient handbook. As you read it, ask yourself, "If I were a patient, would I get the impression that the hospital cared about me as a person?" Do the words used communicate a commitment to the quality of medical and human care? Do the design, layout, and content of the handbook communicate warmth and concern?

Questionnaire

Although it is not necessary to include much narrative copy on a questionnaire, a short statement that expresses your concern for the patient's well-being and your sincere interest in learning how well you have satisfied their needs is appropriate. The message can motivate people to respond.

A core value at Marriott Corporation is guest satisfaction. This is such a pervasive value that Marriott officials have invested heavily to make certain that they receive the feedback from guests that will help them monitor the degree to which each of their 170-plus properties is successful in meeting guest expectations.

For years, a Marriott slogan was "We Do It Right." Communicated in advertisements, on the covers of matchbooks, on brochures and buttons, this slogan reinforced Marriott's pledge and commitment to please its guests. The slogan eventually found its way onto the front cover of their questionnaire. "We Do It Right. Right?" was the question asked of guests. The questionnaire sat atop the dresser, inviting a response.

Then one day, the title was changed. From the powerful statement followed by a challenging question, it became a gentle inquiry from a man recognized as a champion of excellence, Bill Marriott, Jr. On the front of the questionnaire now appeared the question, "Will You Let Me Know?"

Marriott Corporation's Office of Consumer Affairs monitors the impressive volume of questionnaires processed every week. Soon after the change, the number of questionnaires increased, and Marriott officials think that this one change in title has as much to do with the increased response rate as any other factor. Is it any wonder? Before the change, a guest was challenged to disagree, whereas the new questionnaire was significantly more solicitous. Since the change, Mr. Marriott has received approximately 750,000 responses to his printed question each year.

It is important to take heed of this lesson and to make certain that the messages used on your questionnaire are geared to create action. Do not challenge your guests to disagree and do not devalue the questionnaire by refusing to invest in its design or failing to display it prominently. You need the feedback to make the improvements that will increase levels of satisfaction in the future.

EXTERNAL PUBLICATIONS

Annual Report

If you publish an annual report, do you include messages relating to your commitment to satisfying the needs and expectations of your patients and other guests? Including information about your service initiatives says a lot about the extent of your commitment.

Image Brochures

Brochures can portray the "high touch" that must be a part of the spirit of the culture if the hospital is going to be competitive. "High tech" alone is not as powerful.

If you want people to think of you as a provider of quality services, you must shape their impression of you. The quality of the paper and the printing indicates something about the quality of the diagnosis and treatment in the minds of prospective patients.

Recruitment Brochures

As the ready supply of talent and resources dwindles, recruitment of nurses and other allied professionals becomes increasingly important. If you publish a recruitment brochure, does it reflect your standards of quality and your dedication to people—both those who consume your services and those who deliver them? A brochure alone will not recruit the prospective candidate. Yet, if it does a good job of clearly communicating your organizational values, you can arouse the interest of those who share similar values.

Medical Staff Directory

Many hospitals publish a medical staff directory, but most are unimaginative. A directory of physicians can become an important promotional piece. Produced effectively, it can assist you in recruiting business for your physicians. Unless the list of your medical staff is simply too long, feature each physician with a biographical sketch describing his or her certifications, educational background, and other relevant information. A photograph may even be included.

A directory is a useful service to patients (and referring physicians), as well as to your own physicians.

Newsletters/Magazines

There are numerous newsletters and magazines available for purchase, or published internally, that create a sense of who you are and what you stand for. Your primary reason for sending these newsletters to households in your service area is to shape your image in the minds of the consumer. Although the overall content may be directed at health and wellness issues, does it communicate the humanistic side of your business as well? Most of the newsletters and magazines available for purchase allow you to customize several pages with your own copy. When editing this copy for publication, make certain that you communicate your capability to cure and your capability to care. Remember that all things being equal, it is better to promote your ''high tech'' capabilities and reinforce the quality of the services you deliver. There is no reason, however, why you cannot convey that message in a caring manner.

Newsletters for Physicians' Office Staffs

Important constituents to whom you should direct attention are the staffs of physicians' offices. You can strengthen the relationship between your physicians' employees and the hospital by keeping in regular contact with them. Although this should be done in person on a regular basis, a publication sent to them periodically is another tangible sign of your support. The publications can be as rudimentary or as sophisticated as your budget will allow. A one-page memo filled with hospital developments, continuing education opportunities, marketing tips, practice management advice, and other tidbits of information (especially the kind that can be passed along to the physician to reinforce patient/guest communication and relations) is of great value. An alternative to developing and printing this yourself is to purchase in bulk one of the professionally produced practice management newsletters. These newsletters can be printed with the hospital's identity on the masthead.

Issues-Oriented Newsletter

Although almost every kind of consumer publication, from tabloid to digest, has rolled off the presses recently, few resemble the community newsletter that is published by Waukesha Hospital System in Waukesha, Wisconsin. Created 12 years ago as a fund-raising piece, it has now been transformed into a position paper. Published once a month and distributed at no charge to the news media, government leaders, opinion and business leaders, physicians, dentists, and employees, *Direction* is filled with news on state and federal health care issues. The publication is another way to educate people about some of the complex issues facing the industry and the hospital.

OTHER INTERNAL PUBLICATIONS

Official Communications

Most hospitals produce a great deal of written material for wide distribution, both internally and to external publics. All carry important messages about what you value and why.

Memos

The memos and other official announcements dispatched from the executive office are often prepared so routinely that little consideration is given for what might be communicated "between the lines."

One of the best examples of how official communications can distort and contradict the professed values of the organization is offered in Exhibit 18-2. This is an actual memo (although the identity has been changed) to the managers and supervisors of a hospital, announcing that "the time has finally come" for a long-anticipated layoff. The grapevine heard of the action under consideration, which created a pervasive sense of insecurity. Top administration decided it was time to clear the air, so they distributed a memo. If you think it a bit irregular and strange that they chose to deliver this message in a written memo rather than verbally, you are probably astute enough to figure out that there was more wrong with this organization than their method of communication.

What was wrong with the memo in Exhibit 18-2? By reading it, do you get the feeling that the administration of the hospital truly cares about its employees? Do you think they give their management any credit? How often do you think they express appreciation to managers and employees? How often do you predict that they actually mingle and mix with the troops? The administration of this hospital hides within the secure confines of their executive suites. They let the words on paper do their communicating. Yet, they proclaim a sincere belief in, and devotion

Exhibit 18-2 Inter-Office Memo

GENERAL HOSPITAL

To: Department Director
From: Joe Smith
Date: December 15, 1986
Re: Staffing

As you know, hospital layoffs are a regular occurrence around the country. We have not found it necessary to initiate a major reduction in force in the past, in spite of the fact that our patient days have been steadily declining. Fortunately, we had the foresight to realize that the reimbursement changes imposed by the Medicare program several years ago would force us to change the ways in which we delivered our services. We responded by diversifying and, as a result, have done relatively well financially. This is due in no small part to you. However, with the prediction that we may have as few as 100,000 patient days in 1987 (as compared with 132,000 two years ago), there is a general consensus that we should tighten up. Management has not been established as a target as of yet. Staffing, however, must be justified from the ground up.

In order to do this in as professional a manner as possible, a committee has been established to review staffing by department. Meetings will be scheduled during the next three weeks. You will be contacted by Jim Jones or myself shortly.

---

to, values that are without a doubt some of the most beautifully composed, fundamentally sound, and humanistically oriented that have ever been published. When it was suggested that perhaps they should get out, and wander a little more, exercise their vocal chords, peer into the eyes and touch the lives of those people they employ, a few embarrassed snickers were heard before one person was bold enough to admit: ''We can't do that. The employees will be paranoid that something is wrong.''

Although a memo is an uncaring way to communicate sensitive information, this memo could be written in such a way to convey a different message. Why deliver a slap in the face when a pat on the back would make the blow a bit easier to take? Many deficiencies are apparent in this memo, but consider how including this one paragraph below might have altered the tone of the memo and made it a little more positive.

> ''Even in light of this decrease in patient days, our statistics declined more slowly than all other hospitals in our service area. We are well aware that the strength of this hospital is due in great part to dedicated efforts of our management team and employees, for which we are thankful.''

It is not necessary to sugarcoat all of your communications. It is important, however, to be very aware of the powerful—and sometimes distorted—messages conveyed by certain words and certain punctuation. If some leaders find it difficult to express themselves effectively, a skillful and trusted secretary can be given the responsibility to call major distortions to the attention of the author.

Letters of Appreciation

Letters of appreciation often come from patients. Yet, there is no reason why letters of appreciation cannot come from the administrator, president of the medical staff, or chairman of the board. Typically, these letters are in response to a specific event, such as the accomplishment of a hospital goal, or a season's greeting at Thanksgiving, Christmas, or during National Hospital Week. An example of a letter written by an administrator to his staff appears in Exhibit 18-3.

Official communications can be sent to thank publicly and reinforce the efforts of employees. Executives should take every advantage to communicate their sincere appreciation and to acknowledge the dedication and spirit of employees. When census is high and tempers are short, a message from the top can be especially meaningful.

Promotional Ideas

Many hospitals look for ways to use their guest relations slogan or theme in publications and on such specialty items as key rings, pencils, notepaper, and other tokens. De Kalb General Hospital in Atlanta reinforced its guest relations principles creatively in 1984 by publishing a 12-month calendar. Using the theme of its ''I am the Link'' guest relations program, the calendar featured a photograph and a monthly reminder on every page.

Special Edition Newsletters

Many hospitals have renamed their employees' newsletters after their guest relations program. Others have introduced new publications solely dedicated to guest relations. It is not necessary to spend a lot of money on these publications. Obviously, photographs are reproduced with greater clarity when they are professionally printed, but if you want to distribute a regular guest relations update, this can be done at minimal cost by typing it, using Clip-Art or other illustrations, and then photocopying it.

Exhibit 18-3 Letter of Appreciation

June 12, 1987

Dear Employees:

Many times over the past 8 years, I have had former patients approach me to pass on a compliment about their stay. It happens at parties, at Rotary meetings, at church, here at the hospital—just about anywhere. I have always thought it was a bit strange that people would go to such great lengths to seek me out and express their feelings about the care they received at General Hospital. It seems that almost everyone ends their comments with the statement, "Your employees really cared—thanks."

I must admit that after awhile, it is easy to take these comments somewhat for granted. When you are respected in your community for being an institution that provides quality care, you naturally expect that people will feel this way. I would accept these compliments as if they were mine to accept.

Two weeks ago, I was one of your patients and the experience reminded me that those compliments are not the result of what I do—but rather what each and every one of you does. Overnight, I relinquished the control of my daily life and placed my care in your hands and those of my physicians. I was the recipient of your care and concern and I felt secure and comforted.

You cared and it made a big difference to me and to my family. I wish I could thank each and every one of you personally. May I simply instead express my heartfelt appreciation to each of you in this letter.

In your job here at General Hospital, you may have direct patient contact or you may be one of the many important people behind the scenes. Yet, each of you contributes to the care which is delivered and the services which are rendered. My experience reminded me that the only reason General Hospital is so great is because its employees are so great!

Best regards,

Bob Evans

ADVERTISING

Advertising is a form of external communication that can be a potent force in shaping images and reinforcing your values to the public. Is the advertising agency you work with aware of your values? Does the promotion reflect those?

There are two kinds of advertising. Image advertising is designed to do just what the name implies—to strengthen your image in the minds of the consumer. Product advertising is typically used to create awareness and demand for specific services, although it can also elevate the overall image of your facility in the process. If you are attempting to create awareness and demand for a new hospital service, you will probably find image advertising to be ineffective.

A few hospitals have resolved the dilemma between image and product advertising by capturing the essence of "high touch" in their *product* advertising. Those who have effectively managed this creative challenge have learned through follow-up research that consumers consider their hospital both a "high tech" and "high touch" provider.

The legitimacy and value of pure image advertising, as opposed to specific product advertising, are still under debate because generally, image advertising does not succeed in stimulating demand. When significant dollars are spent on advertising, boards of trustees in particular want a quantifiable return on their investment. For that reason, image advertising has lost favor in comparison with product advertising, especially that which contains direct response mechanisms, such as telephone numbers or mail-in response cards. Product advertising in both the print and broadcast media, such as for a physician referral service, may result in over 100 telephone calls a day to the referral line. If it is really effective, product advertising may stimulate 800 calls, as it did within a 24-hour period for one hospital in Hawaii. These calls were tangible evidence that the advertising accomplished its intended objective.

Shaping institutional image and customer perceptions about overall quality, competency, and caring is a much more protracted and complex process. One hazard of image advertising is that it can elevate expectations of service to an unattainable level. In these instances, image advertising is a worthless investment, because every unhappy customer who leaves your hospital will contradict your message with potent word-of-mouth advertising of his or her own. Every radio spot heard, billboard seen, and television commercial viewed will irritate and stimulate the customer's resolve to counter your assertions.

Some hospital radio spots promote and promise that if you appear in their emergency room, you will be seen within 60 seconds. That is an inviting message to those who have minor emergencies and decide to treat them like trauma. However, if patients' definition of "being seen" are different from yours and they wait 90 minutes following their initial assessment by a triage nurse, you will have unhappy customers who will believe that you deceived them. The system does not need to be corrected, but the copy should be carefully worded to convey that "being seen" may not mean "being treated."

In addition, the sum and substance of previous image advertising has been, "We Care," to which many respond, "Who Cares?" Presenting your friendliness, concern, compassion, and respect requires intimate, human interaction. It is difficult to sense those qualities over the radio or television. Even those Madison Avenue magicians who have adroitly stimulated viewers' tear ducts by simultaneously orchestrating the collision of hearts with the sudden crescendo of Pacobel's Canon in D succeed in presenting short-lived illusions. At the height of the "high touch" trend, the advertising industry produced some heavy-duty "kill 'em with kindness" promotions that were hard to believe and somewhat counterproductive. These have been toned down recently without obscuring their humanistic messages. Many of these advertisements now focus on issues that are on the minds of consumers, such as quality, and creating impressions of medical competence, with the human touch still figuring prominently in the message.

For example, radio spots used by health maintenance organizations to promote *personal* attention became very popular as consumers grew increasingly disgruntled at being "just a number" and finding that managed care options did not permit them to establish a relationship with one physician. Image advertising can strike responsive chords as well, if it is used to educate people about the way things really are, the way they used to be, and the way they will be again.

SUMMARY

External and internal communications help shape images and communicate values to a variety of important audiences. Target your publications and promotions so that they strengthen and reinforce the image you so strongly desire to create through your service management efforts.

NOTE

1. Kim Painter, "Patients Want Physicians in White," *USA Today* (January 2, 1987): D1.

Chapter 19

Differentiation: Competitive Positioning

More than one nurse has been assaulted by a patient's angry demand for service: "I'd be treated a lot better at the Holiday Inn, and for a lot less, too." Like it or not, the patient has naïve expectations that are frequently shaped by previous experiences in hotels. The analogy may cause nurse and administrator alike to bristle in anger, but it cannot be dismissed.

In 1982, Ernest Van Den Haag wrote an article for *Fortune* entitled "How to Make Hospitals Hospitable." His solution to the demeaning and dehumanizing treatment routinely accorded hospital patients was to create a new kind of "medical hotel." Part of his assessment of hospitals, following his experience in three major university-affiliated hospitals, is as follows:

> In these hospitals, patients willing and able to pay for pleasant accommodations must often stay in quarters that make an average Holiday Inn seem palatial by comparison. The rooms are cramped and often have peeling paint and minuscule bathrooms, which invariably lack a tub. The beds are narrow and uncomfortable. The mattresses and pillows are sheathed in plastic on which patients slide around, feeling hot and uncomfortable. While patients are in principle free to bring their own pajamas, in practice they will almost always end up in those skimpy and demeaning hospital gowns because there is no provision for laundering personal clothing. Telephones and TV sets are usually provided, but there are no radios, reading lamps, vases for flowers, or writing materials. Rather modest hotels routinely offer these facilities.
>
> Even more distressing than the lack of physical amenities is the character of the service. Information about the most basic matters—the latest temperature reading, when the doctor will come, why one procedure or another is scheduled—is routinely withheld, and a patient who acts as though he has a right to know about such matters is made to feel

like a pest. Meals must be ordered from a limited menu 24 hours in advance—something even a healthy person might be reluctant to do. There is no food service on demand; everybody must eat at the same time. Wine, beer, hard liquor, and tobacco are banned.

Why should a hospital not rival a hotel, offering as much luxury as patients are willing to pay for? Why must we all be equal when ill, as we are in death?[1]

In 1982, the author's very suggestion that hospitals could and should change brought vehement protests from many health care practitioners. Resistance to reform, fueled by defensiveness and self-justification, was strong. It was an outright insult to be compared to a hotel. Yet, once the shield of righteous indignation was permeated, changes began to occur. Modest changes occurred first. Hospitals called patients guests before they began treating them as guests, but the evolution ultimately did take place over several years. Van Den Haag's perceptions of what a hospital could and should be like have now been realized in many hospitals throughout the United States. Although the respected Cornell University School of Hotel Management has yet to institute a curriculum specifically for hospital administrators, hospitals are seeking guidance from the hotel industry and other service businesses in an effort to distinguish their services.

The airline industry has a saying that there is no commodity as perishable as an airline seat. If it is not filled when the plane takes off, the empty seat becomes a loss for the airline that can never be recouped. Hotel beds are almost as perishable as airline seats. For these reasons, many hotel chains and airlines have implemented frequent guest/flier programs to build brand loyalty and increase the probability that travelers will fly on their plane and retire to their hotel during their next visit. Beyond that, attentions are focused on ways to make the customers more comfortable, the service more convenient, and the satisfaction longer lasting.

Are hospital rooms any less perishable? Not at all. In an effort to fill beds, numerous ploys, gimmicks, and downright brilliant programs have been created. These marketing efforts, both internal and external, parallel similar initiatives within the hotel and airline industries.

This chapter explores many of the methods and approaches now used by hospitals to exceed customer expectations, create differentiation in the marketplace, and stimulate demand. Although many of these initiatives parallel those used in other service industries, the purpose of the discussion is not to suggest that hospitals model themselves after hotels and airlines. The comparisons are useful and can serve as the basis for conclusions about the future of service management and marketing in the health care industry.

BENEFIT SEGMENTATION

In his article, Van Den Haag asked the question: "Why should a hospital not rival a hotel, *offering as much luxury as patients are willing to pay for?"* His question raises an essential point: Some people are willing to pay extra for services that they perceive have extra value. That is why some wealthy people fly in the coach class of an airplane, whereas others with much more modest incomes go first class.

Some hotels have used this principle of value to their advantage by segmenting those audiences willing to pay a premium for premium services and then clustering services to meet their needs. The next time you are in a major hotel, ask the desk clerk if the hotel has a concierge level. If there is such a level and your room is not reserved on it, ask the desk clerk for a pass key so that you can evaluate whether you would like to reserve a room there on your next visit. Once you have completed the tour, ask yourself whether you would be willing to pay additionally for the ambience and amenities offered. Then close your eyes and imagine a similar tour down the south wing of your hospital's third floor. If you were going to create a concierge level, what would you include?

Michael Reese Hospital in Chicago answered that question in the fall of 1986 when they opened Centennial Suites. On this special wing of the hospital, you walk down the corridor that is dimly lit by wall sconces stationed about 20 feet apart. The sound of your footsteps is muffled by thick corridor carpet. You pass a man who clearly resembles a room service waiter in a hotel. Placed on his shoulder is a tray adorned with china, glassware, and a small bud vase with a single rose. You enter a bright, cheerful room. A velour bathrobe hangs in the closet, and a bouquet of flowers sits next to the videotape recorder on the dresser. On the writing desk is a folder containing stationary and a pen. Fluffy towels hang on the rods in the bathroom, and a basket containing a shower cap, bar of soap, and small bottles of shampoo and lotion is to the side of the sink. Bedside secretarial services, transcription, and word processing are provided for those patients who cannot leave the office behind. The Centennial Suite rooms have been specially decorated and the services specially designed to meet the needs of those who prefer to pay more money for a little extra attention, a pleasant ambience, and a few additional services.

Service "above and beyond" is the pledge of those stationed on the Centennial Suites, and on more than one occasion they have demonstrated that no request is too great to meet. For example, one patient who had suffered a mild heart attack was disturbed to discover that his television would not pick up New York Stock Exchange transactions. The concierge arranged to have another television installed to accommodate his request. Although *complete* bedrest may be what doctors prefer for their patients, they also realize the importance of market transactions for some patients. Relegating them to game shows and soap operas may cause greater stress than a volatile market.[2]

The Methodist Hospital, located in the heart of Houston's medical center district also provides a variety of hotel services to its patients and guests. Doormen welcome those who pass through the entrance of this 1181-bed hospital. Bellmen carry the patients' luggage directly to their rooms because most patients are preadmitted. The hospital is staffed with concierges who provide other services for patients and families.

Luxury suites have been cropping up in hospitals throughout the country and represent one of the truly distinctive ways in which a hospital can respond to the segmented needs of the patient population. Transforming rooms into two-room suites and private single rooms is quickly becoming an attractive strategy to recruit patients who do not mind paying between $30 and $150 a day additional for these special rooms. The list of special services and amenities provided in hospital luxury suites is limited only by your imagination. Many hospitals provide on-floor admitting; in-room electrocardiograms, blood tests, and urinalyses; a special menu; food served on fine china with crystal and silver accessories; a concierge (special patient representative) to coordinate all nonmedical services; and primary nursing care. Some hospitals even offer limousine services to and from the hospital to these special guests.

The hotel industry's influence on hospitals has not been limited to the design of decor, the amenities of luxury suites, or the stationing of concierges throughout the facility. Monogrammed mints and candies are being distributed on the patient's pillow or nightstand by housekeepers. However, given the fact that approximately 20 percent of all patients are diabetic and others are on medically restricted diets, this touch may be ill-advised and, at the least, difficult to monitor. Another word of caution is also offered. One hospital distributed mints with a card that read, "You're worth a mint at General Hospital." Upon receiving their bills, the patients probably understood why!

If the patient's tooth is not sweet, but his or her stomach growls for attention, some hospitals are staffed to satisfy this need by offering extended room service hours. In addition, as early as 1983, 42 percent of the 2,100 members of the American Society of Hospital Service Administrators reported having some type of upgraded or gourmet meal service. This number has risen rapidly as food service departments have become more aggressive and progressive.[3]

Special food services make service distinctive at Suburban Hospital in Bethesda, Maryland. When officials there transformed an old surgical floor into luxury suites, they contracted with a local restaurant in Washington, D.C., to provide evening meals for patients and their families. Likewise, if fast food fare will make the patient happier, food service personnel will order in a "Big Mac." As long as it is not medically unadvisable or nearly impossible, hospitals such as Suburban are catering to the whims and requests of patients.[4]

It is important to keep in mind that interior decor and extra touches are of minor importance if your services do not meet the primary needs and expectations or if the perceived quality of your product is not at an acceptable level. But the special services offered, from chauffeured limousines to gourmet meals to concierges, represent benefits that will satisfy the needs and preferences of specific patient segments.

DIFFERENTIATION

Benefit segmentation, with the goal of appealing to a specific group of people with common interests, values, and/or expectations, is not the only impetus for creating hotel-like services and appearances within hospitals. Hotel services can also help create an image of responsiveness. If quality is indistinguishable but acceptable, a hospital can utilize special services for the purpose of differentiation.

Some years ago, as you traveled down America's highways, you saw roadside motels with neon signs advertising "Free TV." When these enticements lost their novelty, motels changed their signs to read "Color TV." The advent of cable television brought a new announcement: "Free HBO." Differentiating one motel from another down the road became a function of finding value-added amenities to lure the weary traveler off the road and into the parking lot.

Hospitals should take cues from the roadside motels and recognize that there are a few amenities that travelers and patients alike value. Although the daily charge for a hospital room far exceeds even the most luxurious hotels, most hospitals still insist on charging their guests for basic television and telephone services. Obviously, room rates in hospitals and hotels are not computed on the same basis, but despite the justifiably high costs of delivering health care, most patients are not necessarily sympathetic to pricing rationales. Patients often compare their hospital charges to hotel charges and resent the extra charge levied for television and telephone. This reaction is reminiscent of the "good old days" when service was something for which you did not have to pay additional money.

In part, the resentment caused by high medical costs is fueled by the guest's irritation at being "nickled and dimed to death." Hospitals are beginning to respond to this perception, and some have turned it into a distinguishing feature of their promotion. Methodist Hospital of Peoria, Illinois, did. In one of their print advertisements the copy reads:

> From time to time, you may ask for little things, such as aspirin or
> hand lotion, and we're happy to provide them—at no charge."

This simple statement has a powerful effect on many patients. Their reaction: "Well, it's about time."

If you have a contract with an outside company for television service, investigate the capital investment and maintenance costs of providing free television service. If at all possible, release your patients from the obligation to pay for a service that can mean the difference between total boredom and mild amusement. If the television rental provides a source of income to your volunteers, ask them to consider other income sources and to provide television as a *service* to your guests. They may lose significant revenue, but it is a small price to pay for the good will that is created.

Of course, you can go a step farther. Contracting for cable channels is not inexpensive, but it is an attractive service. If you provide basic television service at no additional charge, many patients are not opposed to paying extra for in-room movies. Many of the VIP suites in hospitals are equipped with in-room VCRs, and patients are able to borrow video cassettes for their viewing enjoyment.

You do not necessarily have to transform your existing rooms into deluxe suites to achieve a first-class appearance. You can upgrade patient rooms by selecting color-coordinated bed and bath linens, cubicle curtains, window treatments, patient apparel, hospitality kits, and food service items in thousands of well-researched combinations. The Impressions System, developed by American Hospital Supply, uses a proprietary software system to explore hundreds of product combinations, color schemes, and pricing structures to create a custom-designed image for a hospital. The program was developed specifically to help hospitals visually portray their philosophies of personalized, caring patient service.

The cleanliness of the room plays an important role in shaping impressions. The patient expects a clean room and a clean hospital. And because the hospital housekeepers spend significant time with the patient while cleaning the room, their attention to detail is observed by patients. Although housekeepers in hotels are not usually observed by guests, they are no less attentive to detail. In fact, Marriott Hotel officials ensure that each guest room will be spotlessly cleaned by maids because they have specified 66 tasks to do in cleaning the room—from dusting the tops of all pictures to making sure the telephone books and Bibles are in good condition. I was sitting in my hotel room one night when I noticed a folded card under the bed. I picked it up and saw that it read: "Yes, we clean here daily too!" In part, Marriott's obsessiveness emanates from a belief that quality of service lies in the details. You cannot argue with success![5]

The personal appearance of employees also plays a role in image building. First impressions count, and it is for this reason that you find most hotel employees in uniforms.

Do the employees of your admitting office look professional? One way to enhance the professional presentation of this staff is to provide uniforms that give a "front desk" appearance. Just ask officials of Pacifica Community Hospital in

Huntington Beach, California, what outcomes are created when you outfit your staff in uniforms. They will tell you that doing so not only impresses patients and visitors but also enhances the confidence of the employees. The front desk employees at Pacifica wear gray tailored business suits with a skirt or slacks, a blazer, a burgundy or rose-colored print blouse, and a burgundy bow tie. Gray or neutral hose can be worn with low-heel, closed-toe pumps. The hospital provides uniforms at no charge to employees and pays for dry cleaning; the employees purchase only their shoes. In addition, Pacifica holds professional image and makeup seminars for their personnel. Employees have been very receptive to their new ''look,'' having received many compliments from patients and visitors during the 2 years they have been wearing the uniforms. The compliments have helped build the employees' sense of self-esteem. Pacifica is currently developing hotel-like uniforms using the color scheme of the hospital decor for members of the dietary, ICU, ER, and housekeeping departments.

AGGRESSIVE HOSPITALITY

Guest Relations Managers

Most hospitals employ individuals who represent patients as their advocate or ombudsman. These two titles suggest an almost adversarial relationship, raising the questions: ''Why should a patient need an advocate?'' and ''Is the system for or against him or her?'' For this reason, these titles are being replaced with such terms as ''concierge,'' ''customer service representative,'' or ''guest relations manager.'' In their expanded roles, they provide special services to guests and their family members, in addition to other important functions described in Chapter 11.

Although it is not unusual to find several patient representatives in a large hospital, Beth Israel Medical Center in New York City has recently exceeded the norm in an effort to support its staff and practice aggressive hospitality. Fourteen guest relations managers are employed by this 934-bed facility. Each nursing floor has a team of two guest relations managers who assist in the admission and discharge of patients and visit patients at least every other day. Their duties are to prevent problems from arising and to do whatever they can to make patients' stays as pleasant and comfortable as possible.[6]

Other hospitals employ persons in this capacity, but what makes Beth Israel Medical Center unique is that they recruit guest relations managers from the hospitality industry. On their staff are former employees of the Plaza Hotel and Hertz Corporation and a flight attendant from People Express. The number of guest relations managers employed by the medical center is an indication of its commitment to the concept of special service to guests.

Admission and Discharge

First and final impressions are acknowledged to be the most lasting. Stumbling at the starting gate can make getting back on the right foot especially difficult, and a final bad experience can sour an otherwise positive stay. For these reasons, it is important that strong and positive impressions are created when the patient interacts with the admitting department and business office.

By comparison, the checkin and checkout procedures in hotels are relatively easy and hassle-free, requiring minimal effort. To register requires the provision of little information, and checkout takes little time. Yet, as easy as these procedures have become, hotels are always seeking ways to expedite them. The Chicago O'Hare Marriott Hotel has found a way to check in guests even before they step into the hotel lobby. A desk clerk, equipped with registration forms and a telephone, rides the hotel's airport courtesy van to speed up the process for guests arriving from O'Hare airport. By the time guests reach the hotel, all they have to do is pick up their keys. The checkout process has undergone major changes, with express checkout offered to those preferring to avoid the lines at the cashier's station. The hotel bill is slipped under the guest's door, and the guest can review the charges in the early morning and report any errors before dropping the key at the front desk. Other hotels have gone so far as to offer an in-room review of hotel charges over a designated channel on the television set. Charges appear on the screen, and the guest can complete checkout without leaving the room. It is doubtful that hospitals will ever implement this automated and innovative method of handling discharges. Prior review of hospital charges would likely quicken a relapse in even the most healthy patient!

Those who have endured the frustration of the prolonged processes of hospital admission and discharge can appreciate the benefits of programs designed to reduce those hassles. Patients of the Memorial Care Systems of Houston, can skip most of the paperwork associated with a traditional admission process by registering to be a Memorial Preferred Partner. Qualified applicants must be employed full time, carry medical insurance with at least 80 percent coverage, and have a family income of $25,000 or more. Prospective members complete a registration form that requests much of the same information that is required for hospital registration. After a credit check and insurance verification, the applicant receives a Preferred Partner card. By presenting the card at a hospital affiliated with Memorial Care Systems, patients can bypass most of the paperwork and settle quickly into their rooms. No deposit is required. When they leave the hospital, they drop a quick checkout card at the nurses' station, rather than stop at the business office. Members are entitled to a 90-day postponement of their deductible payment and are provided free parking, discounts in the cafeteria, and other services.[7]

To assist patients with the admissions procedure, many hospitals have also instituted in-room admissions. Jewish Hospital in Louisville, Kentucky, offers such a service. Patients who are seriously ill or feel too uncomfortable to wait in the admissions area are escorted directly to their rooms. If they have not been admitted to the hospital previously, an employee will go to their rooms to obtain the required information.

Although most hospital transactions are computerized, it is doubtful that they will ever employ the sophisticated welcoming techniques offered by a few select hotels. The Park Hyatt Hotel in Chicago, for example, maintains more than 25,000 files on its guests and employs Guest Historians who trace and pull files 2 days before a guest's arrival. Their data storage includes specific information on guests' likes and dislikes. The amenities that should be given to arriving guests, such as a champagne bin complete with a selection of fruits, golf balls, and Evian water are stored. Housekeeping requests, ranging from hanger types to hair dryer needs to the desired firmness of mattress, food and beverage preferences, birthdays, anniversaries, and babysitting requirements can also be recorded. The use of artificial intelligence to give the best possible service to guests is becoming more popular.

For obvious reasons, the most notable of which is that a loyal, satisfied patient may not have any reason to return to the hospital for quite some time, computerized profile systems are not on the horizon for hospitals. With the expansion of computer capabilities, however, modified "profile" systems may be developed for future use. This could help to relieve frustration many patients experience if they do need to be readmitted within a short time from their previous discharge. It is very irritating to many patients to discover that, upon readmission, they are treated as total strangers. They must complete information and undergo tests that were requested a short time before. Initiatives to make patients feel less foreign and more welcome will ease the process of re-entry.

Although there is little anyone can do to reduce the sting of high costs, there are ways to lessen the aggravation that patients and their family members experience when settling their bills. Clear explanations of the charges and insurance processing procedures help. Managers at St. Luke's Regional Medical Center in Boise, Idaho, discovered that an insurance assistance program is a measure of good will that goes a long way to build trust and understanding. They initiated their program to help elderly patients complete Medicare or supplemental insurance claims. The appeal of the service was so widespread that they decided not to restrict the service to the elderly. Now all St. Luke's patients and their families can either call for an appointment or simply walk in to see a counselor during office hours. A brochure explaining the program is included in each admission packet.[8]

STIMULATING DEMAND

In some hospitals, those "perishable" beds have been converted to other uses, such as caring for patients who need step-down care. Other hospitals are finding other ways to provide a continuum of care. With the shortened lengths of stay and the incentives to discharge patients earlier from the hospital, most patients are faced with few, if any, options to receive step-down care. Many hospitals have attempted to resolve this dilemma by designating "swing" beds or transferring to skilled nursing facilities those patients who are not well enough to care for themselves at home. Some hospitals have also built or converted buildings (or units) as on-campus lodging for patients' family members, for out-of-town patients receiving outpatient treatments, and for patients who are discharged from the hospital but are not medically able enough to go home. One such facility is found on the campus of Abbott Northwestern Hospital in Minneapolis, Minnesota. The Accommodations Department of Abbott Northwestern offers tastefully decorated rooms that will house up to 125 people for an average charge of $30 a day. Checkout time is flexible, their philosophy being not to put any additional pressure on guests. Guests checking in by 11 P.M. can stay until 11 P.M. the next day before they are charged for another night's stay. A large assortment of foods is available in vending machines, and microwaves and refrigerators are provided in the two lounges. Guests can also check out microwave cookbooks. In addition, the Accommodations Department offers a "Limited Service Option." If guests prefer, they can clean their own rooms and save $5 on the room rate. Vacuums are available on a checkout basis. Department personnel report that outpatients who use the facilities find it therapeutic to do everyday tasks, such as cleaning their rooms and washing their clothes.

It is important to note that the hotel at Abbott Northwestern is a "department" of the hospital. The hotel is offered only to those guests who have business with the hospital and is not promoted to other potential market segments. One problem that hospitals offering on-campus hotel rooms encounter is resistance from area hotel proprietors, who feel that the hospital's not-for-profit status should prevent them from competing for business.

Another well-known medical hotel model was introduced in 1984 at Presbyterian-University Medical Center in Philadelphia. The HotelHospital, located adjacent to the hospital, has 14 private rooms and a few double rooms. Patients who check into this HotelHospital stay an average of 4.8 days. The services provided include 24-hour homemaker services, hotel-like amenities (iron, hair dryer, newspaper), three meals a day selected from a restaurant-style menu, and immediate access to emergency and comprehensive services, if they are necessary. The medical center provides transportation to and from hospital facilities for medically related appointments. The staff at the HotelHospital can assist the discharged patient in securing medical equipment and supplies, as well as consultations for physical, occupational, and/or speech therapy. The staff also provides recreational therapy activities, such as aerobics, games, music, and craft activities. Another popular service provided by the HotelHospital is a "Holiday

From Home; A Home Hotel Program.'' This program provides respite care for individuals who are normally supervised at home by family members.

The HotelHospital has many benefits. The physicians like it because they are able to monitor patient compliance to treatment. Patients like it because they know that their medical supervision will continue following discharge from the hospital. In addition, rooms are reasonably priced. Family members like it because they can begin caring for their loved one while under the supervision of others. And the hospital likes it because it is economical and helps them manage cases.[9]

QUALITY: THE KEY TO DIFFERENTIATION

Programs and marketing strategies borrowed from hotels, airlines, and other industries can assist you in your marketing effort, but you cannot succeed on ambience and amenities alone. As you endeavor to differentiate your hospital from other providers, it is important not to get too caught up in the zeal for hotel-like services. Research substantiates that patients value ''high tech'' over ''high touch.'' The question must be raised: Is there a measurable difference in the perception of quality in the minds of those in the community because of the hotel services offered by the hospital? It is doubtful that perceptions of quality held by many patients are based on hotel services alone. Their naive assumptions about the quality of your services are influenced by demonstrations of ''high touch,'' but what they perceive as medical competence has a greater impact in shaping their preferences of provider. Quality remains the most powerful way to differentiate your services. Without perceived quality few will elect to use your services regardless of how compelling your incentives and advertising are.

Again, one of the best examples comes from the airline industry. A passenger is unlikely to prefer an airline that has a publicized record of safety violations. The lowest fares available will not stimulate demand if the plane is not perceived to be safe. When passengers perceive that the airline's safety record is good, they may still avoid the airline if they have had past negative experiences with it, such as repetitive loss of or damage to luggage. They may further be discouraged from selecting the airline if they have frequently experienced unclean cabins and bathrooms, exceptionally poor food, and discourteous employees. It is only when the airline represents competence, courtesy, and cleanliness that such incentives as free cocktails, wide seats, longer leg room, frequent flier awards, and gourmet meals achieve optimal returns. Aggressive hospitality will be perceived as gimmickry if your community does not perceive that you deliver quality medical care. If the quality perception is strong, however, the hotel services can greatly enhance your position as a leader who is driven by a commitment to satisfaction.

SUMMARY

Many of the programs and services mentioned in this chapter can help a hospital actualize its service strategy. Underlying most of the innovative services that have been developed by other industries is a strong strategy for building customer satisfaction and loyalty and, as a result, gaining greater market share.

NOTES

1. Ernest Van Den Haag, "How to Make Hospitals Hospitable," *Fortune* (May 17, 1982): 123-129.

2. Paul Galloway, "Hospital Chic," *Chicago Tribune* (November 3, 1986).

3. Carol Caprione, "Foodservice: The Right Medicine for an Ailing Hospital," *NRA News* (January 1984).

4. Kathy Fackelmann, "Bethesda, MD, Hospital Turns Old Wings into 13-bed Luxury Unit," *Modern Healthcare* (March 1, 1985): 102-103.

5. Thomas Moore, "Marriott Grabs for More Room," *Fortune* (October 13, 1983): 108.

6. "Beth Israel Hospital: Hiring a Customer-Service Background," *Hospital Guest Relations Report* (January 1987): 1-2.

7. "Houston's Memorial Care System: Special Programs to Tap Special Markets," *Healthcare Marketing Report* (February 1987): 1.

8. "Boise Hospital Initiates Insurance Forms Assistance Program," *Hospital Guest Relations Report* (June 1986): 1-4.

9. "Medical Hotel Increases Discharge Options Under Shortened Length of Stay," *Hospital Guest Relations Report* (June 1986): 5-8.

Chapter 20

New Pathways: Breakthrough Ideas and Innovations

Excellent hospitals take the initiative to reach beyond the ordinary in an attempt to position themselves clearly as ones that are truly service-oriented and customer-driven. A hospital that has invested the time to develop a comprehensive service action plan will be very involved in implementing it for a long time to come. A hospital with an inquisitive culture that encourages people to ask these questions, "How are we doing?" and "In what ways can we do better?," is the one that discovers and implements the innovations that distinguish service.

The new service renaissance is dependent on the use of participative management skills that encourage the internal creation, development, and implementation of new ideas. Great ideas result when the innovative capacity of employees, patients, visitors, physicians, and their office staffs is stimulated. Those organizations that are so rigid that they stifle innovation will be dependent on borrowed ideas and will watch as those who seize opportunity forge ahead.

The human's resolve to invent the better mousetrap is simply the result of the frustration experienced while using an inferior product that does not get the job done. So, too, with the services one consumes. The frustrations that occur as a result of an experience that does not measure up to one's expectation produce fertile ground for innovation. A high and mighty assertion that "If I were running this show, I would . . ." should not necessarily be dismissed. Chances are that someone in your organization has a good idea or two that, when corroborated with others of like mind, could become the breakthrough ideas that will differentiate the services you deliver.

NKC Hospitals in Louisville, Kentucky, have embarked on a quality improvement program that invites all employees to participate in making suggestions and offering ideas that will improve the quality of service delivered. The hospital recognizes employees for making suggestions in a monthly newsletter entitled, "Quality News." Employees are routinely encouraged to identify things that prevent them from doing their jobs effectively.

Employees are brimming with ideas, many of which can propel you to the forefront of service excellence. Employees can develop hundreds of small service improvements that pay big dividends—in satisfied customers and satisfied employees, decreased inefficiencies and costs, and in increased teamwork and productivity.

You must be driven by a desire to learn from your customers and to translate the information they offer into ideas that will enable you to better meet their needs. The customer requirements committee at NKC Hospitals seeks feedback from groups of customers; specifically patients, physicians, and departments to define their requirements of quality. The goal is to have customers define the "drivers" of quality. An external research firm was hired to define the most important drivers of quality by asking questions of patients and families. The physician liaison staff has conducted more than 600 interviews with physicians to identify problems and opportunities. Departments are asked to identify their needs that must be met to facilitate internal service delivery. The collection of this feedback enables the hospital corporation to make improvements that will impact the quality of service. Quality improvement teams (QIT) are used to study specific problems and to suggest solutions.

Encourage your customers to offer service improvement ideas as well. They confront problems within the system and are often very creative in developing solutions. Over the past few years, I have received a half-dozen calls and letters from former patients who, following their hospitalizations, went to the drawing board and came up with clever innovations. They have designed such items as a more discreet hospital gown, a pouch in which to leave a quarter for the volunteer who may happen by with the morning paper while the patient is away for tests, and a four-page "amusement booklet" containing crossword puzzles and brain teasers to help patients pass the time of day.

Consider implementing—or improving on—these other innovative ideas:

- Tune in to a small but valuable touch by providing AM-FM radios for patients and headsets for those in semiprivate rooms.
- Arrange with your local publisher, a local florist, or durable medical equipment supply firm, to provide complimentary copies of the newspaper, and consider offering your guests the additional choices of *The Wall Street Journal* and *USA Today*.
- Circulate bookcarts, and stock them not only with the best sellers but also with helpful health education materials. The latter selections will help patients focus attention on an important aspect of the healing process— education.
- When patients have been hospitalized for prolonged periods of time, offer simple, but much-appreciated gestures, such as free parking passes or tokens to metered parking lots to their close family members.

- Conduct regular support group sessions for families of critically ill patients, in which they can express concerns to staff and offer suggestions and insights on how the hospital can improve its services.

You must always weigh the cost of a proposed service against its value. However, even if the cost of the service does not exceed the benefit, it is best not to be too tightfisted. Some organizations are unrelenting in their preoccupation with the bottom line. As a result, they dampen any ideas that can spur innovation. You can be fiscally prudent and maintain a respectable level of risk aversion without stifling innovation, but it takes some work. If you seek justification, remember that benefits are often intangible and difficult to quantify.

Some hospitals are so caught up in the traditions of the past that they are paralyzed. To create superior service, the constraints on idea generation must be unleashed. Encouraging an organization to be more innovative is a slow process. Managers must first learn to focus their gaze outward onto tomorrow's horizon of opportunity. As ideas incubate, they crystallize. The resulting crystals form the prisms that create many brilliant ideas.

SUMMARY

Just as a baby learns to crawl before walking, and then takes faltering steps before he or she achieves a degree of stability, you will likely find that the process of generating ideas will be slow in the beginning. How can you provide better service to guests? How can you create more loyal and lasting relationships with your customers? How can you strengthen the bonds that unite physician and hospital in a common purpose? It is usually the organizations that "think big" and "dare to be different" that are most adept at identifying and implementing the small changes that add up to measurable differences in the minds of the guests. If that is true, then it stands to reason that small innovations arising from early attempts to think beyond the ordinary will ultimately nurture an organizational mindset that will create new pathways in customer service.

In some markets, doing 1,000 things 1 percent better can provide incremental improvements that will sustain the competitive advantage and improve patient care. Harnessing creative talent and capturing opportunities to make improvements in the way service is conceptualized, managed, and delivered are answers to the excellence challenge. Devotion to innovation will produce the sought-after results.

Keep asking the questions!

Vendors of Guest Relations Products, Seminars, and Consulting Services

The following list of vendors has been compiled from known sources and direct mail brochures that have been received over the years. Several of the companies and individuals listed below provide comprehensive consulting services; others offer limited lines of products or seminars. Most of these vendors have experience in health care settings.

A.K. Jackson and Associates
46 3rd St.
P.O. Box 1662
Hickory, NC 28603
(704) 328-8968

Abington Memorial Hospital
1200 York Rd.
Abington, PA 19001
(215) 576-2200

Advantage Media, Inc.
11312 Santa Monica Blvd., Suite 2
Los Angeles, CA 90025
(213) 477-6538

Advantage Customer Relations System
603 First St.
Oceanside, CA 92054
(619) 722-4522

American Hospital Resources
900 Creek Rd.
P.O. Box 99
Downingtown, PA 19335
(215) 269-6952

Bernie Hoffman Associates, Inc.
20755 Greenfield, Suite 601
Southfield, MI 48075
(313) 557-9340

Better Than Money Corporation
9210 East Bloomington Freeway
Bloomington, MN 55420
(612) 884-3311

Betty Wishard and Associates
P.O. Box 9076
Metairie, LA 70055
(504) 832-0058

Center for Continuing Education
University of Georgia
Athens, GA 30602
(404) 542-4766

Continuing Education Services
917 Pleasant Valley Blvd.
Altoona, PA 16602
(814) 944-1535

Corporate Systems and Images
508½ W. Washington St.
South Bend, IN 46001
(219) 323-5771

Creative Media
820 Keo Way
Des Moines, IA 50309
(515) 244-3610

Customer Communication Systems
5327 General Forest Ct.
Nashville, TN 32715
(615) 377-9720

Dartnell Institute of Management
4652 Ravenswood Ave.
Chicago, IL 60640
(312) 561-4000

Development Dimension International
1225 Washington Pike
Pittsburgh, PA 15343
(414) 257-0600

DiversiHealth
920 S. 107th Ave., Suite 200
Omaha, NE 68114
(402) 393-6057

Dome Learning Systems
550 North Broadway, Suite 700
Baltimore, MD 21205
(301) 955-7632

Einstein Consulting Group
York and Tabor Roads
Philadelphia, PA 19141
(214) 456-7890

Forbes Health Systems
500 Findley St.
Pittsburgh, PA 15206
(412) 665-3553

Health Management Inc.
1828 L St. N.W., Suite 908
Washington, DC 20030
(202) 887-8110

Health Central Institute
2810 57th Ave., North, Suite 240
Minneapolis, MN 55430
(612) 574-7850

Health East Communications
Commerce Plaza, Suite 020
5100 Tilghman St.
Allentown, PA 18104

Hermann Hospital
1203 Ross Sterling Ave.
Houston, TX 77030
(713) 797-4540

Hospital Learning Centers, Inc.
6240 Laurel Canyon Blvd., Suite 100
North Hollywood, CA 91606
(818) 980-0292

Hospital Training Systems
645 Seabreeze Drive
Seal Beach, CA 90740
(213) 594-9030

Human Resource Strategies
2233 Wisconsin Ave., Suite 222
Washington, DC 20007
(202) 944-8010

Interact Performance Systems
7434 S. State St., Suite 204
Midvale, UT 84047
(801) 562-9429

Interact Performance Systems
300 West Owens Drive, Suite 350
Santa Ana, CA 92706
(714) 835-3671

K.E. Peterson & Associates
Merged with Laventhol & Horwath
300 South Riverside Plaza
Chicago, IL 60606
(312) 648-0555

Louis A. Weiss Memorial Hospital
4646 N. Marine Drive
Chicago, IL 60640
(312) 878-8700

Management Communication Associates
645 Los Altos Ave.
Long Beach, CA 90814
(215) 494-4871

Management Training Consultants
360 Rine Hill Rd.

Wakefield, RI 02879
(401) 783-0693

Media Collaborative
50 Milk St., 15th Floor
Boston, MA 02109
(617) 377-9720

Mediatec
1150 Foothill Blvd.
La Canada, CA 91011
(818) 790-9450

Memorial Health Systems, Inc.
205 W. Jefferson
South Bend, IN 46601
(219) 287-5009

Memorial Sloan-Kettering Cancer Center
1275 York Ave.
New York, NY 10021
(212) 207-3455

Miranda Associates, Inc.
818 18th St., N.W., Suite 1060
Washington, DC 20006
(202) 857-0430

Northeast Georgia Medical Center
743 Spring St., N.E.
Gainesville, GA 30505
(404) 535-3392

Organization Development Group
Division of Fairlane Health Services
   Corporation
Suite 1002 West
One Parklane Blvd.
Dearborn, MI 48126
(313) 271-6550

Pacific Southwest Airlines
9850 Carroll Canyon Rd.
San Diego, CA 92131
(619) 586-6714

Performance Improvement Affiliates
Subsidiary of North Mississippi Health
   Services, Inc.
830 South Gloster St.
Tupelo, MS 38801
(601) 841-1717

Performance Programs International
1131 Vine St.
Gainesville, GA 30501

Personal and Professional Development, Inc.
712 S. Milwaukee Ave., Suite 10-A
Wheeling, IL 60090
(312) 459-6686

PRO-MED Learning Systems
P.O. Box 36264
Lakewood, CO 80236
(303) 986-8487

Pro-Med Learning Systems
8120 West Baker
Lakewood, CO 80227
(303) 922-4339

Sandy Corporation
1500 West Big Beaver Rd.
Troy, MI 48084
(313) 649-0800

Travenol Management Services
1 Baxter Parkway
Deerfield, IL 60015
(312) 948-2769

University of Cincinnati
Division of Continuing Education
350 French Hall
Cincinnati, OH 45221

Vernine and Associates
P.O. Box 10925
Knoxville, TN 37919
(615) 424-8888

Victoria International Corporation
100 Boylston St.
Boston, MA 02117
(617) 247-2424

Walter Jonas and Associates
5438 Hyde Park Blvd.
Chicago, IL 60615
(312) 955-5035

Wellness Learning Systems
Division of Mark-Maris, Inc.
2280 Main St.
Buffalo, NY 14214

PATIENT SATISFACTION MEASUREMENT SERVICES

Endresen Research
4 West Blaine
Seattle, WA 98119
(206) 285-1771

EPPSTAT
P.O. Box 1452
Anderson, SC 29622
(803) 261-1000

National Research Corporation
Gold's Galleria
1033 O St.
Lincoln, NE 68508
(800) 228-3984

Press, Ganey Associates, Inc.
P.O. Box 1064
Notre Dame, IN 46556
(219) 232-3387

SRI Gallup
300 South 68th St.
Lincoln, NE 68510
(800) 221-8702

ENVIRONMENTAL DESIGN

Baxter Hospital Supply
Impressions Program
1450 Waukegan Rd.
McGaw Park, IL 60085
(312) 473-0400

Jain Malkin, Inc.
7606 Fay Ave.
La Jolla, CA 92037
(619) 454-3377

Medicor
Medline Industries
1 Medline Place
Mundelein, IL 60060-4480
(800) 245-1670
(312) 949-3003

NEWSLETTERS

Hospital Guest Relations Report
St. Anthony Hospital Publications
Suite 001
801 Pennsylvania Avenue, S.E.
Washington, DC 20003

"GRIP"
The Einstein Consulting Group
York and Tabor Roads
Philadelphia, PA 19141

"The Doctor's Office"
Wentworth Publications
1858 Charter Lane
Lancaster, PA 17601

"Practice Marketing & Management"
Professional Communications, Inc.
5799 Tall Oaks Road
P.O. Box 9036
Madison, WI 53715

PATIENT APPAREL

Ramsey Designs, Inc.
Box 163, Route 9G
Germantown, NY 12526
(518) 828-4443

Suggested Readings

Aagaard, T.L. *Effective Patient Relations*. Kansas City, Mo.: Midwest Medical Books, 1986.

Aburdene, Patricia, and Naisbitt, John. *Re-Inventing the Corporation*. New York: Warner Books, 1985.

"Administrators Invest More Money in Design to Remain Competitive." *Hospitals*, June 16, 1985, p. 82.

"A High-Powered Pitch to Cure Hospitals' Ills." *Business Week*, Sept. 2, 1985.

Albrecht, Karl. *The Creative Corporation*. Homewood, Ill.: Dow Jones Irwin, 1987.

Albrecht, Karl, and Crego, Edwin T., Jr., "What Every Customer Wants," *Perspective* 13, no. 3, pp. 3–5, 31–32.

Albrecht, Karl, and Zemke, Ron. *Service America*. Homewood, Ill.: Dow Jones Irwin, 1985.

Alexander, Thomas, and Terry, Kathleen. "Quality Circles in Hospitals." *Hospital Forum*, May/June 1982, pp. 29, 31–32.

"A Little TLC Goes a Long Way in Oklahoma Hospitals." *Hospitals*, November 5, 1986, pp. 64–69.

Alff, Joseph. "Rx: Caring." *Michigan Hospitals*, August 1985, pp. 25–28.

Alpern, Barbara. *Reaching Women*. Chicago: Pluribus Press Inc., 1987.

Arnold, Danny R.; Capella, Louis M.; and Sumrall, Delia A. "Organizational Culture and the Marketing Concept: Diagnostic Keys for Hospitals." *Journal of Healthcare Marketing*, March 1987, pp. 18–28.

Austin, Nancy, and Peters, Thomas. "A Passion for Excellence." *Fortune*, May 13, 1985, pp. 20–32.

Austin, Nancy, and Peters, Thomas. "Treating the Customer Like a King." *Industry Week*, June 24, 1985, pp. 42–44.

Austin, Nancy, and Peters, Thomas. *A Passion For Excellence*. New York: Warner Books, 1986.

Barker, Michelle. "People-Oriented Design." *Hospital Forum*, July/August 1985, pp. 35–36.

Benner, Susan. "Peters' Principles: Secrets of Growth." *Inc.*, July 1983, pp. 34–39.

Bennett, Addison C. *Improving Management Performance in Health Care Institutions*. Chicago: American Hospital Publishing, Inc., 1978.

Block, Peter. *The Empowered Manager*. San Francisco: Jossey-Bass Publishers, 1987.

Braskamp, Larry A., and Maehr, Martin L. *The Motivation Factor—A Theory of Personal Investment*. Lexington, Mass.: Lexington Books, 1986.

Bronkesh, Sheryl. "What Can Hospitals Learn from Banks & Airlines? Plenty." *Hospital Marketing & Public Relations*, November/December 1983, p. 3.

Brown, Stephen W., and Morley, Andrew P. *Marketing Strategies for Physicians*. Oradell, N.J.: Medical Economics Books, 1986.

Brozovich, John D. "Managing Change Through Values." *Healthcare Executive*, March/April 1986, pp. 45–47.

Bubell, Victor. *Handbook of Modern Marketing*. New York: McGraw Hill Book Company, 1986.

Buckley, Jerry; Carey, John; and Smith, Jennifer. "Hospital Hospitality." *Newsweek*, February 11, 1985, pp. 78–79.

Burda, David. "Five Future Areas of Liability Risks Haunt Providers." *Hospitals*, November 20, 1986, pp. 48–52.

Burns, Norman R. "Courtesy, Attitude, Respect, Enthusiasm = C.A.R.E." *Michigan Hospitals*, August 1985, pp. 29–31.

Cane, William J. "We're All Losers in the Nurses' Revolt." *Medical Economics*, May 25, 1987.

Caprione, Carol. "Foodservice: The Right Medicine for an Ailing Hospital." *NRA News*, January 1984, pp. 21–24.

Carlzon, Jan. *Moments of Truth*. Cambridge, Mass.: Ballinger Publishing Company, 1987.

Clarke, Roberta, and Kotler, Philip. "Creating the Customer Responsive Organization." *Healthcare Forum*, May/June 1986, pp. 26–30, 32, 35, 36.

Clarke, Roberta, and Kotler, Philip. *Marketing for Health Care Organizations*. Englewood Cliffs, N.J.: Prentice-Hall, 1986.

Coddington, Dean C.; Palmquist, Lowell E.; and Trollinger, William V. "Strategies for Survival in the Hospital Industry." *Harvard Business Review*, May–June 1985.

Cohen, Michael T. "Training Employees for On-The-Job Survival." *Personnel Administration*, November 1985, pp. 24, 28, 30.

Coile, Russel C. *The New Hospital*. Rockville, Md.: Aspen Publications, 1986.

Coleman, Lynn G. "No Silver Lining Expected to Brighten Airlines' Stormy Skies." *Marketing News*, September 25, 1987, p. 1.

"Confronting Organizational Culture." *Healthcare Forum*, November/December 1986, p. 38.

Consumer Complaint Handling in America: An Update Study Part I, A How-to-Do-It Manual for Implementing Cost-Effective Consumer Complaint Handling Procedures (revised). Technical Research Program Institute, September 30, 1985.

Consumer Complaint Handling in America: An Update Study Part II, Complaint Handling Practices of Business, State/Local Government and Private Voluntary Agencies; and a Review of Recent Studies. Technical Research Program Institute, March 31, 1986.

"Consumers Ask MDs to Select Hospitals." *Hospitals*, March 5, 1986, pp. 68, 70.

"Consumers' Gripes About Hospital Services Drop," *Hospitals*, April 5, 1986, pp. 60, 62.

Corson, Robert. "Finding the Fifth 'P'." *Profiles in Hospital Marketing*, July 1984, pp. 64–65.

Crosby, Phillip B. *Quality Without Tears*. New York: McGraw-Hill Book Company, 1984.

Cunningham, Lynne, and Ross, Karen. "Aggressive Hospitality." *Southern Hospitals*, January/February 1986, pp. 30–32.

Curtin, Leah. "Client, . . . Loosely, a Customer." *Nursing Management*, July 1985, pp. 7, 8.

Curtin, Leah. "Courtesy: Rescuing Patients from the Me-Generation." *Nursing Management*, May 1986, pp. 7–9.

Curtin, Leah. "Guest Relations and Private Obligations." *Nursing Management*, May 1986, pp. 40–42.

Darling, LuAnn W., and Luciano, Kathy. "The Physician as a Nursing Service Customer." *The Journal of Nursing Administration*, June 1985, pp. 17–20.

Deal, Terrence; Kennedy, Allan; and Spiegel, Arthur. "How to Create an Outstanding Hospital Culture." *Hospital Forum*, January/February 1985.

Deal, Terrence, and Kennedy, Allen. *Corporate Cultures*. Reading, Mass.: Addison-Wesley Publishing Company, Inc., 1982.

Desatnick, Robert L. *Managing to Keep the Customer*. San Francisco: Jossey-Bass Publishers, 1987, p. 20.

DeWolf, Linda. "Focus Groups: Assessing Patient Satisfaction & Targeting New Services." *Hospital Topics*, March/April 1985, pp. 32–34.

Dillion, Theresa, and Woods, James. "The Performance Review Approach to Improving Productivity." *Personnel*, March 1985, pp. 20–27.

Dobson, Grant; Heffring, Michael; Neilsen, Joan; and Szklarz, Marie. "High Tech, High Touch: Common Denominators in Patient Satisfaction." *Hospitals and Health Services Administration*, March/April 1986, pp. 80–93.

"Doctors Being Taught a New Bedside Manner." *Chicago Sun Times*, May 1, 1983, p. 12.

"Doctors Urged to Work to Restore Lost Public Confidence in Medical Profession." *FAH Review*, July/August 1984, pp. 28, 32.

Dunlop, Richard. "Hospitals Try to Heal Themselves." *American Way*, March 1982, pp. 33, 34.

Easterbrook, Gregg. "The Revolution in Medicine." *Newsweek*, January 26, 1987.

Eickhorn, Suzanne. "A Hospital Humanizes Patient Care." *Hospital Forum*, May/April 1985, pp. 55–57.

Eisenberg, Barry, and Gardella, Maria. "Assessing Readiness for Guest Relations Programs." *Hospitals*, April 16, 1985, pp. 128, 132.

Ethiel, Nancy. "Guest Relations Program Fulfills Great Expectations." *The Volunteer Leader*, Spring 1986, pp. 10–11.

Evans, N. "More on Guest Relations." *Hospital Forum*, January/February 1984, pp. 50–51.

Feler, Armando; Fochman, David; and Stukenborg, George. "The Ideal Physician: Implications for Contemporary Hospital Marketing." *Journal of Healthcare Marketing*, June 1986, pp. 17–25.

Fincham, Jack E., and Wertheimer, Albert J. "Predictors of Patient Satisfaction for a Health Maintenance Organization." *Journal of Health Care Marketing*, September 1986, pp. 5–11.

Finn, David W., and Lamb, Charles W., Jr. "Hospital Benefit Segmentation." *Journal of Health Care Marketing*, December 1986, pp. 26–33.

Fisher, Susan. "Marketing in Academic Health Centers." *Journal of Healthcare Marketing*, September 1986, pp. 49–51.

"Five Myths About Democracy in the Workplace." *Training*, August 1984, pp. 8, 10, 13.

"Floridan VIP Suites." *Healthcare Marketing Report*, February 1984, p. 6.

"Follow-Up Determines Success of Guest Relations Efforts." *Hospitals*, November 16, 1985, p. 60.

Franklin, William. "Six Critical Issues for the 80's." *Administrative Management*, January 1982, pp. 24–27, 54.

Friedman, Emily. "Room at the Top." *Healthcare Forum*, January/February 1986, pp. 18–21.

Friedman, Emily. "What Do Consumers Really Want?" *Healthcare Forum*, May/June 1986, pp. 19–24.

Fritz, Rita. "Guest Relations Challenges Management." *Small or Rural Hospital Report*, March/April 1985.

Fritz, Rita. "Developing a Consumer-Driven Hospital—Four Fatal Flaws." *Healthcare Forum*, May/June 1986, pp. 39–40.

Fritz, Rita, and Miller, Grace. "Guest Relations as Corporate Strategy." *Hospital Forum*, January/February 1984, pp. 52–54.

Gaida, Kathleen A.; Johnson, Eugene M.; and Schueing, Eberhard. *Profitable Service Marketing*. Homewood, Ill.: Dow Jones Irwin, 1986.

Galloway, Paul. "Hospital Chic." *Chicago Tribune*, November 3, 1986, Section 5, pp. 1, 3.

Garfield, Charles. "Peak Performance for Managers." *Sky*, July 1985, pp. 18, 20, 23.

Garside, Pamela; Rice, James; and Slack, Richard. "Hospitals Can Learn Valuable Marketing Strategies from Hotels." *Hospitals*, November 16, 1981, pp. 95, 97, 98, 100, 102, 104.

Gekas, Alexandra. "Customer-Oriented Management Important to Hospitals, Survey Finds." *The Hospital Manager*, May/June 1985, pp. 5, 6.

Gekas, Alexandra. "Good Patient Relations Can Help Abate Potential Risk Situations." *Hospitals*, March 16, 1978, p. 58.

Gekas, Alexandra. "Good Patient Relations Crucial to Hospital Survival." *Cross Reference on Human Resource Management*, September/October 1983, pp. 1–2.

Goldsmith, Martin, and Leebov, Wendy. "How to Create a More Consumer-Oriented Workforce." *Personnel Administration*, October 1984, pp. 99, 100, 105, 106, 108.

Goldsmith, Martin, and Leebov, Wendy. "Does Your Customer Relations Program Have What It Takes"? *The Hospital Manager*, January/February 1985, pp. 23–25.

Gombeski, William R.; Stone, Cheryl E.; and Weaver, Frank J. "Improving Patient Services Through a Professional Shopper Program." *Journal of Healthcare Marketing*, September 1986, pp. 64–68.

Grahm, Judith. "Quality Gets a Closer Look." *Modern Healthcare*, February 27, 1987.

Greenfield, Meg. "The Land of Hospital." *Newsweek*, June 30, 1986, p. 74.

Guarriello, Donna Lee. "Nurses Don't Get Mad; They Get Even." *Medical Economics*, May 2, 1983, pp. 67–70.

Guest, Robert; Hersey, Paul; and Blanchard, Kenneth. *Organizational Change Through Effective Leadership*. Englewood Cliffs, N.J.: Prentice-Hall, Inc., 1977.

Haas, Robert W.; Oulken, Herve; and Wotruba, Thomas. "Marketing Factors Affecting Physician Choice as Related to Consumers' Extent of Use and Predisposition Toward Use of Physician Services." *Journal of Healthcare Marketing*, Fall 1985, pp. 7–17.

Hafer, John, and Joiner, Carl. "Nurses as Image Emissaries: Are Role Conflicts Impinging on a Potential Asset for an Internal Marketing Strategy?" *Journal of Healthcare Marketing*, Winter 1984, pp. 25–35.

Harju, Mark, and Inguanzo, Joe. "Creating a Marketing Niche." *Hospitals*, January 1, 1985, pp. 62, 64, 67.

Harju, Mark, and Inguanzo, Joe. "Are Consumers Sensitive to Hospital Costs?" *Hospitals*, February 1, 1985, pp. 68–69.

Harju, Mark, and Inguanzo, Joe. "What Makes Consumers Select a Hospital?" *Hospitals*, March 16, 1985, pp. 90, 92, 94.

Harju, Mark, and Inguanzo, Joe. "How Do Consumers Receive Local Health Care Information?" *Hospitals*, April 1, 1985, pp. 74–76.

Harju, Mark, and Inguanzo, Joe. "Consumer Satisfaction with Hospitalization." *Hospitals*, May 1, 1985, pp. 81–83.

"Have a Good Rest in the Hospital." *New England Journal of Medicine*, May 1984, p. 24.

Hawes, Jon M., and Rao, C.P. "Using Importance-Performance Analysis to Develop Health Care Marketing Strategies." *Journal of Healthcare Marketing*, Fall 1985, pp. 19–25.

Hays, Michael D. "Consumer Base Quality Perceptions on Patient Relations, Staff Qualifications." *Modern Healthcare*, February 1987, p. 33.

Heskett, James L. *Managing in the Service Economy.* Boston: Harvard Business School Press, 1986.

Hickey, Kevin. "Managing Organizational Values." *Cross Reference on Human Resource Management*, May/June 1983, pp. 2–3.

Hickman, Craig, and Silva, Michael. *Creating Excellence—Managing Corporate Culture, Strategy and Change in the New Age.* New York: New American Library, 1984.

Higgins, Adele. "Cost-Reduction Pressures Force Hospitals to Innovate." *San Diego Daily Transcript*, March 27, 1985, p. 1.

Hogan, Norma Shaw. *Humanizing Health Care.* Oradell, N.J.: Medical Economics Company, 1980.

"Hospital Valets Give Patients a Guest Reception." *Hospitals*, August 1, 1983, p. 66.

"Hospitals, Physicians in the Competitive Era: Learning to Live in New Environment." *FAH Review*, July/August 1984, p. 12.

Hostage, G.M. "Quality Control in a Service Business." *Harvard Business Review*, July/August 1975, pp. 98–106.

Jenna, Judith K. "Toward the Patient-Driven Hospital, Part I." *Healthcare Forum*, May/June 1986, pp. 8–18.

Jenna, Judith K. "Toward the Patient-Driven Hospital, Part II." *Healthcare Forum*, July/August 1986, pp. 55–59.

Jensen, Joyce. "Advertising Helps More Consumers Select Hospitals." *Modern Healthcare*, April 12, 1985.

Jensen, Joyce, and Miklovic, Ned. "Fewer Consumers Report They Have Physicians Who Provide Routine Care." *Modern Healthcare*, January 3, 1986, pp. 88, 89.

Jensen, Joyce. "Women Generally Select Their Family's Physician." *Modern Healthcare*, January 31, 1986, pp. 60, 61.

Jensen, Joyce, and Miklovic, Ned. "Consumer Satisfaction with Physicians Is High." *Modern Healthcare*, February 14, 1986, pp. 62, 63.

Jensen, Joyce. "Women Pick the Providers Who Treat Their Illnesses, Those of Their Children." *Modern Healthcare*, May 9, 1986, p. 66.

Jensen, Susan. "Patient Relations as Customer-Oriented Management." *Texas Hospitals*, September 1984, pp. 20–22.

Johnson, Donald E.L. "Hospitals Emphasize Guest Relations." *Modern Healthcare*, December 1980, p. 42.

Johnson, Barbara. "Hospital 'Hotels'; The Time Has Come." *Michigan Hospitals*, August 1985, pp. 7–9, 11.

Kaiser, Leland. "The Emerging Hospital/Employee Relationship." *Human Resource Management*, January/February 1985, pp. 17–18.

Kaiser, Leland. "Organizational Mindset." *Healthcare Forum*, January/February 1986, pp. 50–53.

Kaiser, Leland. "Kaiser on Innovation." *Healthcare Forum*, January/February 1987, pp. 16–21.

Kazemek, Edward, and Peterson, Kristine. "Improving Complaint Management Skills." *HFMA Journal*, October 1987, pp. 123–124.

Keely, Charles. "The Gourmet Hospital." *PSA*, March 1985, pp. 62–65, 111.

"Key to Successful Guest Relations: Service Management." *Healthcare Marketing Report*, November 1986, pp. 17, 18.

Kilman, Ralph. "Culture." *Psychology Today*, April 1985, pp. 63–68.

Kleinfield, N.R. "A Push to Market Health Care." *New York Times*, April 16, 1984, pp. 25, 28.

Knight, Gordon F. "Employee Complaints: Open Door Is Not Enough." *Michigan Hospitals*, August 1985, pp. 32–33.

Koepp, Stephen. "Why Is Service So Bad?" *Time*, February 2, 1987, p. 51.

Kosterlitz, Julie. "The Hospital Business." *AHA National Journal*, October 11, 1985, pp. 1–8.

Kotler, Philip. "Idea Management." *Healthcare Forum*, March/April 1986, pp. 45–48.

Kotulak, Ronald. "Hospitals Find a Cure for Gripes," *Chicago Tribune*, November 22, 1985.

Kresgoski, Ronald, and Scott, Beverly. *Quality Circles*. Chicago: The Dartnell Corporation, 1982.

Krupat, Edward. "A Delicate Imbalance." *Psychology Today*, November 1986, pp. 22–26.

Kurman, Marsha, and Leebov, Wendy. "Diffusing Resistance to Guest Relations." *The Hospital Manager*, May/June 1986, p. 4.

Larsen, Dave. "Hospitals Put Warmth in Patients' Stay." *Los Angeles Times*, May 4, 1984, pp. 1, 10–11.

Lee, Gerald. "Patient Representation: Now More Than Ever." *Michigan Hospitals*, August 1985, pp. 19–21, 23.

Levitt, Theodore. "After the Sale Is Over." *Harvard Business Review*, September/October 1983, pp. 87–93.

Levitt, Theodore. *The Marketing Imagination*. New York: The Free Press, 1983.

Lewin, Tamar. "Hospitals Pitch Harder for Patients." *New York Times*, May 10, 1987, Section 3, pp. 1, 28.

Lewis, Robert. "When Guests Complain." *The Cornell HRA Quarterly*, August 1983, pp. 23–25.

Love, John. *McDonald's Behind the Arches*. New York: Bantam Books, 1986.

Lovelock, Christopher H. *Services Marketing*. Englewood Cliffs, N.J.: Prentice-Hall, 1984.

Lu, Elizabeth. "More Hospitals Turn to Hospitality as Front-Office Elixir." *Los Angeles Times*, January 13, 1986, pp. 6, 8.

"Luxury Amenities at Nevada Hospital Attract Patients, Staff." *Contract*, February 1984, pp. 94–96.

Lyons, R.D. "Cleveland Clinic for the World's Elite." *New York Times*, May 8, 1984, p. 16.

MacHaffie, Reginald. "Make Your Patients Feel You Really Understand Them." *Physician's Management*, November 1982, pp. 151–154, 158.

MacStravic, Robin Scott. *Marketing Healthcare*. Rockville, Md.: Aspen Publishers, 1977.

MacStravic, Robin Scott. "My Personal Hospital." *Modern Healthcare*, July 1984, pp. 182, 184, 187.

MacStravic, Robin Scott. "Promises, Promises . . ." *Hospital Forum*, March/April 1985.

Magill, Judith, and Scheuerman, Janet. "Friends' Recommendations Pull More Patients to Emergi-Centers." *Modern Healthcare*, June 1984, pp. 70, 72.

Malkin, Jain. "Psychology: Implications for Health Care Design." *Hospital Physician*, August 1983, pp. 96, 99.

Malkin, Jain. "The Body Language of Office Decor." *San Diego's Business Quarterly for the Medical Community*, Fall 1984, p. 1.

McCord, Robert. "Seven Essential Elements of a Successful Practice." *Physician's Management*, May 1984, pp. 60–67.

McGregor, Douglas. *The Human Side of Enterprise*. New York: McGraw-Hill, Inc., 1986.

McKenna, Regis. *The Regis Touch*. Reading, Mass.: Addison-Wesley Publishing Company, Inc., 1986.

Mickus, Raymond, and Shortell, Stephan. "Standing Firm on Shaky Ground." *Healthcare Forum*, January/February 1986, pp. 55–58.

Mills, David. "Dose of Smiles Is Latest Prescription for Hospitals That Vie for Patients." *Wall Street Journal*, September 24, 1987.

Mitchell, Mary. "The New Bedside Manner." *Columbus Monthly*, December 1985, pp. 99–110.

Naisbitt, John. *Megatrends*. New York: Warner Books, 1982.

Orlikoff, James E., and Snow, Anita. *Assessing Quality Circles in Health Care Settings*. Chicago: American Hospital Publishing, Inc., 1984.

"Out in Front." *Healthcare Forum*, May/June 1986, p. 42.

Painter, Kim. "Patients Want Physicians in White." *USA Today*. January 2, 1987, p. D1.

Patient Representative In Contemporary Health Care. Chicago: National Society of Patient Representatives of the American Hospital Association, 1985.

Peters, Thomas. "Common Courtesy: The Ultimate Barrier to Entry. Part I." *Hospital Forum*, January/February 1984, pp. 10–16.

Peters, Thomas. "Common Courtesy: The Ultimate Barrier to Entry. Part II." *Hospital Forum*, March 1984, pp. 51–56.

Peters, Thomas. *Thriving on Chaos*. New York: Alfred A. Knopf, 1987.

Peterson, Kristine E. "Lessons in Customer Service: Health Care Manager's Notebook." *Hospital Forum*, January/February 1984, pp. 17–20.

Peterson, Kristine E. "First Impressions from Foundations." *The Journal for Hospital Admitting Management*, Spring 1985, pp. 1–3.

Peterson, Kristine E. "Practice Expansion—Your Business Depends on Patient Relations." *Primary Care Technology*, September/October 1985, pp. 5, 20.

Peterson, Kristine E. "Innovative Imaging: What You Can Do to Create a Competitive Edge." *Administrative Radiology*, December 1986, pp. 74–76, 78, 80, 82.

Peterson, Kristine E. "How Do You Rate in Customer Relations?" *Provider*, February 1987, pp. 22, 24–25.

Peterson, Kristine E. "Internal Marketing: Closing the Loop." In *Reaching Women*, by Barbara Alpern. Chicago: Pluribus Press, Inc., 1987.

Pinchot, Gifford, III. *Intrapreneuring*. New York: Harper & Row Publishers, 1985.

Pope, N.W. "Mickey Mouse Marketing." *American Banker*, July 25, 1979, pp. 18–27.

Pope, N.W. "More Mickey Mouse Marketing." *American Banker*, September 12, 1979, pp. 22–27.

Powills, Suzanne. "Florida Hospital Uses Nursing Staff to Market Services to Community." *Hospitals*, June 1, 1985, p. 46.

Powills, Suzanne. "Hospitals Call a Marketing Time-Out." *Hospitals*, June 5, 1985, pp. 50–55.

Powills, Suzanne. "Marketing: Consumer Gripes About Hospital Service Drops." *Hospitals*, April 5, 1986, p. 60.

Press, Irwin. "The Predisposition to File Claims: The Patients' Perspective." *Law Medicine & Health Care*, April 1984, pp. 53–62.

Press, Irwin, and Smith, Dixie. "Premedical Students as Patient and Family Liaisons in the Emergency Department: A Strategy for Patient Satisfaction." *Journal of Emergency Nursing*, January/February 1986, pp. 23–25.

"Product Line Management." *Healthcare Forum*, September/October 1986, pp. 11–14.

Ranelli, Edward. "Health Care Marketing—A Service Marketing Approach." In *Health Marketing Quarterly*, edited by William Winston, 3, Winter 1985, pp. 7–12.

Reynolds, Barbara. " 'Gall Bladder in 322A' Now Has a Real Name." *USA Today*, August 11, 1986, p. 9A.

Reynolds, Peter C. "Imposing a Corporate Culture." *Psychology Today*, March 1987, pp. 33–38.

Rice, J.A.; Slack, R.S.; et al. "Hospitals Can Learn Valuable Marketing Strategies from Hotels." In *Services Marketings: Test, Cases & Readings*, edited by C.H. Lovelock, 119–125. Englewood Cliffs, N.J.: Prentice-Hall, 1984.

Richman, Dan. "Nursing: An Endangered Profession." *Modern Healthcare*, March 27, 1987, p. 33.

Ries, Al, and Trout, Jack. *Marketing Warfare*. New York: McGraw-Hill, Inc., 1986.

Riffer, Joyce. "The Patient as a Guest: A Competitive Strategy." *Hospitals*, June 16, 1984, pp. 4, 8, 51, 55.

Robinson, Donald. "Investor-Owned Hospitals: Rx for Success." *Readers Digest*, April 1983.

Rodgers, Buck. *The IBM Way*. New York: Harper and Row Publishers, 1986.

Rose, J.C. "Marketing New Food Services." *Hospitals*, August 1, 1983, pp. 64–66.

Rosenthal, T.L. "VIP Program Improves Admissions, Public Relations. *Patient Accounts*, May 1984, p. 3.

Rudnick, John D., Jr., and Routledge, Jack. "Employee Recognition Reinforces Guest Relations." *The Hospital Manager*, November/December 1985.

Schier, Mary Jane. "Course Teaches 'All Little Things' Important to Patients." *Houston Post*, August 20, 1979, p. 10.

"Service Marketers Must Balance Customer Satisfaction Against Their Operational Needs." *Marketing News*, October 10, 1986, pp. 1, 14.

"Service with a Smile? That's Not Nearly Enough." *Hospitals*, November 5, 1986, pp. 80–81.

Shafer, Dennis W. "Managing the 'Fifth P' Leads to Teamwork." *Marketing News*, November 7, 1986, p. 12.

Shaffer, James C. "Seven Emerging Trends in Organizational Communication." *IABC Communication World*, February 1986.

Smith, Charolette. "Recognition-Motivation Program Aims @ Cost Containment and Better Customer Relations." *Journal of Hospital Admitting*, Spring 1985, p. 6.

Smith, Robert. "Patient Opinions Help Place Hospital Services in Perspective." *Hospitals*, August 16, 1977, pp. 65–66, 68.

Strum, D.W., and Studin, I. "R&D: Implementing Guest Relations." *Hospital Forum*, January/February 1984, pp. 47–49.

Super, Kari. "Memorial Hospital Emphasizes Guest Relations to Attract Patients." *Modern Healthcare*, August 29, 1986, pp. 42–44.

Super, Kari. "Providers Realizing Importance of Quality Service." *Modern Healthcare*, October 10, 1986, p. 112.

Super, Kari E. "Many Nurses Taking a New Course: How To Take Care of Hospital Image." *Modern Healthcare*, February 13, 1987.

T.A.R.P. "Measuring the Grapevine—Consumer Response and Word-of-Mouth." Study conducted for Corporate Consumer Affairs Department of the Coca-Cola Company by T.A.R.P., August 1983.

T.A.R.P. Working Paper. "The Bottom-Line Implications of Unmet Customer Expectations and How to Measure Them." June 1983.

"The Emerging Leaders: Seeding the Healthcare Frontier." *Healthcare Forum*, May/June 1986, pp. 48–61.

Thomas, Laurita, and Berry, Lana. "Employees 'Capture the Spirit' at UM." *Michigan Hospitals*, August 1985, pp. 13–16.

Toufexis, Anastasia. "No More Mickey Mousing Around." *Time*, March 11, 1985, p. 54.

Uttal, Bro. "Corporate Culture Vultures." *Fortune*, October 17, 1973, pp. 66–72.

Uttal, Bro. "Companies That Serve You Best." *Fortune*, December 7, 1987, pp. 98–101, 104, 108, 112, 116.

Van Den Haag, Ernest. "How to Make Hospitals Hospitable." *Fortune*, May 17, 1982, pp. 123–126, 129.

Verzillo, Jeanette. "A Program for Caring." *Supervisor Nurse*, July 1980, pp. 10–12, 15–16.

"VIP Suites Make Patient's Outlook More Positive." *Texas Hospitals*, February 1984, p. 28.

Wallace, Cynthia. "Hospital's 'Personalized' Care Unit May Boost Share, Patient Satisfaction." *Modern Healthcare*, January 3, 1986, pp. 36–38.

Waterman, Robert H., Jr. *The Renewal Factor*. New York: Bantam Books, 1987.

Winston, William J. *Health Marketing Quarterly*. New York: The Hawthorn Press, 1985.

Winston, William J. *Professional Practice in Health Care Marketing*. New York: The Hawthorn Press, 1986.

"Women as Healthcare Consumers." *Healthcare Forum*, January/February 1986, pp. 22–24.

Wright, Wayne L. "Escape From Mediocrity." *Personnel Administrator*, September 1987, p. 109.

Yoshihara, Nancy. "Nordstrom—Chain Sets Itself Apart with an Old-Fashioned Service Policy." *Los Angeles Times*, September 30, 1984, Section V.

Zemke, Ron. "Why More Firms Stress Customer Service Training." *Training/Human Resources Development*, May 1981.

Zenger, John. "Leadership: Management's Better Half." *Training*, December 1985, pp. 44–47, 52, 53.

Index